INTRODUCTION TO INDIAN BUDDHISM

INTRODUCTION TO INDIAN BUDDHISM

K S Dwivedi

MD PUBLICATIONS PVT LTD
NEW DELHI
www.mdppl.com

Published by :

MD Publications Pvt Ltd
"MD House", 11, Darya Ganj,
New Delhi - 110 002
Phone : +91-11-45355555
E-mail : contact@mdppl.com
Website: www.mdppl.com

ISBN: 978-81-7533-304-8

Published and Printed by Mr. Pranav Gupta on behalf of MD Publications Pvt Ltd at Mohit Enterprises, Delhi.

PREFACE

In India, Buddhism started with the life of Lord Buddha. He was born as prince Siddartha in the royal family of the Shakya Kingdom. However, he left his home in the search of the real meaning of life. After spending a number of years in asceticism and meditation, he finally attained enlightenment under the Bodice tree in Gaya, Bihar. By 3rd century BC, the religion spread all over South Asia, through the Mauryan Empire.

Buddhism was spread in India throughout the north in the areas where Buddha and his disciples traveled and was firmly rooted in this area. But it was not until the 3rd century BC that Buddha's teachings began to spread to other lands and cultures. A king of the Mauryan Dynasty, by the name of Ashoka, became the greatest patron and factor in the spread of Buddhism the world has ever known. With the arrival of Turks in India, the remaining monasteries in plains were also reduced to ruins. That time saw Buddhism, as an organized religion, practically vanishing from India. Bhutan and Sikkim, the only independent Himalayan kingdoms, tribal groups in the mountains of northeast India and Sri Lanka were the only places where Buddhism still thrived. Approximately thirty years later, around 1956, Buddhism again surfaced in India. Dr. Bhimrao Ambedkar, leader of the Untouchables or Harijans in India, adopted Buddhism to escape from the barriers created by the Hindu caste system.

Buddhism began a steady and dramatic comeback in India during the early twentieth century, spurred on originally by a combination of European antiquarian and philosophical interest and the dedicated activities of a few Indian devotees.

The foundation of the Mahabodhi Society (Society of Great Enlightenment) in 1891, originally as a force to wrest control of the Buddhist shrine at Gaya from the hands of Hindu managers, gave a large stimulus to the popularization of Buddhist philosophy and the importance of the religion in India's past.

A major breakthrough occurred in 1956 after some thirty years of Untouchable, or Dalit agitation when Bhimrao Ramji Ambedkar, leader of the Untouchable wing within the Congress announced that he was converting to Buddhism as a way to escape from the impediments of the Hindu caste system. He brought with him masses of Untouchables-also known as Harijans or Dalits-and members of Scheduled Castes who mostly came from Maharashtra and border areas of neighboring states and from the Agra area in Uttar Pradesh. By the early 1990s, there were more than 5 million Buddhists in Maharashtra, or 79 percent of the entire Buddhist community in India, almost all recent converts from low castes.

I am very grateful to Mr. Pranav Gupta, Director of MD Publications Pvt Ltd, New Delhi, for his kind cooperation and support for this book.

K S Dwivedi

CONTENTS

1

The Life and Teachings of the Buddha

The founder of Buddhism was an historical person, Siddhatta Gotama who lived in North India from 563 BCE to 483 BCE. His father was Suddhodana the ruler of the Sakyas a people inhabiting a country which lay on the border between modern Nepal and India. At the time of his birth his mother Mahamaya was on a journey and he was born in a park at Lumbini on the full moon day of the month of April-May in the year 563 BCE. A commemorative pillar was erected on the spot by King Asoka some three centuries later.

Several legends are *Digha Nikaya* to the birth of Sidhatta, including a prophecy by the Brahmin Asita that he would either be a great ("universal") ruler or a fully enlightened teacher. It is said that Suddhodana wanted his son to become a monarch rather than a great religious teacher, and accordingly brought him up in the lap of luxury with the training befitting a future king. But very little is known of the early life of Sidhatta. No indication of his future destiny is recorded other than a reference to an incident when as a child he went into a meditative trance while seated in an open field watching an agricultural festival. When he was sixteen Sidhatta was married to Bhaddakacana (also known as Yasodara).

The events that forced his decision to renounce the life of luxury he was leading and take to the religious life occurred when he was about 29 years of age. It is claimed that at this time he encountered the famous four signs, that of an old man, of a sick man, of a corpse and of a religious recluse, and that these led him to question the unsatisfactoriness of life and the need to find a way of escape from its travails. The misery and brevity of human existence struck him with force, and also the desire to find a solution to the problems of life. But the critical event was the birth of his first child, a son who was named Rahula. When the child was born Gotama realised that if he were to assume the role of a parent he would never leave the household life in this quest for the meaning of life, and accordingly he decided to renounce the household life.

Fearing that a public announcement would bring pressure to change his mind, he left his palace with only his charioteer accompanying him, donned the garments of a recluse and went into the homeless life. Gotama thus became a *samana (sramana)* or religious mendicant. The samanas were people who devoted their entire time to the search for religious truth. They did not adhere to the prevailing religious orthodoxy of the day, the Brahmanical religion based on the ancient Vedas. They were highly individualistic and engaged in a variety of practices.

The next seven years of Gotama's life were devoted to his quest. He became the pupils of the leading religious teachers of his day, such as Alarara Kalama and Uddaka Ramaputta. They were the leading exponents of meditation of the day, and Gotama mastered all the meditation techniques they could teach including the development of the *jhanas*. Since these did not provide the solution he was seeking, he continued in his search. By this time his wandering had taken him south of the Ganges River. He now formed an association with five other samanas, who were more inclined to the practice of austerities. But even these did not satisfy Gotama. He now continued his search alone.

His search finally ended on the full moon day in the month of Vesakha (April-May) in the year 528 BCE when he meditating under an Asattha or Pippala tree (*ficus religiosa*) near Uruvela (now known as Buddha-Gaya). He had become the Buddha (a term meaning the "Enlightened One"), by which title he was henceforth to be universally known. The tree has come to be known as the Bodhi (or Bo) tree, and is regarded as a symbol of the Buddha's enlightenment. After considerable thought he decided to proclaim his discovery for the benefit of mankind. His hesitation arose from the complexity of the system he had discovered, and its opposition to the comfortable beliefs which then as now appeared to offer an easier solution to the spiritual needs of people.

The first proclamation of the *Dhamma* took place at the deer-park in Isipatana close to the city of Sarnath (near modern Benares) to the five former ascetic companions, who became the Buddha's first disciples. From that day on until his death some 45 years later the Buddha travelled around Northern India tirelessly proclaiming his message. The five ascetics became the first members of the Buddhist *Sangha* (or Community of disciples) which have survived to this day in unbroken succession. The exact chronology of the Buddha's ministry has not been recorded and cannot be reconstructed. His more important discourses are preserved, but while they indicate the circumstances leading to each discourse, and often the place of its delivery, there is generally no indication of the date or even year of the discourse.

From the places mentioned in the discourses it is possible to reconstruct the area of the Buddha's travels. This was confined mainly to the middle Gangetic plain with Kapilavatthu to the North, Uruvela to the South, and Campa to the East. The Western extent is not certain, some suttas being delivered not far from the modern Delhi. This area straddled the Ganges River, and included parts of two important kingdoms in the Buddha's time. These were Kosala which was located north of the river Ganges with Savatthi as its capital, and Magadha which was to the South of Kosala with Rajagaha as its capital. The Buddha became well known in both these kingdoms and their capital cities. There are legendary accounts of visits of the Buddha to places as far away as Sri Lanka, and even to heavenly domains, but these have no historical basis.

The Buddha and his followers initially followed the wandering life of the *samanas*, but soon developed the habit of staying at least part of the year in a monastery. The period of monastic sojourn came to be known as the "rains retreat" *(vas)* because it coincided with the Indian monsoon. The monasteries were donated by wealthy lay followers. In the early years the Buddha spent his rains retreats south of the Ganges River mainly at Rajagaha, but gradually moved north. In the later years the most frequently visited location was Savatthi, where the Buddha spent 23 of the last 25 rains retreats. The very last rains retreat was spent at Vesali when the Buddha was on his last journey from Rajagaha to Savatthi.

The Buddha's death (*pariNibbana*) took place at a place called Kusinara mid-way between Vesali and Savatthi. While some debate may attach to the exact dates of the Buddha's life there can be no doubt about the historicity of the Buddha. The Buddha's teaching, unlike that of many other founders of religious systems, was so unique, original and consistent that it could only have been the work of a single person. The Buddha did not appropriate on himself the role of a God or of a prophet of God, in order to validate his teachings. His teachings were derived from his own unaided efforts.

Recently discovered archaeological evidence corroborates the accounts in the texts. These include the discovery of urns with inscriptions indicating that they were the receptacle for the relics of the Buddha. King Asoka's pillars, though a few centuries after the death of the Buddha also identify the places associated with the life story of the Buddha. The most recent discoveries have been archaeological remains authenticating the birthplace of the Buddha as Lumbini. There is a detailed account of the last days of the Buddha in the Mahapari*Nibbana* sutta, but no such detailed information is available for any other part of his life. After his death the relics of the Buddha was distributed and stupas were built over them.

THE BASIC TEACHING OF THE BUDDHA

Buddhism recognises no creeds whose uncritical acceptance is expected of its followers. Instead the Buddha enunciated certain basic laws and truths whose veracity he invited his followers to test for them. One of the traditional epithets of the *Dhamma* is "ehipassiko" (meaning literally "come and see") which is an appeal to the empirical verification of the *Dhamma*. In his very first discourse the Buddha identified Four Noble Truths as forming the core of the *Dhamma*. These four Truths have since become a convenient way of stating the fundamentals of the *Dhamma*. They are often regarded as the most basic teaching of the Buddha. The Buddha also identified three fundamental characteristics (*tilakkhana*) of the *Dhamma*.

These basic tenets the Buddha presented in several ways. Two such presentations have become well known. These are the Three Signata (*tilakkhana*), perhaps better rendered as the three basic laws, and the Four Noble Truths. The acceptance of the validity of these laws and truths, if only in the first instance as a working hypothesis, is the *sin qua non* of a Buddhist. In addition the Buddha proclaimed several other doctrines, the most important being those of karma and re-birth.

The validity of such doctrines is more difficult for an ordinary person to verify, but their dogmatic acceptance is not expected as a fundamental requirement of those who go for refuge to the "Three Gems" of Buddhism. The three signata and the four truths form the core of the *Dhamma*. They are at the same time both alternatives and complements to each other. It may however be appropriate to consider them separately.

THE THREE FUNDAMENTAL LAWS OF THE BUDDHA

The three signata refer to the three essential marks or characteristics of all "compounded" things, animate or inanimate, microscopic or macroscopic. Because of the universality of their applicability they could be considered as having the force of universal laws. These characteristics are impermanence (*Anicca*), unsatisfactoriness (*Dukkha*), and insubstantiality (*Anatta*). As these translations of the basic Pali terms are only approximate, a further elaboration of these basic concepts of the *Dhamma* is necessary.

1. *Anicca*. The law of impermanence asserts that all phenomena are subject to constant change, to rise and fall, and no permanent states, either physical or animate, exists. The dynamic nature of phenomena is today a commonplace of science. But until quite recently many physical features of the universe were considered immutable, and in the human plane the belief in enduring states or characteristics is still an article of faith in many religious systems. The law of *Anicca* establishes impermanence as the basic universal law.
2. *Dukkha*. The law of *Dukkha* states that all complexes of phenomena are in the final analysis unsatisfactory. It means that no compounded thing or state could be considered as a universal norm of goodness or beauty. It imparts the normative dimension into the consideration of objective reality which is the hallmark of the *Dhamma*. The law of *Dukkha* is usually considered in relation to the human situation, and here unsatisfactoriness manifests itself as "suffering", which is the popular rendition of the term. It is in this sense that it constitutes the first of the four Noble Truths.
3. *Anatta*. The third law states that there is no permanent essence, "self", ego, or soul in phenomena. The term originates as the negation of the concept of *atta* (*Atman*) which was the equivalent in the old Brahmanical religion of the Buddha's day to what other religions have called the "soul". The Buddha advanced psycho-physical explanation of the individual which leaves no room for a soul. The Buddha recognised that the delusion of self or ego was one of the most powerful of human instincts, and at the same time one of the most potent sources of ignorance and wrong action. In applying the *Anatta* doctrine to the phenomena of the external world some care mush be exercised.

Early Buddhism did not deny the reality of the external world. It argued that the phenomena of the external world could be broken down into its constituent components, and that nothing else other than these components existed. It was only in this sense that the phenomena of the external world were declared to be empty (sunna). Some schools of Mahayana Buddhism have taken the doctrine of emptiness (sunnata) to imply a denial of the reality of the external world. This interpretation is foreign to early Buddhism. Early Buddhism only asserts that there is no fixed essence or being in phenomena, but only a process of becoming bhava.

THE FOUR NOBLE TRUTHS

The four noble truths result from the application of the three basic laws to the human condition. The Buddha frequently asserted that he was interested in the problem of the alleviation of human suffering: "Only one thing do I teach, suffering, and how to end it". His approach to the problem of suffering was similar to that of the physician to his patient. He first diagnoses the malady, and then seeks the cause of the malady, next finds out whether a cure is possible. Finally he prescribes the medicine. The four truths correspond to the four steps of this diagnostic-curative procedure.

1. The Truth of Suffering.

This truth affirms that the law of *Dukkha* is applicable to the human condition:

"Birth is suffering, decay is suffering, death is suffering; sorrow, lamentation, pain, grief, and despair are suffering. To be separated from the pleasant is suffering; to be in contact with the unpleasant is suffering; in short the five aggregates of existence connected with attachment are all suffering".

The validity of the truth of suffering need not be belaboured here; it is essentially a matter for personal verification. The truth of *Dukkha* refers not to the on-existence of the pleasurable and the joyful, but to the very incompleteness and finitude of that enjoyment. The imputation of pessimism sometimes made of early Buddhism is without foundation; suffering in the Buddhist sense encompasses what is usually termed "evil" in other religo-philosophical systems, and the existence of evil, caused either by chance events or by deliberate ill-will is not seriously denied.

2. The Truth of the Cause of Suffering.

The proximate cause of suffering is craving (*tanha*), but the root cause of ignorance (*avijja*). The objects of craving are manifold: sensual pleasure, material possessions, glory, power, fame, ego, craving for re-birth, even craving for *Nibbana* (nirvana). There are various degrees of craving from a mild wish to an acute grasping (upadana). Craving is the proximate cause of suffering and is itself caused by other conditioning factors. The full formula of causation is contained in the Buddhist formula of dependent origination, where the causes for existence and suffering are traced back through a chain of twelve links, back to ignorance.

3. The Truth of the Cessation of Suffering.

This growth constitutes the "good news" of Buddhism. The cause of suffering could be counteracted. This truth affirms that a way out of suffering exists, which if followed will lead the individual to a state of non-suffering called *Nibbana*, perhaps better known by the Sanskrit form of the term, Nirvana. If the first truth could be considered to have a taint of "pessimism", this truth has the full flavour of "optimism".

4. The Truth of the Path to Enlightenment.

The Buddhist path to enlightenment is that discovered by the Buddha through his own personal effort and practice. It has been called the Middle Path (majjima paipada) because it is a *via media* between the extremes of self-indulgence and self-mortification. Both extremes of practice were common in the Buddha's day (as indeed they are in out own). The Buddha calls such extremes vain, profitless and ignoble. The path of the Buddha avoids two kinds of activity usually considered essential for salvation by many religious systems. These are: (1) prayer to supra human powers and agencies, and (2) elaborate rites and rituals. On the contrary these are considered as being positive impediments on the path to the cessation of suffering and the gaining of insight and wisdom.

While the Four Noble Truths and the Three Laws of Existence contain the kernel of the Buddha's teaching, and were proclaimed by the Buddha in his very first discourse, there are many other doctrines that are central to a philosophical system which is as deep as that of Buddhism. A few of these aspects of the teaching will be mentioned here and a few of these will be considered in detail elsewhere.

THE GOAL OF BUDDHISM AND THE MEANING OF LIFE

The Buddhist goal is the achievement of human perfection, which should be the real purpose of life. It is in this sense that life has meaning, and which should inform the most salient aspects of human activity. A person who has made good progress along the Buddhist path would have reached a high degree of happiness, contentment and freedom from fear. Sometimes material affluence is seen as the goal of many persons, but these do not necessarily bring about the happiness which the Buddha sought to promote.

Many religions look upon the present life as a ground for laying the foundation in a future life after physical death. Some Buddhists also adopt this attitude and try to secure a good rebirth or even *Nibbana* without residue. Exhortations from the Buddha could be produced to this effect. But the Buddha also affirms that we must make use of the present life, of which we are sure, and that the pursuit of the Noble Eightfold Path is the best way of doing so regardless of any consequences that may happen after death.

THE THEORY OF CAUSALITY

One of the central doctrines of Buddhism is that all phenomena owe their origin and existence to pre-conditioning factors. Everything is the result of some cause or other working on the thing concerned. This is a view that is also shared by modern science, for without the operation of systematic causes much of the achievement of modern science may not be possible. But whereas science generally restricts this principle to physical phenomena and events, in Buddhism the theory of causation considers causation as a central characteristic of all phenomena, even non-physical ones which do not form the subject matter of scientific enquiry. The Buddhist theory of causation should be distinguished from the theory of the "First Cause" which is often used by theists to prove the existence of God. The theory of the first cause asserts that since God is identified as the first cause (all others being "created" by God) there is no need to explain the existence of God. Buddhism does not agree with this position and considers it as another instance of sophistry ("eel-wriggling") to which theists resort to sustain their absurd views.

THE DOCTRINE OF DEPENDENT ORIGINATION

This is one of the cardinal discoveries of the Buddha during his enlightenment. It is presented as a list of twelve bases which are causally linked to each other. Since the links from a closed circle we can break into the chain at any point. The order in the traditional list is as follows: (1) Ignorance, (2) Volitional formations (*sankhara),* (3) consciousness, (4) mind-and-form, (5) sense-bases, (6) contact, (7) feeling, (8) craving, (9) clinging, (10) becoming, (11) birth, (12) old-age-and-death. There are various ways of interpreting this chain, but we shall not deal with them here.

The traditional interpretation of this is that it represents three phases often interpreted as lifetimes. The first phase (the past) is comprised of links 1 and 2; the second (the present) of links 3 to 10, and the third (the future) of links 11 and 12. In the ongoing process what if the present becomes and past and what is the future becomes the present. A detailed explication of this famous formula is not attempted here.

EMPTINESS AND NON-SELF .

The doctrine of "emptiness" (sunyata) is more associated with Mahayana than with Theravada. If it represents another term for the *Anatta* doctrine described earlier it presents no new problem. However some Mahayana interpretations tend towards philosophical idealism and towards the Hindu notion that the world is an illusion (maya) but such an interpretation cannot be entertained by Basic Buddhism.

HUMANISM AND RATIONALISM

Basic Buddhism has some affinity with Western notions of humanism and rationalism. However these terms are used in a variety of contexts, with humanism associated with theistic notions on the one hand and extreme secular-materialist notions on the other. But if humanism means what it should mean, that is the primacy of the human as against the Divine, and then it conforms to the Buddhist approach. With rationalism as the application of reason and the scientific method to investigation there is much in common. One of the basic sutta of the Buddha, the Kalama Sutta given in the Anguttara Nikaya is rightly regarded as the Buddhist charter for free inquiry.

THE BUDDHIST PATH

The Buddha's path of practice is called the Noble Eightfold path. The eight components of this path, as presented in traditional order, could be briefly described as follows:

1. Right View (Understanding) - This is the right way of interpreting and viewing the world. It involves the realisation of the three signata in all phenomena, and of the Four Noble Truths as being applicable to the human condition. More generally it involves the abandonment of all dogmatically held wrong views.
2. Right Intention (Thought) - The Buddha argued that all human thought and action spring from basic "intentions", "dispositions", or "roots", which are capable of deliberate cultivation, training and control. The three roots of wrong, unwholesome or "unskilful" action are: Greed, Aversion and Delusion. The right intention which the Buddhist path requires is an intention which is free from these roots. The Buddha called the intention "that is free from greed and lust, free from ill-will, free from cruelty".
3. Right Speech - Since speech is the most powerful means of communication, the Buddha emphasises the cultivation of right modes of speech. These have been described as

avoiding falsehood and adhering to the truth; abstaining from tale-bearing and instead promoting harmony; refraining from harsh language and cultivating gentle and courteous speech; avoiding vain, irresponsible and foolish talk, and speaking in reasoned terms on subjects of value. Naturally right speech includes in the modern context right ways of communication whatever the medium used.

4. Right Action - This refers to wilful acts done by a person, whether by body or mind. Under the former it involves such forms of ethical conduct as not killing (or harming) living beings, theft, sexual wrong-doing, etc. On the positive side right action, also called wholesome deeds (*kusalakamma*), involves acts of loving-kindness (*metta*), compassion (*karuna*), sympathetic joy (*mudita*), generosity (*caga*), etc.
5. Right Livelihood - This involves not choosing an occupation that brings suffering to others, e.g. trading in living beings (including humans), arms, drugs, poisons, etc.; slaughtering, fishing, soldiering, sooth-saying, trickery, usury, etc. This provides the economic blueprint for a truly Buddhist society.
6. Right Effort - This has been described as "the effort of avoiding or overcoming evil and unwholesome things, and of developing and maintaining wholesome things" (Nyanatiloka). Right effort enables an individual to cultivate the right frame of mind in order to accomplish the ethical requirements under right speech, right action and right livelihood. It is generally presented as a factor of mental training, enabling individuals to develop the sublime states of loving-kindness (*metta*) compassion (*karuna*), sympathetic joy (*mudita*), and equanimity (*upekkha*). However it has a general applicability and the effort could be directed to all wholesome activities.
7. Right Mindfulness - This is the basic Buddhist technique of cultivating awareness. The classic sutta on the subject is the satipahana sutta. Although viewed as a meditation component in fact right awareness has a wider applicability.

8. Right Concentration - This is the concentration of mind associated with wholesome consciousness which could be achieved through the systematic cultivation of meditation. Progress along this line is indicated by the achievement of the different levels of "absorption" (*jhanas*).

Of these eight components of the Path, the first two have usually been grouped under wisdom (*panna*), the next three under morality (*sîla*), and the last three under mental development (*bhavana*). This classification is not quite satisfactory, but it does present a broad grouping that is useful in many contexts. The first of these components (right view) is generally considered the most important, but there is no particular order of importance of the path that can be called "meditation". However in course of time the component of mental development came to be regarded as meditation. In view of the importance *Digha Nikaya* to meditation, particularly in Western practice it is necessary to examine this subject in the special subsection. This is done in the following section.

THE ROLE OF MEDITATION

We have seen that the Buddhist path consists of wisdom/ knowledge, ethical conduct, and mental development. Some teachers put an almost exclusive emphasis on the last of these (calling it "meditation") as the route to the other two. Because of the widespread propagation of this view in the West it is worth considering it in some detail. The widely held picture of meditation in the West is one where the meditator sits in silent company, usually in the "lotus position", and is engaged in inward contemplation.

The session may last from a half-hour to several hours. It is generally a congregational activity but it is usually presided over by a teacher who determines the duration of the session and may give directions as to how the activity is to proceed. Practitioners are encouraged to engage in the activity individually at home if congregational meditation is not possible. Often special meditation retreats are held lasting from 3 to 14 days in which up to 12 hours a day may be devoted to meditation activities. Because of the long periods involved sitting meditation is alternated with "walking meditation", sometimes also with yogic exercises.

Often silence is enforced during the retreat (called the Rule of Golden Silence), and the teacher has individual meetings with each participant during which the individual practitioner's "progress" is probed and special instructions given. The teacher is very often looked upon as a "guru" as in the Hindu tradition. This type of meditative exercise is often represented as the exclusive way to "practice" Buddhism. We shall use the term "stylised meditation" to designate this kind of meditation. Meditation on the other hand has always been a valid part of Buddhist practice (note however that is a part, nor the whole of it).

The task is then to differentiate genuine Buddhist meditation from stylised meditation. Buddhist mediation is the practice of the last two components of the eightfold path (*sati* and *samadhi*) in the "right"(*samma*) manner. The Pali term that is used to denote stylised meditation is *bhavana.* This term is not used with great frequency in the Pali Canon and when used is associated with mental development from whatever kind of activity that will improve the mind. Stylised meditation is derived from meditation practices in the principal Asian Theravada countries, viz. Sri Lanka, Burma and Thailand each of which has developed their own meditation traditions.

In spite of the diversity within each country a few broad generalisation may be possible. In Sri Lanka the primary focus of Buddhist practice has been on the cultivation of *panna* and in the development of ethical practice (*sîla*). Meditation has not occupied great prominence and has been undertaken on an individual basis, rarely performed in a congregational setting. In this the Sri Lankan Buddhists have generally followed the instructions on meditation given in the Visuddhimagga of Buddhaghosa which was composed in that country. Where meditation has been used as the principal focus in Sri Lanka it has been practised by reclusive forest monks with little contact with the rest of the *Bhikkhu-Sangha* or the laity.

The country from where stylised meditation was introduced into the West is Thailand. Here the "forest" orders have enjoyed much more status than elsewhere. They tend to look on stylised meditation as the key to the entire Buddhist practice including the achievement of wisdom and morality. This system attaches much importance to the *jhanas* which is considered almost indispensable to enlightenment. There is little attempt at sutta-study except those relating to meditation. While this kind of meditation may suit the lifestyle of forest monks it is their importation into the general community, especially of lay persons, that is questionable. If the Sri Lankan and Thai modes of meditation can be taken as occupying two ends of a spectrum the meditation practice of Burma occupies an intermediate position.

Here meditation is taken more seriously than in the Sri Lankan tradition but some of the excesses of the Thai forest traditions are avoided. Buddhist meditation of whatever type takes two principal forms - the cultivation of calm and tranquillity (*samatha bhavana*) and the cultivation of insight (*vipassana bhavana*). The efficacy of meditation in promoting calm and tranquillity is indisputable. In fact it is for this reason that it is also adopted by some non-Buddhist schemes such as Hinduism and "transcendental meditation". But its use as a method of achieving insight into reality it may be questioned. True insight comes only we understand that the three signata underlie all phenomena.

In meditation one may realise this within in the ambit of ones own experience, but it will not lead one understand the universality of these traits. Thus meditation has to be supplemented by other methods such as the first two components of the Buddhist path. The classic discourse on which the theory of meditation is based is the Satipahana Sutta, which occurs twice in the Canon. Here the Buddha identifies four methods (or foundations) of meditation. These are the contemplation of the body (*kayanupassana*), of feeling (*vedananupassana*), of the mind (*cittanupassana*) and finally that of the *Dhammas* (*Dhammanupassana*).

Some preconditions are laid down in the Sutta before these contemplations are attempted. One is that the practitioner should have "overcome in this world covetousness and discontent" (*vineyya loke abhijja domanassa*). In the case of lay persons this does not require complete withdrawal from the world, but the development of a sufficient degree of detachment from it. The Satipahana cannot be attempted by those completely given to greed. The second is that the contemplations should be done in an empty room (*sunnagara*) or if outdoors at the root of a tree. This rules out the congregational sessions in which stylised meditation takes place.

The contemplation of the body, with the initial focus on the breath, is the initial contemplation that is taught by most teachers. The Buddha used it purely as the starting point of his sequence of contemplations, and he even recommends the "lotus position" in which to undertake the contemplations, which is a classic yogic stance. The Buddha extended the traditional Vedic meditation concerns by extending the contemplation to other physical postures and awareness of other bodily actions, and finally to the contemplation of the foulness of the body. The progress of the meditation from the body to feelings is also relatively easy for many practitioners. The next stage of the contemplation of the mind is relatively more difficult.

The objective here is to achieve one-pointedness of mind. This is relatively difficult because of the propensity of the mind to shift quite fast. The last one requires contemplation of the *Dhammas*. In the Buddha's time when the corpus of *Dhamma* was memorised, this contemplation was the only way of acquiring the knowledge of the *Dhamma*. Today the situation is somewhat different and this particular foundation of mindfulness could be acquired by discursive study. The view that the awakening of wisdom can only come through intense meditation is not only found in schools like Zen but is also held by some teachers of Theravada.

However meditation in Buddhism is primarily a method of mental training. It could be used to calm the mind, to instil tranquillity, and to set the stage for the realisation of true insight. In fact fascination with meditation can be a distraction from the true path. A capable exponent of early Buddhism David Maurice puts this quite well: "There is meditation at the very beginning of the practice but the practice is to get away from meditation". Even though stylised meditation may not be necessary it is necessarily harmful. It could suit the temperament of some people, especially those who desire a strict discipline. On the other hand what we have termed Buddhist meditation is something that anyone can do with profit. It may not lead to the final goal in itself, but it could be a great help in the fulfilment of the other components of the path.

THE BUDDHIST ATTITUDE TO GOD

It is first of all necessary to establish what is meant by the term "God". This term is used to designate a Supreme Being endowed with the qualities of omnipotence and omniscience, who is the creator of the universe with all its contents, and the chief law-giver for humans. God is generally considered as being concerned with the welfare of his human creatures, and the ultimate salvation of those who follow his dictates. God is therefore a person of some kind, and the question whether such an entity exists or not is fundamental to all theistic systems. In contrast to this notion of a personal God some modern theologians have interpreted the term "God" as representing some kind of abstract principle of good (or "ground of being").

This view was first developed in the ancient Indian *Upanishads* where God is equated with an abstract principle (*Brahman*). The ancient Indian philosophers could entertain such a view because they also had a theory of karma which really does away with the need for a personal God. Buddhists too have a theory of karma, which is different from that of the Hindus, and which even more unequivocally dispenses with the need for a Deity. The use of the term "God' to denote an abstract reality by monotheistic theologians who have no theory of karma is difficult to justify; one suspects that this is merely a device to explain away the contradictions that arise from the notion of a personal God. In fact the actual practice of theistic religion proceeds as if God is a real person of some kind or other.

Just as Buddhism rejects the notion of a Supreme God it also rejects the notion of an abstract God-principle operating in the universe. The notion of *Brahman* (in the neuter) is not discussed at all in the Buddhist texts, and even in India it may well be a post-Buddhist development resulting from the attempt to reconcile the belief in God (s) with the powerful critique of the Buddha. It is therefore the attitude of Buddhism to the notion of a supreme personal God animating the Universe that we must consider. One popular misconception of Buddhism must be dismissed at this point. This is view that the Buddha is some kind of God figure.

In the Theravada tradition the Buddha is regarded as a supremely enlightened human teacher who has come to his last birth in samsra (the Buddhist cycle of existence). Even Mahayana traditions which tend to think in terms of transcendental Buddhas do not directly make a claim for Buddha as God. Thus the Buddha cannot be considered as playing a God-like role in Buddhism. In the Buddhist texts Maha Brahma is the equivalent of God and is represented as claiming the following attributes for himself: "I am Brahma, the Great Brahma, the Supreme One, the Mighty, the All-seeing, the Ruler, the Lord of all, the Maker, the Creator, the Chief of all appointing to each his place, the Ancient of days, the Father of all that is and will be."

The Buddha dismisses all these claims of Maha Brahma as being due to his own delusions brought about by ignorance. Maha-Brahma is seen simply a *deva* unenlightened and subject to the samsric process as determined by his kamma (cf the Brahmajla and the Agganna Suttas). In the Khevadda Sutta he is forced to admit to an inquiring monk that he is unable to answer a question that is posed to him, and advises the monk to consult the Buddha. This clearly shows the Brahm acknowledges the superiority of the Buddha. In the West a number of "arguments" have been adduced to prove or disprove the existence of God. Some of these were anticipated by the Buddha.

One of the most popular is the "first cause" argument according to which everything must have a cause, and God is considered the first cause of the Universe. The Buddhist theory of causation says that every thing must have preconditions for its existence, and this law must also extend to "God" should such an entity exist. But while the "first cause" claims that God creates everything, it exempts God from the ambit of this law. However if exemptions are made with respect to God such exemptions could be made with respect to other things also hereby contradicting the principle of the first cause.

But the argument which the Buddha most frequently uses is what is now called the "argument from evil" which in the Buddhist sense could be stated as the argument from *Dukkha* (suffering or unsatisfactoriness). This states that the empirical fact of the existence of *Dukkha* cannot be reconciled with the existence of an omnipotent and omniscient being that is also all good. The Buddha argues that the three most commonly given attributes of God, viz. omnipotence, omniscience and benevolence towards humanity cannot all be mutually compatible with the existential fact of *Dukkha*.

THE BUDDHIST ATTITUDE TO MAN

In considering the Buddhist view of man we are essentially looking at the psychological postulates of Buddhism which has sometimes been described as a psychological system. Given the meaning normally *Digha Nikaya* to Psychology this is too narrow a description of psychology. Buddhism deals with many other matters which are not normally included in psychology. But there is a psychological dimension to Buddhism. This is because of the great concern which Buddhism has with the mind and with the training of the mind. In this sense Buddhism is unique amongst the world religions. The first stanza of the well-known book of Buddhist aphorisms the *Dhammapada* sums up very well the primacy that Buddhism gives to the mind:

Monopubbagama Dhamma manoseha manomaya

Manasa ça paduhena bhasati va karoti va

Tato na Dukkhamanvet cakka va vahato pada

Mind is the forerunner of all states, mind-based and mind-made are they

If one speaks or acts with an evil mind

Suffering results, just as the wagon wheel follows the ox drawing it

Similarly good thoughts lead to good actions.

Most religious systems decompose the individual into a body and a soul. In this division the body includes what Buddhists (and modern psychologists) would regard as the mind. Very often in this scheme the mind is located in the heart. There is no location given for the soul. It is in fact a mysterious entity created by God. While the physical body perishes at death the soul goes either to Heaven or to Hell where it is reunited with a body (perhaps similar to the old one) and continues its existence as one of sensuous conform or of torment depending on the destination.

The Buddha dispensed with this scheme which was similar to the system advocated in the old Vedas. Instead the Buddha identified five constituents of the empirical person, the first of which (*rûpa*) was physical and the last four (collectively called *nama*) were mind components. These five components have been called Groups of existence or Five Aggregates (*pancakkhanda*). These are:

1. Corporeality (*rûpa*). This is the physical basis of existence. The five sense organs (eye, ear, nose, tongue and body) are especially important in generating the various signals which are processed by the mind (which is also recognised as an organ in is own right).
2. Feeling (*vedana*). Feelings are a by-product of the contact between the organs of the physical body and the external world. They are classified in various ways - wholesome

and unwholesome, gross and subtle, painful and pailful, etc.

3. Perception (*sanna*). This is how the mind processes the feelings that its sense organs transmit. No two individuals have the same perception of the same feelings they may experience.
4. Formations (*sankhara*). The formations are the deliberative acts of the individuals. it is often referred to as karmic formations.
5. Consciousness (*vinnana*). This is the condition of being aware of the environment in which the individual exists.

While corporeality is readily understood the other four components are more subtle. Three of these, viz. feeling, perception and consciousness, are known to modern psychological science, and the Buddhist interpretation does not differ substantially from the scientific one. But the concept of "formations" is not known to modern psychology. At the same time there is nothing in conventional psychology that denies its existence. Here the Buddhist view transcends that of the conventional analysis of mental components.

KNOWLEDGE, WISDOM AND ENLIGHTENMENT

The Buddha traced the root cause of suffering to ignorance; so the search for enlightenment is the supreme activity for the Buddhist. The activity proceeds at both the intellectual and the intuitive levels. Pure intellectual understanding is not sufficient, although it is often a very good starting point. When enlightenment is attained pure intellectual understanding is transcended by an intuitive grasp of the truths of the Universe. If knowledge is the outcome of "intellectual" activity, a person's fund of knowledge at any moment of time is made up of a number of beliefs that he considers valid.

The Buddha was quite clear on what he considered legitimate to believe in. In his discourse to the Kalamas (a people who were confused by the diversity of viewpcints they were confronted with) the Buddha said:

"Come, O Kalamas, do not accept anything from mere hearsay, or from what you have been told, or because it is mentioned in sacred teachings, or because of logic merely, or because of its methods, or in consideration of plausible reasoning, or by tolerating views based on speculation, or because of its appearance of its possibility and because `your teacher is venerable'. But when you, Kalamas, realize by yourself that views are unwholesome, faulty, condemned by the wise, and that they lead to harm and misery when practised and observed, then Kalamas, you should reject them".

This is the criterion of acceptability which the Buddha wanted to apply to all claims, including his own. In Buddhism there cannot be room for blind faith, and all propositions, religious or otherwise should be subjected to analysis and practice. The reference to "mere logic" and "plausible reasoning" in the quotation given serves as a caution concerning some extreme forms of "rationalism" which argue that "pure reason" is sufficient to establish the truth of metaphysical propositions (like that of the existence of God). Deductive methods are useful, but as they can only bring out what is already contained in the premises of the argument, they cannot be used as a vehicle for the discovery of new truths. Rightly has the Kalamasutta been termed the Buddhist charter of free enquiry?

As a result of the Buddha's rational and tolerant attitude early Buddhism never had concepts like heresy, apostasy and blasphemy (and this is true of all subsequent Buddhist schools). In many theistic systems imprisonment, torture and death have been inflicted on people who have refused to bow before dogma. In Buddhist epistemology three levels of understanding are recognised. These are (using the Pali terminology): *Ditthi* ("views"), *nana* ("science"), and *bodhi* ("wisdom"). *Ditthi* refers to views accepted more or less dogmatically. Not all such beliefs are necessarily harmful, because some people could be motivated to act wholesomely even though motivated by incorrect views. But more usually such "views" can be extremely harmful.

The Buddha did not consider knowledge consisting of *Ditthi* to be useful in the longer term. *Ditthi* is often contrasted with scientifically based knowledge, which results from thinking, from learning and from mental development. This is usually terms *nana* or *panna*. The acquisition of this kind of knowledge is useful, and is not discouraged; but it alone will not lead to enlightenment. This is clearly seen in the case of many eminent scientists, who have progressed far in the acquisition of particular kinds of knowledge, but have not been able to outgrow the dogmatic views inculcated in early childhood.

True enlightenment can arise out of the third kind of knowledge, consisting of wisdom (*bodhi*) and insight (*vipassana*). This results from the intuitive realisation of the Buddhist laws and truths after the successful traverse of the Middle Path. The enlightenment process involves the breaking of the ten fetters (*sayojana*) that bind people to the phenomenal world. These are the five lower fetters of personality belief, sceptical doubt, clinging to rite and ritual, sensuous craving and ill-will, and the five higher fetters of craving for "fine material" existence, craving for "immaterial existence", conceit, restlessness, and ignorance.

THE DOCTRINES OF KARMA AND REBIRTH

The Buddhist doctrine of kamma [karma] ("deeds", "actions"), and the closely related doctrine of rebirth, is perhaps the best known, and often the least understood, of Buddhist doctrines. The matter is complicated by the fact that the other Indian religious traditions of Hinduism and Jainism have their own theories of Karma and Reincarnation. It is in fact the Hindu versions that are better known in the West. The Buddhist theory of *kamma* (to give the Pali word) and rebirth are quite distinct from their other Indian counterparts. In Buddhism the law of kamma is the moral law of causation - good actions give good results and vice versa.

It is the quality of an act which determines its consequences. But what determines the karmic quality of a deed? In Hinduism it is the correct performance of a person's "duty", especially his caste duties that counts. Early Buddhism, which recognised no caste distinctions, evaluates the karmic quality of an act in terms of moral and ethical criteria. In particular it is the mental factors which accompany the commission of deed that determines its consequences or "fruits" (*vipaka*). All negative kamma (i.e. those leading to bad consequences) arise from the three roots of unwholesomeness. These are greed (*lobha*), aversion (*dosa*), and delusion (*moha*). Accordingly good kammic results follow from deeds that spring from generosity (*raga*), loving-kindness (*metta*) and wisdom (*vijja*).

The Buddha emphasised that it is the mental factors involved, rather than the deeds themselves, that determine future consequences. Thus the same deed committed with different mental factors will have different consequences. Likewise purely accidental deeds *may* have neutral consequences; however if the accident occurred because insufficient mindfulness was exercised it could have adverse results for the person responsible for it. The theory of kamma presupposes that individuals have "free will". Everything that happens to an individual is not the fruit of some past kamma. In fact the experiences that involve an individual may be of three kinds: some are the result of past action, some are deliberately committed free acts; and the remainder could be due to chance factors operating in the environment.

The doctrine of kamma is not a theory of predestination of any kind. One common misunderstanding is not to distinguish between the action and its results - between *kamma* and *vipaka*. It must also be mentioned that the fruiting of an act may be postponed, and that it is possible to reach enlightenment - the goal of the Buddha's path - before all the previous *kammas* have yielded their results. The Buddhist theory of rebirth asserts that the fruits of some kamma may manifest themselves in "future lives". This brings us to the Buddhist theory of rebirth. Similar concepts occur in other religious systems - e.g. the Platonic theory of the "pre-existence of the soul" and the Hindu-Jain theory of re-incarnation. Such reincarnation theory involves the transmigration of a soul. In Buddhism, however, it is the unripened karmic acts outstanding at the death of an individual which conditions a new birth.

The last moment of consciousness too is also a conditioning factor, but it is the store of unripened kamma generated by volitional acts (the *sankharas*) of previous existences which generates the destiny of the new individual. A newly born individual needs not only the genetic blueprint derived from the genes of the natural parents, but also a kammic blueprint derived from the volitional acts of a deceased person. The question has been posed whether the new individual is the same as the old individual whose kamma it has inherited. The Buddha's answer to this question was somewhat enigmatic: "It is not the same, yet it is not another" (*na ca so, na ca anno*). To understand the Buddha's reply we have to investigate the criteria which establish personal identity. Is the child the same as the adult it later becomes? In the Buddhist sense we are making two observations at two points of time in a constantly changing psycho-physical entity.

For legal and conventional purposes some arbitrary criteria are used, such as physical continuity over time, or the retention of memory. These define only a conventional person. Just as it is a conventional or "fictional" person who lasts continuously from birth to death, so it is just such a conventional person who persists from one life to another. In the Buddhist view of rebirth the only links between two successive lives is the karmic residue carried over and an element of consciousness, called the re-linking consciousness: (*paisandhi vinnana*), which momentarily links the two lives. In Buddhism there is no conception of a transmigrating soul which inhabits successive material bodies until it unites with God.

Buddhism uses the Pali term *sasara* to denote the "round of births" in various planes of existence governed by the law of kamma. The acceptance of the validity of the hypothesis of sasara is very difficult for some people, while for others it is the most natural of hypotheses. Some features of the observable world suggest it. In the Culakammavibhanga Sutta the Buddha is asked: "What are the reason and the cause for the inequality amongst human beings despite their being human?" (The context making it clear that it is inequality at birth that is meant). The Buddha answered: "Beings inherit their kamma, and it is kamma which divides beings in terms of their inequality". The theistic hypothesis cannot give a rational answer, except in terms of an iniquitous and unjust "God".

Some support for the theory of rebirth comes from reports of recollections of past lives, whether spontaneously or under hypnosis, which have been reported from all parts of the world. While many such reports may be mistaken or even fraudulent, some are undoubtedly genuine. According to Buddhism individuals can develop the power of "retrocognition" (i.e. the ability to recall past lives), but the development of such supernormal powers is usually the accompaniment of progress along the spiritual path of enlightenment. IT may be possible that some karmic factors may predispose some individuals towards such experiences.

However parapsychological experimentation is still in its early stages, and many people have no personal recollection of their own previous lives. For such individuals the dogmatic acceptance of the doctrines of kamma and rebirth is not expected. The central tenets of Buddhism relate not to any abstract theories about rebirth or karma but to the interpretation of human experience which is within the capacity of every person to verify. This verification can be undertaken, not in terms of an abstract cycle of lives, but also in terms of the one life we are all familiar with. The Buddhist *sasara* is to be seen in every moment of existence, as well as the whole "cycle of births".

One would expect that in the Kalama Sutta, the discourse in which the Buddha decries the acceptance of theories on the basis of authority (which was quoted earlier), that he would address himself to the question of belief in the doctrine of kamma and rebirth. This he does. Referring to the "four-fold confidences" which the "noble person" (*ariya puggala*), i.e. the person who follows the path of the Buddha, attains to, the Buddha states:

"`If there is the other world and if there is the fruit and result of good and bad deeds, then there is reason that I shall be reborn into the state of bliss, the celestial world, on the dissolution of the body, after death.' This is the first confidence that he attains.

"`If, however, there is no other world and if there is no fruit and no result of good and bad deeds, then I shall myself lead he a happy life, free from enmity, malice and suffering in this very life'. This is the second confidence that he attains."

Thus even the extreme rationalist who would suspend judgement on the truth of the sasaric hypothesis (i.e. the doctrines of karma and rebirth) would find that the Buddha-*Dhamma* would not have lost its rationale. He can aspire to the second confidence of the "noble person" and make the one life that he is sure of, a happy one.

BUDDHIST COSMOLOGY AND NIBBANA

The Buddhist scriptures contain a cosmology of the Universe which provide an interesting contrast to the cosmologies of other religions (e.g. that of the Bible) and even the modern scientific cosmology (on which there is no complete agreement). The cosmological claims in the Buddhist scriptures should not be seen as an accurate description of the physical universe, but as establishing the stage on which the great sasaric drama is enacted. While considering this cosmology we may also consider the important concept of *Nibbana* which is the state of final release. The latter term is better known in its Sanskrit version as "Nirvana". We shall use the Pali term because the concept of Nirvana is also used in other Indian religions notably Jainism.

We may first consider the planes of existence which form the arenas for samsaric existence. The number of planes recognised depends on the fineness with which they are classified. In the earlier more succinct listing only 3 states of existence are mentioned. These are:

1. The sensuous realm (*kama loka*). This is the physical world as accessible to be person who entirely on the physical stimuli, without subjecting these stimuli to a refined degree of conscious mental processing.
2. The fine-material realm (*rupa loka*). This is the same physical world as it is perceived by the active meditator.
3. The immaterial world (*arupa loka*). This is the physical world as it is apprehended by the advanced meditator who realises the "emptiness" of the phenomena that assail the senses of the ordinary person.

The last two realms of existence are meditative stages. In the Buddhist literature there are other ways of classifying meditative states, including some such as those that are induced by *vipassana* (insight) meditation which differ is some details from the *aurpa-loka*, but we need not be concerned here; they are dealt with fully in manuals dealing with Buddhist meditation. The two contemplative states of existence are subjective and would not fall into what is considered by cosmology in the modern scientific sense. Some consider the realm of *Nibbana* as also falling into the "meditative states", but this is regarded as something completely outside all planes of existence The first realm, the *kama-loka,* clearly deals with actual realms of existence, which is the only realm for those not subject to some degree of enlightenment, and even in the case of the latter still provides the physical dimension of existence.

It is this realm that could be compared to other cosmologies, whether held by scientists or religionists or ordinary people. A word may be said about the Buddhist views on the phenomenal worlds which constitute the arenas of sasaric existence, and of the concept of *Nibbana* [Nirvana] (the state of final release) which is the antithesis of sasara. These views contained in early Buddhist writings should not be looked upon as dogmas whose acceptance is expected of Buddhists. Many of them are beyond the capacity of unenlightened people to verify. Some of them are burrowed from the prevailing cosmological views in the India of the Buddha's time, and would have been used by the Buddha as illustrations to clarify his own theories.

In the Pali literature five "planes of existence" characterised in varying degrees of unsatisfactoriness are recognised. These are (in increasing order of "suffering"): (1) the sphere of the plane of the *devas* ("shining beings" often translated as "gods"); (2) humans; (3) The spirit world; (4) the animal world; (5) the lower world (duggati, niraya) often translated as "hells". According to the law of kamma beings could be born into any of these planes of existence, but the sojourn in any of these destinations is never permanent. There is no necessary "progression" from the lower to the higher levels. The cycle of rebirth in these various states of existence could be terminated only on the achievement of *Nibbana* (which itself is not included in the sasaric planes). *Nibbana,* the final liberation, can only be achieved by beings in the first two planes of existence, but more usually only by humans.

In some of the earliest strata in the Pali Canon only three spheres of existence are recognised. These are: (1) the sensuous world (*kama loka*); (2) the fine material world (*rûpa loka*); and (3) the immaterial world (*arûpa loka*). Here the "sensuous world" comprises all the realms of physical existence, and the other two correspond to states of meditation. In the later literature (especially in the *Abhidhamma*), the "planes of existence" are further subdivided, and some 32 planes of existence are recognised. There are three ways of interpreting these "planes of existence":

1. They could be actual physical locations somewhere in the physical universe.
2. They could be forms of psycho-physical existence which could be reached from any given physical location depending on mental disciplines exercised.
3. Some states belong to the first type and others to the second type.

The earliest interpretation leans towards the second given above, but the 32-fold classification favoured by many modern exponents of Buddhism leans towards the third, which of course implies that some states must correspond to the first. This raises the question of Buddhist cosmology on which something needs to be said. In terms of physical location the planes of existence could be located anywhere in the Universe. That the Buddhist view of the physical world is not much different from that of modern science is brought out clearly in this quotation:

"As far as these suns and moons revolve shedding their light in space, so far extends the thousand-fold universe. In it there are thousands of suns, thousands of moons, thousands of inhabited worlds of varying sorts.... This is the thousand-fold minor world system (*culanika lokadhatu*). Thousands times the size of the thousand-fold minor world system is the twice-a-thousand Middling World System (*Majjima lokadhatu*). Thousands of times the size of the Middling World System is the thrice-a-thousand Great Cosmos (*maha lokadhatu*)."

With such a multiplicity of inhabited worlds it is possible to interpret the planes of existence in realistic terms. But the interpretation in terms of psychological and meditation states may be the more appropriate. Heavens and hells are not specific locations with pleasant or unpleasant experiences, but they could be experienced even in the human earthly form. The claim that "devas" exist should not be taken as a concession to theism. Even though this term is commonly translated as "gods" it does not imply the existence of divine authority. The devas are a category of beings, subject to their own *kammas* formations and reverting to human or other form after the expiry of their *kammas*, and quite incapable of granting concessionary prayers addressed to them.

In the Buddhist scheme all of the leading deities of the Hindu pantheon, including Maha Brahma, the "creator" of the universe in the Hindu scheme, are reduced to the status of devas with only a transient existence in the deva-sphere. This treatment of the powerful Gods of the Brahmanical system, to whom the sacrifices and prayers of the system were directed, instead of being a support of theism was a powerful critique of this system. As against the varied planes of sasaric existence the Buddha postulated the existence of a state called *Nibbana* [nirvana] which serves as the *summum bonum* of Buddhism. This, the most difficult of Buddhist concepts, cannot really be grasped unless some considerable progress has been made on the Buddhist path. It is usually described in negative terms.

It is the "Unborn, Unoriginated, Uncreated, Unformed"; it is the complete annihilation of all defilement; it is the complete destruction of the five components of beings; it is a situation where no *kammas* are being formed or previous *kammas* fruited; it is the extinction of the three roots of unwholesome action (greed, aversion and delusion); it is the end of rebirth itself. Two misconceptions of nirvana may be mentioned - one, entertained by the materialist, is that it implies nothingness; the other, entertained by the theist, is that it involves merger with a higher entity. The Buddha answered both questions "Does the arahant exist after death?" and "Does the arahant not exist after death?" It is only the limitation of our conceptualisation process that leads us to pose such questions.

Sometimes a distinction is made between "sasaric Buddhism" and "nibbanic Buddhism". It is claimed that in the former the aim is improvement in sasara, while in the latter it is the attainment of *Nibbana.* It is also claimed that the former should be the aim of the lay Buddhist and the latter that of the Buddhist monk. However even in the Buddha's day many monks did not attain *Nibbana,* while there was never advanced the claim that a lay person could not attain to the nibbanic state. The true position is that each person should proceed along the Buddhist path according to his own capacities and priorities.

The lay person is neither at a disadvantage nor at an advantage relative to the monk (*Bhikkhu*) when it comes to the question of progress along the path. The lay Buddhist and the *Bhikkhu,* because of their differing life styles, will apply the

Dhamma to different areas. In particular the lay person can engage in activity aimed at the social and economic upliftment of suffering humanity to a greater extent than the *Bhikkhu*, while the latter will concentrate more on personal advancement through the development of meditation and the keeping of the strict moral code expected of the *Bhikkhu Sangha*.

BUDDHISM AND THE MODERN WORLD

The Buddha delivered the fundamental principles of *Dhamma* some 2500 years ago. Initially it spread over most of Asia in some form or other, but since then it has been declining until it now has much less adherents than the other main religions. There have also been many changes in several other areas and it might to appropriate to consider the Buddhist position with regard to some of them.

THE DHAMMA AND THEISTIC RELIGION

Theism essentially means the service of an unseen God. Since this God never addresses individuals directly, but through "prophets" there has never been a shortage of the latter. And when the rival prophets make irreconcilable and conflicting claims, and impose mutually inconsistent rites, rituals, and codes of behaviour on their followers, it is not difficult to see in these a potent cause of conflict. Indeed a large part of the violence and crimes we see in history has been caused by the attempt of the followers of one "prophet of God" to impose dominion over those of another.

In the modern world the bulk of the people owe formal allegiance to Christianity and Islam, religions which arose long after the death of the Buddha. They are offshoots of another religion Judaism which has remained confined to a small ethnic group. All three religions affirm the existence of an all-powerful creator God. The Buddha had long ago repudiated the notion of a supreme creator God.

Both Christianity and Islam have been fundamentally intolerant religions dedicated to the goal of converting others, and persecuting those of different faiths. In the last century or so, Christianity has been forced to give up some of its traditional methods of persecution but it has not abandoned its evangelical zeal. Islam continues very much in the way it has even though conquest by the sword is becoming less easy. As a result of these attitudes Buddhism has not been able to penetrate into those countries where Christianity and Islam have established themselves historically. Buddhists should seek to spread its message of religious tolerance and the peaceful dialogue between religions. Whether it will succeed in this has still to be seen.

THE DHAMMA AND MATERIALISM

The great development in the last century has been the rise of materialism. Quite apart from philosophical system that have extolled materialism there has also been a growth of materialist objectives in many people. Philosophical materialism may not be very detrimental to Buddhism because much of the argument which materialists have directed at religion has been against theistic religion. However political movements which have formally proclaimed materialism as their creed have acted against religions, and Buddhism has suffered perhaps relatively more from such movements.

What is unsatisfactory if philosophical materialism is that it often denies the existence of absolute, objective moral standards? Buddhism of course insists on the existence of such a moral code. The failure of materialism is been mainly due to its lack of a universal norm of goodness, truth and justice. The increase in the materialist motivation of people has been seen even in people who would consider themselves as being religious. Where this leads to an increase in greed it would reduce the ability of these people to practice Buddhist values. However Buddhism is not against the growth of material affluence provided that it results from the pursuit of right livelihood. But much of the pressures that result from the scamble to reach the top of the economic pile often lead to an abandonment of the principles of right livelihood.

The growing conflicts of the modern world arise from a continuous proliferation of greed and craving. The ethical systems of both the leading forms of theism and materialism encourage and endorse this tendency by giving a license to humans to prevail over other forms of life, and encouraging the "prudent" and ceaseless accumulation of material wealth as an individual and social blessing. While such ethical systems may have given a measure of material affluence to their followers, this material gain has been at the cost of seriously heightening conflict within these societies as well as in the world at large, even endangering the very future of mankind itself. The Buddhist ethic, which involves the pursuit of a middle policy, by dampening the acquisitive instinct, could offer mankind with a viable and more appropriate alternative.

THE DHAMMA AND SCIENCE

The *Dhamma* is closely related to what is understood by Science or Philosophy. Science investigates the nature of phenomena, and some of the latest discoveries in the areas of the physical and the psychological sciences are in conformity with Buddhist principles. However Science has a self-imposed limitation - it has no procedure to move from the positive to the normative. The *Dhamma* can make this transition, and thus has the ability to transcend Science. It is also in this sense that the *Dhamma* can be considered a Philosophy. However a substantial part of philosophy in the west since the time of Aristotle has been concerned with metaphysical speculation. The Buddha however looked on most such metaphysical speculations as being baseless and unprofitable, and very often a cloak for ignorance.

An outstanding feature of the modern world has been the triumph of science and the explosion of knowledge. These have posed a serious challenge to theistic religion. Many of the dogmas that lie at the basis of revelatory religions have been exploded by scientific developments. While one section of theists have been busy in reinterpreting the old dogmas in "metaphysical" terms (a hopeless task as it has proven to be), and other group of "fundamentalists" have turned their backs on scientific discovery and by boldly using modern methods of propaganda and psychological conditioning have tried to reassert the old dogmas in all their simplicity.

These developments have raised the real possibility of a return to the "dark ages". Materialism seems to have been better in coping with scientific discovery, but has been totally helpless in evaluating correctly the uses to which such discovery has to be put. Buddhism on the other hand has been able to reconcile scientific discovery with its basic laws, and the path of practice that Buddhism proclaims has provided a norm for the optimal use of man's ever increasing knowledge. For neither the Buddhist there is no conflict between the claims of science and religion (as there is for the theist) nor a quandary as to how knowledge could be applied for the betterment of man (as it is for both the materialist and the theist).

BUDDHISM AND HUMANISM

The primary appeal of Buddhism was to the dignity of man, not the glory of God. In this sense the *Dhamma* is primarily a humanistic philosophy. In describing Buddhism as humanism some care must be taken in defining the latter term. Theists have defined humanism broadly as embracing "any attitude exalting man's relationship to God, his free will, and his superiority over nature". Such definitions leave out an essential quality of humanism, viz. the primacy of man and the inconsequence of God. There is no implication in Buddhism that human beings have some prior claim over other forms of living beings, or for that matter over "nature", as is implied in the definition of humanism quoted. Buddhists however hold that of all forms of existence possible, the human form is the one most conducive to deliverance.

These aspects of Buddhist humanism make the *Dhamma* once again unique. Another aspect of Buddhist humanism is that it makes an individual the master of his own destiny. On his death-bed when asked by his followers as to whom they should follow when he was gone, the Buddha replied: "Be ye a lamp (*dîpa*) unto yourselves; work out your own salvation with diligence". The Pali word *dîpa* also means an island, and the Buddha's final exhortation could also be rendered as "Be ye an island unto yourselves..." etc. In either case the fundamental idea is that of self-reliance rather than reliance on an external agency.

The *Dhamma*, as could be reconstructed from the Pali Canon remains the source of the Buddha-word. The follower of the Buddha would need to understand this, if need be with the help of a teacher but be alone has to practice it. In this respect it may be mentioned that the Mahayana Schools of Buddhism have introduced the notion of salvation by the grace of beings called "*Bodhisattvas* ", i.e. beings who have achieved enlightenment but postponed their entry into Nirvana in order to help others to get there through their grace. This notion is foreign to early Buddhism or to present-day Theravada Buddhism.

THE RELEVANCE OF BUDDHISM

In the modern world Buddhism has to contend with two broad alternatives to itself. These are theism and materialism. Paradoxically the Buddha had to contend with the very same ideologies in his own day. And now as then Buddhism offers the better alternative for the realisation of the greater happiness of all beings inhabiting the world (and not just humans alone). The relevance of Buddhism for the contemporary era would depend on its ability to meet the challenges posed by the contemporary world better than the rival ideologies of theism and materialism and very often a combination of the two.

The unbridled exploitation of the earth's resources, almost amounting to a rape of these resources, has been another example of this greed. Buddhism teaches that man should live in harmony with the Universe. We have seen the extinction of many species of birds, animals and fish, and the threat of extermination of many more, because of the dominance of theistic and materialistic ethics, which has consistently refused to conceded the "right to life" to non-human forms of existence.

It is only a step from this position to the exploitation of natural resources to the extent that eco-systems have been destroyed beyond repair, and has put into question the long-term possibility of survival.

The lack of tolerance of diverging viewpoints has been one of the most potent causes of misery and war. Even though we would like to think that the worst excesses of sectarian conflict are behind us, we have no real ground to such optimism. The world needs a measure of Buddhist tolerance. It has been said that the flavour of the *Dhamma* is the flavour of freedom (*vimutti*). The freedom that is meant here is primarily the freedom of the mind unburdened by crippling dogma (be they of ego or of God); but such mental freedom is the basis of all other freedom, even those of the more "worldly" kind, like political, social or economic freedom.

In a world where freedom is constrained in many ways the liberating effect of the *Dhamma* is sorely needed. True freedom cannot be attained until the mind is set free. The *Dhamma* actually provides a therapy for the freeing of the mind from mental defilement. Modern society seems to have aggravated rather than lessened the need for mental purification and calm. The pace of change has quickened, and external pressure on individuals increased. A balanced mind, created by a true understanding of the world and man's place in it, coupled with the practice of the Buddha's path, could serve as a radical new therapy.

The importance of the Buddhist principle that a person should be free to believe according to one's freely formed and informed opinions, can hardly be overstated. The current practice of indoctrinating children with the religious views of their parents is one that comes to mind. Many religious organisations carry this process into formal schooling, and reinforce it later by using the latest technology of the information revolution. It then becomes a veritable "brain-washing" no less insidious because it has the full approval of the establishment.

The right of a child to have its mind free of religious indoctrination until it can made a decision on this vital matter in full maturity with all the information at its command, is a right that is rarely mentioned, but one in which Buddhists can take a lead. Basic Buddhism is relevant for the problems of modern society in several other ways. But it must be remembered that the traditional practices of Buddhism in several of its schools, including to some extent in the Theravada tradition, departs considerably from the principles enunciated by the Buddha. Here too what is needed is a return to the principles and practice of basic Buddhism.

2

Early Buddhism

Buddhism is a religion based on the teachings of Siddhârth Gautam Buddh, who lived between 566 and 486 BCE. Originating in India, Buddhism gradually spread throughout Asia to Central Asia, Sri Lanka, Tibet, Southeast Asia, as well as the East Asian countries of China, Mongolia, Korea, Japan, Vietnam, Cambodia and Laos. With over 375 million followers, Buddhism is a major world religion. The aim of Buddhist practice is to end the suffering of cyclic existence, *samsara* (Pali, Sanskrit), by awakening the practitioner to the realization of true reality, the achievement of liberation nirvana and Buddhahood.

To achieve this, one should act according to the laws of Karma: perform positive wholesome actions, avoid negative harmful actions, and purify and train the mind. Buddhist morality is underpinned by the principles of harmlessness and moderation. Mental training focuses on moral discipline (*sila*), meditative concentration (*samadhi*), and wisdom (*prajnâ*).

Buddh, (known as Buddha in the western world), is a word in ancient Indian languages including Pâli and Sanskrit which means "one who has awakened". It is derived from the verbal root "budh", meaning "to awaken" or "to be enlightened". The word "Buddha" denotes not just Siddhartha Gautama, but a type of person, of which there have been infinite ones throughout the course of cosmic time. The historical Buddha is simply one member in the spiritual lineage of Buddhas. A Buddha is anyone who has fully awakened to the true nature of existence, liberated from the cycle of birth, death and rebirth, has eradicated all negative qualities and developed all positive qualities, including omniscience.

The principles by which a person can achieve enlightenment are known as the Buddhadharma, or simply the Dharma, meaning (in this context) "law, doctrine, or truth". Legend has it that Buddha was born around the 6th century BCE. His birthplace is said to be Lumbini in the Shâkya state, one of a small group of old Hindu oligarchic republics. His father was a (Hindu) king, and Siddhârtha lived in luxury, being spared all hardship. A a seer predicted that Siddhartha would become either a great king or a great holy man; because of this, the king tried to make sure that Siddhartha never had any cause for dissatisfaction with his life, as that might drive him toward a spiritual path.

Nevertheless, at the age of 29, he came across four sights; an old crippled man, a sick man, a decaying corpse, and finally a wandering holy man. These four sights led him to the realization that birth, old age, sickness and death come to everyone, not only once but repeated for life after life in succession since beginningless time. He decided to abandon his worldly life, leaving behind his wife, child and rank, etc. to take up the life of a wandering holy man in search of the answer to the problem of birth, old age, sickness, and death. Indian holy men (*sâdhus*) often engaged in a variety of ascetic practices designed to "mortify" the flesh. It was thought that by enduring pain and suffering, the *âtman* or "soul" became free from the cycle of rebirth. Siddhârtha proved adept at these practices, and was able to surpass his teachers. He and a small group of companions set out to take their austerities even further.

After nearly starving himself to death with no success, Siddhârtha began to reconsider his path. Taking a little buttermilk from a passing goatherd, he found a large tree (now called the Bodhi tree) and set to meditating. He developed a new way of meditating, which began to bear fruit. His mind became concentrated and pure, and then, six years after he began his quest, he attained Enlightenment, and became a Buddha. It is said that after his enlightenment, the Buddha was wondering whether or not he should teach the Dharma.

He was concerned that, as human beings were overpowered by greed, hatred and delusion, they wouldn't be able to see the true Dharma which was subtle, deep and hard to understand. A god, Brahma Sahampati, however, interceded, and asked that he teach the Dharma to the world. With his great compassion, the Buddha agreed to become a teacher. At the Deer Park near Benares in north India he delivered his first sermon to the group of five companions with whom he sought for enlightenment before. They, together with Buddha, formed the first *Sangha*, the company of Buddhist monks. It has also been advanced that the influence of Jain culture and philosophy in ancient Bihar gave rise to Buddhism. Buddhist scriptures describe various penances (tapas) undertaken by Gautama Siddhartha which appear identical to Jain penances. Buddhist writings reflect that Jainism was an already established faith- rather than a newly founded or reformist one- by the time Buddha lived. The Majjhima Nikaya relates instances of Buddha seeking converts from the apparently sizeable Nigantha (Jain) community. Both philosophies continue to share similar Prakrit terminology for important themes and teachings.

PRINCIPLES OF BUDDHISM

Buddhists seek refuge in what are often referred to as the Three Jewels. These are the Buddha, the Dharma (or *Dhamma*), and the "Arya" (noble) *Sangha* or community of monks and nuns. While it is impossible to escape one's Karma or the effects caused by previous thoughts, words and deeds, it is possible to avoid the suffering that comes from it by becoming enlightened. In this way, dharma offers a refuge. In all forms of Buddhism, refuge in the Three Jewels is taken before the *Sangha* for the first time, as a part of the conversion ritual. The main goal of Buddhism is to escape from the suffering of cyclic existence.

The Four Noble Truths: The Buddha taught that life was dissatisfactory because of craving, but that this condition was curable by following the Eightfold Path. This teaching is called the Four Noble Truths:

- *Dukkha*: All worldly life is unsatisfactory, disjointed, containing suffering.
- Samudaya: There is a cause of suffering, which is attachment or desire (*tanha*) rooted in ignorance.
- Nirodha: There is an end of suffering, which is Nirvana.
- Marga: There is a path that leads out of suffering, known as the Noble Eightfold Path.

Noble Eightfold Path: In order to fully understand the noble truths and investigate whether they were in fact true, Buddha recommended that a certain lifestyle or path be followed which consists of:

- Right Understanding
- Right Thought
- Right Speech
- Right Action
- Right Livelihood
- Right Effort
- Right Mindfulness
- Right Concentration

The Eightfold Path essentially consists of meditation, following the precepts, and cultivating the positive converse of the precepts (e.g. benefiting living beings is the converse of the first precept of harmlessness). The Path may also be thought of as a way of developing Sîla, meaning mental and moral discipline.

The Five Precepts: Buddhists undertake certain precepts as aids on the path to coming into contact with ultimate reality. Laypeople generally undertake five precepts. These are:

- To refrain from harming living creatures (killing).
- To refrain from taking that which is not freely given (stealing).

- To refrain from sexual misconduct.
- To refrain from incorrect speech (lying, harsh language, slander, idle chit-chat).
- To refrain from intoxicants which lead to loss of mindfulness.

One of the distinguishing features of the Buddhist precepts is that they are wider-ranging in implication than the "commandments" of some other religions. The first precept, against killing, for example, forbids the killing of animals as well as humans. In some schools of Buddhism, serious lay people or aspiring monks take an additional three to five ethical precepts, and some of the five precepts are strengthened. Fully ordained monks and nuns of the Theravada school also vow to follow the 227 patimokkha rules. Fully ordained Mahayana monks and nuns follow 348 equivalent rules with an additional set of, generally, 41 *bodhisattva* vows.

According to the Buddhist tradition, all phenomena (dharmas) are marked by three characteristics, sometimes referred to as the Dharma Seals:

Anatta: In Indian philosophy, the concept of a self is called *âtman* (that is, "soul" or metaphysical self), which refers to an unchanging, permanent essence conceived by virtue of existence. This concept and the related concept of Brahman, the Vedantic monistic ideal, which was regarded as an ultimate *âtman* for all beings, were indispensable for mainstream Indian metaphysics, logic, and science. The Buddha however emphasized changeability and not permanence.

He taught that all concepts of a substantial personal self were incorrect, and formed in the realm of ignorance. But in a number of Mahayana sutras, the Buddha is presented as saying that, while the *skandhas* (constituents of the ordinary body and mind) are not the Self, there does truly exist an eternal, unchanging, blissful Buddha-essence in all sentient beings, which is the uncreated and deathless Buddha-nature ("Buddha-dhatu") or "True Self" of the Buddha himself. This immaculate Buddhic Self (*Atman*) is in no way to be construed as a mundane, impermanent, suffering "ego", of which it is the diametrical opposite.

The *Nikâyas* and *Âgamas* scriptures are ambivalent with regard to the Buddha's views on the existence or otherwise of a permanent self (*âtman/atta*). Though he is clearly reported to have criticized many of the heterodox concepts concerning an eternal personal self and to have denied the existence of an eternal self with regards to any of the constituent elements (*skandha*) of a being, nevertheless he is not reported to have explictly denied the existence of a non-personal, permanent self, contrary to the popular, orthodox view of the Buddha's teachings. Moreover, when the Buddha predicates "anâtman" (*Anatta*) with regards to the constituents of a being, there is a grammatical ambivalence in the use of the term.

Anicca: All compounded phenomena (things and experiences) are inconstant, unsteady, and impermanent. Practically everything is made up of parts, and is dependent on the right conditions for its existence. Everything is in constant flux, and so conditions and the thing itself are constantly changing. Things are constantly coming into being, and ceasing to be. Nothing lasts.

Dukkha: Because we fail to truly grasp the first two conditions, we suffer. We desire lasting satisfaction and happiness, but look for it amongst constantly changing phenomena. We perceive a self, and act to enhance that self by pursuing pleasure, and seek to prolong pleasure when the self too is a fleeting phenomenon.

BUDDHA-DHATU ("BUDDHA-PRINCIPLE", BUDDHA-NATURE).

The Buddha's Mahayana doctrines contain a set of "ultimate" (*nitartha*) teachings on the immanence of a hidden core Reality within all sentient beings which is linked to the eternality of the Buddha and Nirvana. This immanent yet transcendent essence is variously called, in the key *Tathagatagarbha* sutras which expound it, the Buddha-dhatu ("Buddha-element", Buddha-nature) or the *Tathagatagarbha*.

This Buddha-dhatu is empty of all that is contingent, painful and impermanent. In the Nirvana Sutra, it is called by the Buddha the "True Self" (to distinguish it from the "false" worldly self of the five *skandhas*).

OTHER PRINCIPLES AND PRACTICES .

Meditation or dhyâna of some form is a common practice in most if not all schools of Buddhism, for the clergy if not the laity. Central to Buddhist doctrine and practice is the law of karma and *Vipaka;* action and its fruition, which happens within the dynamic of dependent origination (*pratîtya-samutpâda*). Actions which result in positive retribution (happiness) are defined as skillful or good, while actions that produce negative results (suffering) are called unskillful actions. These actions are expressed by the way of mind, body or speech.

Some actions bring instant retribution while the results of other actions may not appear until a future lifetime. Rebirth is closely related to the law of Karma. An action in this life may not give fruit or reaction until the next life time. This being said, action in a past life takes effect in this one, making a chain of existence. The full realization of the absence of an eternal self or soul breaks this cycle of birth and death (*samsara*).

THE THREE MAIN BRANCHES OF BUDDHISM .

Buddhism has evolved into myriad schools that can be roughly grouped into three types: Nikaya (also called Hinayana), Mahayana, and Vajrayana. Of the Nikaya schools, only the Theravada survives. Each branch sees itself as representing the true, original teachings of the Buddha, and some schools believe that the dialectic nature of Buddhism allows its format, terminology, and techniques to adapt over time in response to changing circumstances, thus validating dharmic approaches different from their own.

Although Buddhists concur that taking refuge should be undertaken with proper motivation and an understanding of the objects of refuge, the Indian scholar Atisha identified that in practice there are many different motives found for taking refuge. His idea was to use these different motivations as a key to resolving any apparent conflicts between all the Buddha's teachings without depending upon some form of syncretism that would cause as much confusion as it attempted to alleviate.

The various motives for taking refuge are enumerated as follows, typically introduced using the concept of the "scope" (level of motivation) of a practitioner:

- Worldly scope: to improve the lot of this life - this is not a Buddhist motivation.
- Low scope: to gain high rebirth and avoid the low realms.
- Middle scope: to achieve Nirvana (liberation from rebirth).
- High scope: to achieve Buddhahood in order to liberate others from suffering, the basis of the Mahayana path.

Highest scope is also sometimes included: to achieve Buddhahood as soon as possible - in this life - which is the scope of the highest teachings on the Vajrayana (tantric) path. The Theravada school, whose name means "Doctrine of the Elders", bases its practice and doctrine exclusively on the Pali Canon, which is a collection of what are known as agamas or nikaya sutras. The nikaya sutras are generally considered by modern scholars to be the oldest of the surviving types of Buddhist literature, and they are accepted as authentic in every branch of Buddhism.

Theravada is the only surviving representative of the historical Nikaya branch. Nikaya Buddhism and consequently Theravada are sometimes referred to as Hinayana or "small vehicle", although this is considered by some to be impolite. Native Theravada is practiced today in Sri Lanka, Myanmar, Laos, Thailand, Cambodia and portions of China, Vietnam, and Malaysia. The aim of Nikaya Buddhism is to achieve liberation from rebirth and thus Nirvana.

The Mahâyâna branch emphasizes universal compassion and the selfless ideal of the *bodhisattva*, whose goal is to achieve Buddhahood in order to be of greatest benefit to other sentient beings. In addition to the Nikaya scriptures, Mahâyâna schools recognize all or part of a genre of scriptures that were first put in writing around 1 CE.

These scriptures were written in some form of Sanskrit, except a few manuscripts in Prakrit, and are concerned with the purpose of achieving Buddhahood by following the path of the *bodhisattva* over the course of what is often described as countless eons of time. Because of this immense timeframe, some Mahâyâna schools accept the idea of working towards rebirth in a Pure Land. The Pure Land is normally conceived of as a state which is not enlightenment in itself but which is a highly conducive environment for working toward enlightenment, although some sources indicate that it is synonymous with enlightenment. Native Mahâyâna Buddhism is practiced today in China, Japan, Korea, and most of Vietnam.

The Vajrayâna or "Diamond Vehicle" (also referred to as Mantrayana, Tantrayana, Tantric or esoteric Buddhism) shares the basic concepts of Mahâyâna, but also includes a vast array of spiritual techniques designed to enhance Buddhist practice. Vajrayana Buddhism exists today in the form of two major sub-schools: Tibetan Buddhism and Shingon Buddhism. One component of the Vajrayâna is harnessing psycho-physical energy as a means of developing profoundly powerful states of concentration and awareness.

These profound states are in turn to be used as an efficient path to Buddhahood. In addition to the Theravada and Mahâyâna scriptures, Vajrayâna Buddhists recognise a large body of texts that include the Buddhist Tantras. Native Vajrayana is practiced today mainly in Tibet, Nepal, Bhutan, Mongolia, Leh, Lahaul & Spiti and Sikkim in India, Kalmykia (in Russia), Siberia (in Russia), and - among the Shingon and Tendai schools - in China and Japan.

BUDDHISM AFTER THE BUDDHA .

Buddhism spread slowly in India until the powerful Mauryan emperor Asoka converted to it and actively supported it. His promotion led to construction of Buddhist religious sites and missionary efforts that spread the faith into the countries listed at the beginning of the chapter. After about 500 CE, Buddhism showed signs of waning in India, becoming nearly extinct after about 1200 CE. This was due to Hinduism's revival movements such as Advaita and the rise of the bhakti movement. Some areas of India never parted from Buddhism, including Ladakh and other areas bordering the Tibetan, Nepali and Bhutanese borders.

In China and Japan, it adopted aspects of the native beliefs of Confucianism, Taoism and Shinto respectively. In Tibet, the Tantric Vajrayana lineage was preserved after it disappeared in India. It is said that Kanishka gathered 500 monks, headed by Vasumitra, primarily; it seems, to compile extensive commentaries on the Abhidharma. Scholars believe that it was also around this time that a significant change was made in the language of the Sarvâstivâdin canon, by converting an earlier Prakrit version into Sanskrit.

This event was of particular significance since Sanskrit was the learned language of scholars in India, regardless of their specific religious or philosophical allegiance, thus enabling a far wider audience to gain access to Buddhist ideas and practices. For this reason, all major Buddhist scholars in India thereafter wrote their commentaries and treatises in Sanskrit. Around the 1st century, Buddhism spread from India through successive waves of merchants and pilgrims. It reached as far as Turkmenistan and Arabia to the west, and eastward to Southeast Asia, where the first records of Buddhism date from around 400.

Mahayana Buddhism established a major regional center in what is today Afghanistan, and from there it spread to China, Korea, Mongolia, Japan and Vietnam. In 475, the Indian monk Bodhidharma traveled to China and established the Chan (Chinese; Japanese: Zen), school. During the first millennium, monks from China made pilgrimages to India and wrote accounts of their travels when they returned home. These Chinese travel records constitute extremely valuable sources for information concerning the state of Buddhism in India during the early medieval period.

Vajrayana also evolved at this stage carried from India to Tibet from around 800 by teachers such as Padmasambhava and Atisha. There it initially coexisted with native belief systems such as Bön, but later came to largely supplant or absorb them. An early form of esoteric Vajrayana known as Shingon was also transmitted by the priest Kûkai to Japan, where it continues to be practiced.

There is an active debate as to whether or not Tantrism was initially developed within Buddhism or Hinduism. Buddhist literature tends to predate the later puranic Tantras, and there is some evidence to suggest that the basic structure of tantra depends upon the Mahayana Buddhist philosophical schools. However, it is thought by others that meditative Shiva sects seem to have existed from pre-Vedic times; also, from scriptural citations and study of the Vedas, some say Tantra saw its philosophical basis in the mystical rites and mantras of the Atharva Veda (and later the Hindu Upanishads and Mahayana school of Buddhism).

SCRIPTURES .

The Buddhist canon of scripture is known in Sanskrit as the Tripitaka and in Pâli as the Tipitaka. These terms literally mean "three baskets" and refer to the three main divisions of the canon, which are:

The *Vinâya Pitaka*, containing disciplinary rules for the *Sangha* of Buddhist monks and nuns, as well as a range of other texts which explain why and how rules were instituted, supporting material, and doctrinal clarification. The *Sutta Pitaka* (Pâli; Sanskrit: Sutra Pitaka), containing discourses of the Buddha. The *Abhidhamma* (Skt: Abhidharma) or commentary Pitaka, containing a philosophical systematization of the Buddha's teaching, including a detailed analysis of Buddhist psychology. During the first few centuries after Gautama Buddha, his teachings were transmitted orally, but around the 1st Century CE they began to be written down. The most notable set of texts from the early period is the Pali Canon, which was preserved in Sri Lanka by the Theravâda school. The sutras it contains are also part of the canon of every other Buddhist sect.

Mahâyâna tradition brought with it a collection of new texts, composed in Buddhist Hybrid Sanskrit, many of which were also described as actual sermons of the Buddha. These include the Perfection of Wisdom Sutras, the AvataCsaka, the Lotus Sutra, the Vimalakîrti Sutra, and the Nirvana Sutra. A detailed compilation of Mahayana works is found in the Tibetan canon. This is split into those texts attributed to be authored by the Buddha (Kanjur), and those texts which are understood to be commentaries by Indian practitioners (Tenjur). Vajrayâna practitioners also study the Buddhist Tantras.

Buddhism arose in northeastern India sometime between the late 6th century and the early 4th century BCE, a period of great social change and intense religious activity. There is disagreement among scholars about the dates of the Buddha's birth and death. Many modern scholars believe that the historical Buddha lived from about 563 to about 483 BCE. Many others believe that he lived about 100 years later (from about 448 to 368 BCE). At this time in India, there was much discontent with Brahmanic (Hindu high-caste) sacrifice and ritual. In northwestern India there were ascetics who tried to create a more personal and spiritual religious experience than that found in the Vedas (Hindu sacred scriptures).

In the literature that grew out of this movement, the Upanishads, a new emphasis on renunciation and transcendental knowledge can be found. Northeastern India, which was less influenced by the Aryans who had developed the main tenets and practices of the Vedic Hindu faith, became the breeding ground of many new sects. Society in this area was troubled by the breakdown of tribal unity and the expansion of several petty kingdoms. Religiously, this was a time of doubt, turmoil, and experimentation.

A proto-Samkhya group (i.e., one based on the Samkhya school of Hinduism founded by Kapila) was already well established in the area. New sects abounded, including various skeptics (e.g., Sanjaya Belatthiputta), atomists (e.g., Pakudha Kaccayana), materialists (e.g., Ajita Kesakambali), and antinomians (i.e., those against rules or laws - e.g., Purana Kassapa). The most important sects to arise at the time of the Buddha, however, were the Ajivikas (Ajivakas), who emphasized the rule of fate (*niyati*), and the Jains, who stressed the need to free the soul from matter. Although the Jains, like the Buddhists, have often been regarded as atheists, their beliefs are actually more complicated.

Unlike early Buddhists, both the Ajivikas and the Jains believed in the permanence of the elements that constitute the universe, as well as in the existence of the soul. Despite the bewildering variety of religious communities, many shared the same vocabulary - *nirvana* (transcendent freedom), *Atman* ("self" or "soul"), *yoga* ("union"), *karma* ("causality"), *Tathagata* ("one who has come" or "one who has thus gone"), *buddha* ("enlightened one"), *samsara* ("eternal recurrence" or "becoming"), and *Dhamma* ("rule" or "law") - and most involved the practice of yoga. According to tradition, the Buddha himself was a yogi - that is, a miracle-working ascetic.

Buddhism, like many of the sects that developed in northeastern India at the time, was constituted by the presence of a charismatic teacher, by the teachings this leader promulgated, and by a community of adherents that was often made up of renunciant members and lay supporters. In the case of Buddhism, this pattern is reflected in the Triratna - i.e., the "Three Jewels" of Buddha (the teacher), *dharma* (the teaching), and *Sangha* (the community). In the centuries following the founder's death, Buddhism developed in two directions represented by two different groups.

One was called the Hinayana (Sanskrit: "Lesser Vehicle"), a term given to it by its Buddhist opponents. This more conservative group, which included what is now called the Theravada (Pali: "Way of the Elders") community, compiled versions of the Buddha's teachings that had been preserved in collections called the *Sutta Pitaka* and the *Vinaya Pitaka* and retained them as normative. The other major group, which calls itself the Mahayana (Sanskrit: "Greater Vehicle"), recognized the authority of other teachings that, from the group's point of view, made salvation available to a greater number of people. These supposedly more advanced teachings were expressed in sutras that the Buddha purportedly made available only to his more advanced disciples.

As Buddhism spread, it encountered new currents of thought and religion. In some Mahayana communities, for example, the strict law of karma (the belief that virtuous actions create pleasure in the future and nonvirtuous actions create pain) was modified to accommodate new emphases on the efficacy of ritual actions and devotional practices. During the second half of the 1st millennium CE, a third major Buddhist movement, Vajrayana (Sanskrit: "Diamond Vehicle"), or Esoteric Buddhism, developed in India. This movement was influenced by gnostic and magical currents pervasive at that time, and its aim was to obtain spiritual liberation and purity more speedily.

Despite these vicissitudes, Buddhism did not abandon its basic principles. Instead, they were reinterpreted, rethought, and reformulated in a process that led to the creation of a great body of literature. This literature includes the Pali *Tipitaka* ("Three Baskets") - the *Sutta Pitaka* ("Basket of Discourse"), which contains the Buddha's sermons; the *Vinaya Pitaka* ("Basket of Discipline"), which contains the rule governing the monastic order; and the *Abhidhamma Pitaka* ("Basket of Special [Further] Doctrine"), which contains doctrinal systematizations and summaries.

These Pali texts have served as the basis for a long and very rich tradition of commentaries that were written and preserved by adherents of the Theravada community. The Mahayana and Vajrayana/Esoteric traditions have accepted as Buddhavacana ("the word of the Buddha") many other sutras and tantras, along with extensive treatises and commentaries based on these texts. Consequently, from the first sermon of the Buddha at Sarnath to the most recent derivations, there is an indisputable continuity - a development or metamorphosis around a central nucleus - by virtue of which Buddhism is differentiated from other religions.

THE LIFE OF THE BUDDHA

The teacher known as the Buddha lived in northern India sometime between the mid-6th and the mid-4th centuries before the Common Era. In ancient India the title *Buddha* referred to an enlightened being that has awakened from the sleep of ignorance and achieved freedom from suffering. According to the various traditions of Buddhism, Buddhas have existed in the past and will exist in the future. Some Buddhists believe that there is only one Buddha for each historical age, others that all beings will become Buddhas because they possess the Buddha nature (*Tathagatagarbha*).

The historical figure referred to as the Buddha (whose life is known largely through legend) was born on the northern edge of the Ganges River basin, an area on the periphery of the ancient civilization of North India, in what is today southern Nepal. He is said to have lived for 80 years. His family name was Gautama (in Sanskrit) or Gotama (in Pali), and his given name was Siddhartha (Sanskrit: "he who achieves his aim") or Siddhatta (in Pali). He is frequently called Shakyamuni, "the sage of the Shakya clan." In Buddhist texts he is most commonly addressed as Bhagavat (often translated as "Lord"), and he refers to himself as the *Tathagata,* which can mean both "one who has thus come" and "one who has thus gone."

Traditional sources on the date of his death - or, in the language of the tradition, his "passage into nirvana" - range from 2420 to 290 BCE. Scholarship in the 20th century limited this range considerably, with opinion generally divided between those who believed he lived from about 563 to 483 BCE and those who believed he lived about a century later. Information about his life derives largely from Buddhist texts, the earliest of which were produced shortly before the beginning of the Common Era and thus several centuries after his death.

According to the traditional accounts, however, the Buddha was born into the ruling Shakya clan and was a member of the Kshatriya, or warrior, caste. His mother, Maha Maya, dreamt one night that an elephant entered her womb, and 10 lunar months later, while she was strolling in the garden of Lumbini, her son emerged from under her right arm. His early life was one of luxury and comfort, and his father protected him from exposure to the ills of the world, including old age, sickness, and death.

At age 16 he married the princess Yashodhara, who would eventually bear him a son. At 29, however, the prince had a profound experience when he first observed the suffering of the world while on chariot rides outside the palace. He resolved then to renounce his wealth and family and live the life of an ascetic. During the next six years, he practiced meditation with several teachers and then, with five companions, undertook a life of extreme self-mortification. One day, while bathing in a river, he fainted from weakness and therefore concluded that mortification was not the path to liberation from suffering.

Abandoning the life of extreme asceticism, the prince sat in meditation under a tree and received enlightenment, sometimes identified with understanding the Four Noble Truths. For the next 45 years, the Buddha spread his message throughout northeastern India, established orders of monks and nuns, and received the patronage of kings and merchants. At the age of 80, he became seriously ill. He then met with his disciples for the last time to impart his final instructions and passed into nirvana. His body was then cremated and the relics distributed and enshrined in stupas (funerary monuments that usually contained relics), where they would be venerated.

The Buddha's place within the tradition, however, cannot be understood by focusing exclusively on the events of his life and time (even to the extent that they are known). Instead, he must be viewed within the context of Buddhist theories of time and history. Among these theories is the belief that the universe is the product of karma, the law of the cause and effect of actions. The beings of the universe are reborn without beginning in six realms as gods, demigods, humans, animals, ghosts, and hell beings. The cycle of rebirth, called *samsara* (literally "wandering"), is regarded as a domain of suffering, and the Buddhist's ultimate goal is to escape from that suffering.

The means of escape remains unknown until, over the course of millions of lifetimes, a person perfects himself, ultimately gaining the power to discover the path out of *samsara* and then revealing that path to the world. A person who has set out to discover the path to freedom from suffering and then to teach it to others is called a *bodhisattva.* A person who has discovered that path, followed it to its end, and taught it to the world is called a Buddha. Buddhas are not reborn after they die but enter a state beyond suffering called nirvana (literally "passing away"). Because Buddhas appear so rarely over the course of time and because only they reveal the path to liberation from suffering, the appearance of a Buddha in the world is considered a momentous event.

The story of a particular Buddha begins before his birth and extends beyond his death. It encompasses the millions of lives spent on the path toward enlightenment and Buddhahood and the persistence of the Buddha through his teachings and his relics after he has passed into nirvana. The historical Buddha is regarded as neither the first nor the last Buddha to appear in the world. According to some traditions he is the 7th Buddha, according to another he is the 25th, and according to yet another he is the 4th. The next Buddha, Maitreya, will appear after Shakyamuni's teachings and relics have disappeared from the world.

Sites associated with the Buddha's life became important pilgrimage places, and regions that Buddhism entered long after his death - such as Sri Lanka, Kashmir, and Burma (now Myanmar) - added narratives of his magical visitations to accounts of his life. Although the Buddha did not leave any written works, various versions of his teachings were preserved orally by his disciples. In the centuries following his death, hundreds of texts (called sutras) were attributed to him and would subsequently be translated into the languages of Asia.

THE BUDDHA'S MESSAGE

The teaching attributed to the Buddha was transmitted orally by his disciples, prefaced by the phrase "evam me sutam" ("thus have I heard"); therefore, it is difficult to say whether or to what extent his discourses have been preserved as they were spoken. They usually allude to the place and time they were preached and to the audience to which they were addressed. Buddhist councils in the first centuries after the Buddha's death attempted to specify which teachings attributed to the Buddha could be considered authentic.

SUFFERING, IMPERMANENCE, AND NO-SELF

The Buddha based his entire teaching on the fact of human suffering and the ultimately dissatisfying character of human life. Existence is painful. The conditions that make an individual are precisely those that also give rise to dissatisfaction and suffering. Individuality implies limitation; limitation gives rise to desire; and, inevitably, desire causes suffering, since what is desired is transitory. Living amid the impermanence of everything and being themselves impermanent, human beings search for the way of deliverance, for that which shines beyond the transitoriness of human existence - in short, for enlightenment.

The Buddha's doctrine offered a way to avoid despair. By following the "path" taught by the Buddha, the individual can dispel the "ignorance" that perpetuates this suffering. According to the Buddha of the early texts, reality, whether of external things or the psychophysical totality of human individuals, consists of a succession and concatenation of microelements called *Dhammas* (these "components" of reality are not to be confused with *Dhamma* meaning "law" or "teaching"). The Buddha departed from traditional Indian thought in not asserting an essential or ultimate reality in things.

Moreover, he rejected the existence of the soul as a metaphysical substance, though he recognized the existence of the self as the subject of action in a practical and moral sense. Life is a stream of becoming, a series of manifestations and extinctions. The concept of the individual ego is a popular delusion; the objects with which people identify themselves - fortune, social position, family, body, and even mind - are not their true selves. There is nothing permanent, and, if only the permanent deserved to be called the self, or *Atman*, then nothing is self.

To make clear the concept of no-self (*anatman*), Buddhists set forth the theory of the five aggregates or constituents (*khandhas*) of human existence: (1) corporeality or physical forms (*rupa*), (2) feelings or sensations (*vedana*), (3) ideations (*sanna*), (4) mental formations or dispositions (*sankhara*), and (5) consciousness (*vinnana*). Human existence is only a composite of the five aggregates, none of which is the self or soul. A person is in a process of continuous change, and there is no fixed underlying entity.

KARMA

The belief in rebirth, or *samsara*, as a potentially endless series of worldly existences in which every being is caught up was already associated with the doctrine of karma (Sanskrit: *karman*; literally "act" or "deed") in pre-Buddhist India, and it was accepted by virtually all Buddhist traditions. According to the doctrine, good conduct brings a pleasant and happy result and creates a tendency toward similar good acts, while bad conduct brings an evil result and creates a tendency toward similar evil acts. Some karmic acts bear fruit in the same life in which they are committed, others in the immediately succeeding one, and others in future lives that are more remote. This furnishes the basic context for the moral life.

The acceptance by Buddhists of the teachings of karma and rebirth and the concept of the no-self gives rise to a difficult problem: how can rebirth take place without a permanent subject to be reborn? Indian non-Buddhist philosophers attacked this point in Buddhist thought, and many modern scholars have also considered it to be an insoluble problem. The relation between existences in rebirth has been explained by the analogy of fire, which maintains itself unchanged in appearance and yet is different in every moment - what may be called the continuity of an ever-changing identity.

THE FOUR NOBLE TRUTHS

Awareness of these fundamental realities led the Buddha to formulate the Four Noble Truths: the truth of misery (*Dukkha*), the truth that misery originates within us from the craving for pleasure and for being or nonbeing (*samudaya*), the truth that this craving can be eliminated (*nirodhu*), and the truth that this elimination is the result of following a methodical way or path (*magga*).

THE LAW OF DEPENDENT ORIGINATION

The Buddha, according to the early texts, also discovered the law of dependent origination (*paticca-samuppada*), whereby one condition arises out of another, which in turn arises out of prior conditions. Every mode of being presupposes another immediately preceding mode from which the subsequent mode derives, in a chain of causes. According to the classical rendering, the 12 links in the chain are: ignorance (*avijja*), karmic predispositions (*sankharas*), consciousness (*vinnana*), form and body (*nama-rupa*), the five sense organs and the mind (*salayatana*), contact (*phassa*), feeling-response (*vedana*), craving (*tanha*), grasping for an object (*upadana*), action toward life (*bhava*), birth (*jati*), and old age and death (*jaramarana*). According to this law, the misery that is bound with sensate existence is accounted for by a methodical chain of causation. Despite a diversity of interpretations, the law of dependent origination of the various aspects of becoming remains fundamentally the same in all schools of Buddhism.

THE EIGHTFOLD PATH

The law of dependent origination, however, raises the question of how one may escape the continually renewed cycle of birth, suffering, and death. It is not enough to know that misery pervades all existence and to know the way in which life evolves; there must also be a means to overcome this process. The means to this end is found in the Eightfold Path, which is constituted by right views, right aspirations, right speech, right conduct, right livelihood, right effort, right mindfulness, and right meditational attainment.

NIRVANA

The aim of Buddhist practice is to be rid of the delusion of ego and thus free oneself from the fetters of this mundane world. One who is successful in doing so is said to have overcome the round of rebirths and to have achieved enlightenment. This is the final goal in most Buddhist traditions, though in some cases (particularly though not exclusively in some Pure Land schools in China and Japan) the attainment of an ultimate paradise or a heavenly abode is not clearly distinguished from the attainment of release.

The living process is again likened to a fire. Its remedy is the extinction of the fire of illusion, passions, and cravings. The Buddha, the Enlightened One, is one who is no longer kindled or inflamed. Many poetic terms are used to describe the state of the enlightened human being - the harbour of refuge, the cool cave, the place of bliss, the farther shore.

The term that has become famous in the West is *nirvana,* translated as passing away or dying out - that is the dying out in the heart of the fierce fires of lust, anger, and delusion. But nirvana is not extinction, and indeed the craving for annihilation or nonexistence was expressly repudiated by the Buddha. Buddhists search for salvation, not just nonbeing. Although nirvana is often presented negatively as "release from suffering," it is more accurate to describe it in a more positive fashion: as an ultimate goal to be sought and cherished.

In some early texts the Buddha left unanswered certain questions regarding the destiny of persons who have reached this ultimate goal. He even refused to speculate as to whether fully purified saints, after death, continued to exist or ceased to exist. Such questions, he maintained, were not relevant to the practice of the path and could not in any event be answered from within the confines of ordinary human existence.

Indeed, he asserted that any discussion of the nature of nirvana would only distort or misrepresent it. But he also asserted with even more insistence that nirvana can be experienced - and experienced in the present existence - by those who, knowing the Buddhist truth, practice the Buddhist path.

THE CULTURAL CONTEXT

Buddhism arose in northeastern India sometime between the late 6th century and the early 4th century BCE, a period of great social change and intense religious activity. There is disagreement among scholars about the dates of the Buddha's birth and death. Many modern scholars believe that the historical Buddha lived from about 563 to about 483 BCE. Many others believe that he lived about 100 years later (from about 448 to 368 BCE). At this time in India, there was much discontent with Brahmanic (Hindu high-caste) sacrifice and ritual. In northwestern India there were ascetics who tried to create a more personal and spiritual religious experience than that found in the Vedas (Hindu sacred scriptures).

In the literature that grew out of this movement, the Upanishads, a new emphasis on renunciation and transcendental knowledge can be found. Northeastern India, which was less influenced by the Aryans who had developed the main tenets and practices of the Vedic Hindu faith, became the breeding ground of many new sects. Society in this area was troubled by the breakdown of tribal unity and the expansion of several petty kingdoms. Religiously, this was a time of doubt, turmoil, and experimentation.

A proto-Samkhya group (i.e., one based on the Samkhya school of Hinduism founded by Kapila) was already well established in the area. New sects abounded, including various skeptics (e.g., Sanjaya Belatthiputta), atomists (e.g., Pakudha Kaccayana), materialists (e.g., Ajita Kesakambali), and antinomians (i.e., those against rules or laws - e.g., Purana Kassapa). The most important sects to arise at the time of the Buddha, however, were the Ajivikas (Ajivakas), who emphasized the rule of fate (*niyati*), and the Jains, who stressed the need to free the soul from matter. Although the Jains, like the Buddhists, have often been regarded as atheists, their beliefs are actually more complicated.

Unlike early Buddhists, both the Ajivikas and the Jains believed in the permanence of the elements that constitute the universe, as well as in the existence of the soul. Despite the bewildering variety of religious communities, many shared the same vocabulary - *nirvana* (transcendent freedom), *Atman* ("self" or "soul"), *yoga* ("union"), *karma* ("causality"), *Tathagata* ("one who has come" or "one who has thus gone"), *Buddha* ("enlightened one"), *samsara* ("eternal recurrence" or "becoming"), and *Dhamma* ("rule" or "law") - and most involved the practice of yoga. According to tradition, the Buddha himself was a yogi - that is, a miracle-working ascetic.

Buddhism, like many of the sects that developed in northeastern India at the time, was constituted by the presence of a charismatic teacher, by the teachings this leader promulgated, and by a community of adherents that was often made up of renunciant members and lay supporters. In the case of Buddhism, this pattern is reflected in the Triratna - i.e., the "Three Jewels" of Buddha (the teacher), *dharma* (the teaching), and *Sangha* (the community). In the centuries following the founder's death, Buddhism developed in two directions represented by two different groups.

One was called the Hinayana (Sanskrit: "Lesser Vehicle"), a term given to it by its Buddhist opponents. This more conservative group, which included what is now called the Theravada (Pali: "Way of the Elders") community, compiled versions of the Buddha's teachings that had been preserved in collections called the *Sutta Pitaka* and the *Vinaya Pitaka* and retained them as normative. The other major group, which calls itself the Mahayana (Sanskrit: "Greater Vehicle"), recognized the authority of other teachings that, from the group's point of view, made salvation available to a greater number of people.

These supposedly more advanced teachings were expressed in sutras that the Buddha purportedly made available only to his more advanced disciples. As Buddhism spread, it encountered new currents of thought and religion. In some Mahayana communities, for example, the strict law of karma (the belief that virtuous actions create pleasure in the future and nonvirtuous actions create pain) was modified to accommodate new emphases on the efficacy of ritual actions and devotional practices.

During the second half of the 1st millennium CE, a third major Buddhist movement, Vajrayana (Sanskrit: "Diamond Vehicle"), or Esoteric Buddhism, developed in India. This movement was influenced by gnostic and magical currents pervasive at that time, and its aim was to obtain spiritual liberation and purity more speedily. Despite these vicissitudes, Buddhism did not abandon its basic principles. Instead, they were reinterpreted, rethought, and reformulated in a process that led to the creation of a great body of literature.

This literature includes the Pali *Tipitaka* ("Three Baskets") - the *Sutta Pitaka* ("Basket of Discourse"), which contains the Buddha's sermons; the *Vinaya Pitaka* ("Basket of Discipline"), which contains the rule governing the monastic order; and the *Abhidhamma Pitaka* ("Basket of Special [Further] Doctrine"), which contains doctrinal systematizations and summaries. These Pali texts have served as the basis for a long and very rich tradition of commentaries that were written and preserved by adherents of the Theravada community.

The Mahayana and Vajrayana/Esoteric traditions have accepted as Buddhavacana ("the word of the Buddha") many other sutras and tantras, along with extensive treatises and commentaries based on these texts. Consequently, from the first sermon of the Buddha at Sarnath to the most recent derivations, there is an indisputable continuity - a development or metamorphosis around a central nucleus - by virtue of which Buddhism is differentiated from other religions.

3

The Development of Nikaya Buddhism

For decades, eminent scholars such as Etienne Lamotte and Hirakawa Akira have greatly contributed to our understanding of Mahayana and to the elucidation of its often nebulous origins. However, more recent scholarship has shown that some of their conclusions might have proven indefinite, if not premature. In chapter sixteen of his work, A History of Indian Buddhism from Sakyamuni to Early Mahayana, Hirakawa argues for an originally lay this-wordly, and socially distinct Mahayana Buddhism, and for its stemming from three sources: Nikaya Buddhism, biographies of the Buddha, and lay-administered stupa worship.

While some truth might underlie Hirakawa's enunciated sources of Mahayana, they fail to adequately support his claims that the "Greater Vehicle" was essentially mundane, non-sectarian and lay-oriented. As shall be demonstrated, the situation from which Mahayana arose was not as one-sided as Hirakawa would have it.

Hirakawa's first lists Nikaya Buddhism as one of the origins of Mahayana Buddhism, but he seems to treat both types of Buddhism as separate socio-religious entities. An alternate, some might say more accurate way of approaching the situation would consist in viewing Mahayana as a pan-Buddhist movement, thus pervading all of Nikaya Buddhism.

As Harrison would put it, "all ordained Mahayanists were members of a nikaya, but not all nikaya members were Mahayanists". This would explain the different sectarian influences which one observes when studying the spectrum of Mahayana scriptures.

Hirakawa alludes to this point with reference to transpiring Sarvastivada, Sammatiya and particularly Mahasanghika teachings in Mahayana sutras, but he fails to properly elaborate on the matter. Instead, he resorts to classifying the relation between Nikaya and Mahayana Buddhism as "clearly not a simple one". Hirakawa regards the early Mahayana following as an entity that is relatively distinct from Nikaya Buddhism, and secondly, as a predominantly lay entity.

Numerous scholars, including Etienne Lamotte, have refuted the first clause and its associated implication of a Mayayana-Hinayana divide. For example, Paul Harrison writes that rather than considering Nikaya Buddhism as one of the origins of the Mahayana, he would rather call it its "matrix," thereby postulating a much more intimate and permanent relationship (1995: 59). He goes on to say that there is no strong textual support to uphold the view of Hinayana versus Mahayana friction. Already, Hirakawa's qualification of Mahayana as a lay, this-wordly, and altruistic tradition opposed to a more eremitic, clerical Hinayana tradition concerned with the salvation of one's own salvation looses its footing: its very conceptual framework, which resides in dualistic categorisations, seems inadequate.

Mahayana Buddhism did not develop as an independent sect; rather, it grew within the very bosom of (often monastic) religious communities. If there is to be a cleavage at all, it should therefore be interpreted as a spiritual or doctrinal one rather than a social one. The subject of the disparities between lay and monastic thus becomes a less pressing one. In fact, it is a "non-issue" and as Gombrich argues, if the vision of an organised and distinct order of Mahayanists is a hallucination, there is no need for us to investigate its fictitious historical roots. Whether or not this so-called movement arose out of the lay-administered worship of stupas is impertinent. Nonetheless, this question shall be addressed because of the important volume of debate that has focused on it.

The second clause of Hirakawa's argument, namely that early Mahayana was predominantly of lay character, is another point of contention on which critics have been particularly vociferous. This topic is most comfortably discussed in the context of Hirakawa's third source of Mahayana Buddhism, stupa worship. But before embarking on this discussion, which will constitute the bulk of this effort, it is noteworthy to mention that Hirakawa's second source has been met, at least to my less than exhaustive knowledge, with little resistance. Hirakawa purports that although a great deal of the biographies of the Buddha find their origins in Nikaya Buddhism, the associated genre of literature eventually transcended sectarian lines in a fashion that would inspire the ethos of Mahayana Buddhism.

It is undoubtedly a complex feat to determine if the authors of such texts, often referred to as those of the "vehicle that praised the Buddha," had "pro-lay" and iconoclastic intentions in mind when writing the biographies. It is clear however, that they expound many of the teachings that Mahayana would later consider its own. Nevertheless, if Mahayana grew at the very core of Nikaya Buddhism, it is ultimately irrelevant to underline the fact that biographies of the Buddha were informed by meta-sectarian impulses. Since most recent scholarship considers the claim that Mahayana Buddhism was in its earliest form a distinct social group inaccurate, Hirakawa's buttressing of it with evidence from the biographies of the Buddha is a futile effort.

Hirakawa's third source for the origination of Mahayana Buddhism is perhaps his most controversial. It essentially supports that the Mahayana grew out of an identifiable order of principally lay *bodhisattvas* whose central practice consisted of stupa worship. From this it is inferred that "Mahayana Buddhism was originally concerned with laymen" and that "doctrines for lay *bodhisattvas* play a prominent role in the oldest Mahayana sutras". In addition, it is said that the Mahayana concern with a saviour Buddha can be traced to the worship of sutras. A number of scholars have actually built their reputations around the rebuttal of this thesis. Gregory Schopen for instance, has convincingly argued that the stupa cult was shunned upon by a number of important early Mahayana sutras.

Conversely to Hirakawa, Schopen suggests that early Mahayana revolved around the cult of the book, or text (on the basis of its association to the notion of *dharmkaya*), which was in direct contrast to stupa worship. Indeed, a great deal of early Mahayana sutras advertises the boundless benefits and merits that are gained by memorising, worshiping, or simply reading a sutra. The *Pratyutpanna* Samadhi Sutra, arguably one of the earliest extant Mahayana texts, offers a good case in point:

> If worlds as numerous as the sands of the Ganges Were filled with precious gems and used as a gift, and if someone accepted one verse of this and preached it, the merit of that reverent recitation would exceed the former.

In the same text, *bodhisattvas* are defined, among other things, as having a studious energy that is hard to match; "they immerse themselves in the sutras, they constantly immerse themselves in the sutras". Echoing what has been said with regards to Mahayana's Nikaya origins in the first part of this work, Schopen concludes that, since each text placed itself at the centre of its own cult, early Mahayana (from a sociological point of view), rather than being an identifiable single group, was in the beginning a loose federation of a number of distinct though related cults, all of the same pattern, but each associated with a specific text.

Besides disproving Hirakawa's stupa worship position, Schopen also indirectly negates the possibility of a doctrinally homogeneous early Mahayana which could support the claim that it was a cohesive and distinct school of Buddhism. Furthermore, if Schopen's contention is to be taken as authoritative, the laity would have played a much smaller role than originally proposed. As Williams notes, there is no historical evidence of lay people constructing or preaching new sutras, neither is there evidence of lay doctrinal traditions in Buddhism at the root of Mahayana. Granted, many early Mahayana sutras embrace the role of laity in Buddhism, but the texts themselves remain the product of monks.

Gombrich follows a similar line of argumentation by proposing that the rise of Mahayana is attributable to the use of writing. Early Mahayana texts and doctrine were preserved precisely because they were written down. Only monastic circles had the authority, logistic capacity and organisational skill to hand down Mahayana texts (and by extension, teachings) to future generations. As such, the argument that the Mahayana somehow represented an "underground," subversive, and independent teaching disseminated among the laity remains an unlikely one. Some have argued Hirakawa's position with respect to the alleged lay origins of Mahayana to be anachronistic and indicative of modern trends in Japanese Buddhism.

Paul Williams has written that Japanese scholarship's emphasis on lay orders of *Bodhisattvas* engaged in altruistic activities is reflective of the self-image, interests and concerns of contemporary Japanese Buddhism. Harrison has also quite skillfully paraphrased Tyrell's comment on Adolf von Harnack's work and applied it to the work of Hirakawa, warning us of the potential academic faux pas of "reading back" into history. We must not however revert to the opposite extreme and discount the formative role that the laity played in the development of Mahayana Buddhism. Much like the gap between Mahayana and Nikaya Buddhism has been grossly exaggerated, so has the schism between monastic and lay.

In fact, Harrison, relying mainly on Durt's work, has remarked that the categories of "lay" and "monastic" stem from inappropriate and simplistic Western conceptualisations. The inadequacy derives from the terms *upasaka* and *upasika*. They are usually translated as "layman" and "laywoman" but should refer to "persons hovering just below ordained status, those who are, as it were, semi-ordained". The discrepancy between these terms and those of bhiksu and bikhsuni is much less pronounced then Hirakawa would suggest. The Pratyutpanna Samadhi Sutra actually tends to efface distinctions between monks and the "bodhisattvas wearing white."

The spiritual demands and requirements are equally stringent for both groups and on one occasion, the sutra even interchanges categories when referring to the chief protagonist, Bhadrapala. Whether this inconsistency is deliberate or inadvertent, it reflects Mahayana's inclination towards spiritually categorising its adherents rather than socially segregating them. Rather than reversing the conventional hierarchy and placing the laity above the clergy, Mahayana Buddhism and its glorification of the often lay bodhisattva advertises the absolute worth of bodhicitta and bodhisattvahood. Harrison interprets this as a polemical superseding of the bodhisattva over the Nikayanist sravaka: "That is to say, if even the lay bodhisattva is superior to the ordained sravaka, how much more so the ordained bodhisattva (1995: 67).

Mahayana texts, much like any primary or historical document, must be considered in all their opacity, and as results of complex socio-historical and even religio-political webs; rarely are they directly reflective of the context in which they were written. Before concluding, a brief parenthesis should be made to clarify Hirakawa's position on the soteriological character of Mahayana. Dependant on the misconception of Mahayana as an originally lay movement is the belief that bodhisattvas concede their Buddhahood to save the (lay masses) from which they purportedly came. It has been demonstrated above that the role of the laity and masses in comparison to that of the exclusive clergy in Mahayana was by no means emphatic.

In actuality, *bodhisattvas* are hailed as beings that are distinct from the populace, being extremely talented and having super-human powers. Mahayana thus appears in its elitist garb, starkly contrasting with its usually inclusive (and to some degree, consequently non-ascetical) depiction. As the Pratyutpanna Samadhi Sutra stipulates, "they [bodhisattvas] acquit themselves in debate quite differently from the masses". Throughout the same text, their magical powers are enumerated, thus highlighting their hieratic and supramundane character. As such, Mahayanists might be inclined to worship bodhisattvas and seek deliverance from them, but without going to deeply into the soteriological (and to some extent ontological) paradox of the boddhisattva path, it is sufficient to say that Mahayana is not a "devotional shortcut" as Harrison puts it.

Once again, the Pratyutpanna Samadhi Sutra clarifies the issue: "they [bodhisattvas] never fail to be those among men who are going to achieve the attainment of Buddhahood for them, without ever turning back". The initial message of Mahayana thus clearly resounds: bodhisattvas should not be worshipped and expected to relinquish their spiritual attainments for the deliverance of their devotees. Instead, the Mahayana adherent should strive to become a bodhisattva. Scholarship on the formation of the Mahayana tradition has oscillated back and forth between dualistic categorisations and binary oppositions. Hirakawa for one has sided with a wordly, lay and non-sectarian view of Mahayana.

This view transpires and is simultaneously supported by means of three sources that he enounces as responsible for the rise of Mahayana, namely Nikaya Buddhism, biographies of the Buddha, and stupa worship. The first and second sources have elicited the most scholarly debate, and recent trends tend to indicate that assumptions regarding Mahayana Buddhism are currently in the process of being debunked in favour of more balanced or just interpretations of the tradition. Perhaps it is inappropriate to read so far ahead into the history of Mahayana Buddhism, but it seems that Chang Shang-ying's pilgrimage to Wu-T'ai Shan offers striking insight as to what Mahayana originally was.

The Sung intellectual's experience on the sacred mountain is a genuine encounter with the transcendant, "beyond the distinction between the mundane (lokiya, shih-chien) and the supramundane (lokottara, ch'u-shih-chien). Much like Chang Shang-ying's experience collapses two levels of religious discourse, early Mahayana (whether through texts or practice) seems to collapse the dualisms between laity and clergy, this-wordly and other-wordly, sectarian and homogeneous, via positiva and via negativa, or cultic and non-cultic by paradoxically juxtaposing them. If recent scholarship is indicative of future trends, upcoming scholarship on the origins of Mahayana will hopefully gain inspiration from the subject of its studies and follow suit by avoiding the academic pitfalls or reductionist tribalism and overly simplistic binary oppositions.

So far we have examined the nature and characteristics of the early Buddhist Order. But it may also be helpful to examine how Shakyamuni himself defined who is a priest. First of all, Shakyamuni taught that no form of social distinction-neither class, race, gender nor wealth-should be given any consideration in the priestly order. In his well-known sermon about the eight properties of the oceans, Shakyamuni instructs his priestly disciples:

Just as, monks, whatsoever great rivers there are-namely, Ganga, Yamuna, Aciravati, Sarabhu,Mahi-these, on reaching the mighty ocean, abandon their former names and lineage, and henceforth go by the name of just "mighty ocean," even so, monks, the four castes-namely, the nobles, the brahmins, the merchants and the serfs-on going forth from home to the homeless in the Dhamma-discipline proclaimed by the Wayfarer, abandon their former names and lineage and go by the name of just "recluses who are Sakya sons."

Judging from the openness with which Shakyamuni accepted anyone into his teaching, the total disregard of social distinction or status no doubt permeated the entire community of Buddhists, including lay believers. Blind to social distinctions or status, Shakyamuni attempted to define priests in terms of their spirituality, their character and their action. This was radically different from the traditions of the priestly class of Brahmins, who had to be born into that class. Shakyamuni's position regarding the definition of priesthood is clear from many passages of the early Buddhist texts. For example, in the *Dhammapada,* Shakyamuni teaches: "Not by the tonsure, a shaven head, does a man become a samana, a monk.

How can a man be a samana if he forgets his religious vows, if he speaks what is not true, if he still has desire and greed?" In Sutta-Nipata, Shakyamuni also teaches: "Birth neither Brahmin, nor non-Brahmin, makes; /tis life and conduct moulds the Brahmin true." In light of those passages, to define who is a priest based solely on that person?s position, status or appearance does not accord with the original spirit of Buddhism. Finally it should be noted that Shakyamuni strongly urged lay believers to distinguish bad priests from good ones. In Sutta-Nipata, Shakyamuni explains to the blacksmith Cunda the importance of discerning the true nature of a monk based on his character and action.

He classifies monks or priests into four categories: "Way-conqueror," "Way-herald," "Wayfarer," and "fraud-of-Way." Shakyamuni describes the last category as a priest "Who, cloaked in piety, / Is froward, boaster, cheat /Of clansmen, unrestrained, /A babbler, masked in mode." Shakyamuni then exhorts Cunda as follows: "And the shrewd householder, / Wise Ariyan listener, / Perceiveth them, knows all /As such; and seeing this / His faith wanes not: for how / Could he confound no fraud / With fraud, cleansed with unclean?" Here Shakyamuni encourages his lay followers to develop the wisdom and perception to observe the true nature of crooked monks so that they may protect their faith. Nothing could be further from Shakyamuni's intent than laity bound up in blind, unquestioning obedience to priesthood.

THE MISTRANSLATION OF *SAMGHA* INTO CHINESE AND JAPANESE

Although the scope of my discussion has been limited to early Buddhism in India, I would like to note one important detail about the translation of the term *samgha* into Chinese and then into Japanese. *Samgha* was translated into Chinese as seng-chia. (To be precise, this was a transliteration of the term.) Seng, the Chinese abbreviation of seng-chia, however, came to be used to indicate an individual monk although in India *samgha* never carried this meaning. As I mentioned earlier, in India, an individual monk was referred to as *Bhikkhu* or bhiksu. In the Buddhist texts, the usage of the term *samgha* was strictly distinguished from that of *Bhikkhu* or bhiksu.

The *samgha* was considered one of the three treasures of Buddhism, but an individual monk was never considered an object of veneration as an element of the three treasures. I-Ching, a Chinese Buddhist scholar, after paying visits to many Buddhist sites in India, pointed out to Chinese Buddhists this misapplication of the term *samgha* to individuals. Many scholars acknowledged the error, but they insisted on continuing to use the term to refer to an individual priest or monk. This misuse of the term was simply accepted by the Japanese when Buddhism took root in Japan, as well. The Japanese term so, the Japanese pronunciation of the Chinese seng of seng-chia came to signify an individual priest.

As a result, this mistranslation significantly altered the concept of the three treasures in China and Japan. Particularly in Japan, the term was misused to promote reverence toward an individual priest. It is this misinterpretation that Nichiren Shoshu has been leaning on to dogmatically define its high priest as being part of the three treasures. The treasure of the *samgha* originally referred to the Buddhist Order, which, in the broadest sense, included all Buddhists, both priests and lay believers. The *samgha* was revered especially after Shakyamuni's death precisely because the Buddhist community as a whole fulfilled the important role of preserving and spreading the Buddha's teaching.

In light of those historical facts, as a translator, I personally feel the components of the three treasures would best be translated as the Buddha, the Dharma and the *Samgha* in order to maintain the original meaning and intent of the concept. (The "Law" or the "Teaching" for the Dharma, and the "Order" or "Community" for the *samgha* may be permissible if English terms are preferred for understanding.) But translating the treasure of the *Samgha* as "the treasure of the priesthood" would be, I feel, a gross diminution of the original term, and "the Treasure of the Priest" an outright distortion.

THE BUDDHIST ORDER IN MAHAYANA BUDDHISM

STUPA WORSHIP AND THE RISE OF MAHAYANA BUDDHISM

Shortly before his passing, Shakyamuni prohibited his monks from being involved in his funeral rite. Rather, he encouraged his priestly disciples to focus on their religious practice. In his mind, officiating a funeral service had nothing to do with Buddhism. In Shakyamuni's India, funerals were held by Brahmins or Hindu priests, and early Buddhist leaders often held in contempt the magical incantations recited by Brahmins. It is an ironic reversal of the Buddha's intent that funerals and memorial services have become the primary focus of Buddhism in Japan.

The Japanese Buddhist establishment would not exist today without funerals and memorial services-rites that are virtually unrelated to the original intent of Buddhism. This is why Buddhism in Japan is often referred to as "funeral Buddhism." Shakyamuni died in Kusinagara, and the people who lived there conducted his funeral. His cremated remains were then divided among eight tribes in central India, who constructed stupas (memorial mounds) to house the Buddha's remains. Since lay believers were unable to spend their whole life in scholarship and meditation as were the monks, they soon began to gather around those stupas and worship them, hoping somehow to commune with the Buddha's spirit.

This stupa worship was a simple expression of the laity's sincere devotion to the Buddha, who was symbolically represented by the stupas. This lay movement eventually evolved into Mahayana Buddhism. Mahayana scriptures began appearing around the first century BCE, but the origin of the Mahayana movement that is, worship before the stupa, dates back much earlier. For example, according to one Buddhist text, King Ashoka (r.c. 268-232 BCE) opened the original eight stupas and removed and further divided the Buddha's relics to build many stupas throughout the country. Professor Akira Hirakawa suggests that the king was simply responding to the growing popularity of stupa worship.

BODHISATTVA-SAMGHA

The term Mahayana means "a greater vehicle." The Mahayana Buddhists called Nikaya or Sectarian Buddhism "Hinayana" or "a smaller vehicle." It is not clear if the Mahayana Buddhists applied the term Hinayana to the whole of Nikaya Buddhism, or only to some of its branches such as the Theravada school. But it should be noted that no school of Buddhism referred to itself as Hinayana. Mahayana Buddhism was essentially a lay movement. It encouraged its practitioners to seek their enlightenment through teaching and helping others.

Because of their altruistic orientation, the Mahayana Buddhists referred to themselves as "*bodhisattvas*" (those who seek supreme enlightenment), their teaching as "bodhisattvayana" (the *bodhisattva* vehicle), and their lay Buddhist order as "*bodhisattva-samgha*" or "*bodhisattva-gana*" (group or community of *bodhisattvas*). On the other hand, Nikaya Buddhism was a teaching for monks who would devote themselves to study and meditation for their own salvation. While monks attempted to discipline themselves by following a set of rules or precepts, the Mahayana *bodhisattvas* sought to cultivate wisdom and faith in their own potential to become Buddhas. Those who realized that they have such potential were called *bodhisattvas.*

The Mahayana *bodhisattvas,* therefore, aspired to be equal to the Buddha while monks were content to remain as disciples of the Buddha, rather than striving to achieve the same enlightenment as the Buddha. For this reason, the Mahayana practitioners called the monastic tradition "Buddhism for disciples." Put simply, Mahayana Buddhism appealed to ordinary people and their lives, while Nikaya Buddhism was monastic and therefore withdrawn from the everyday world. One reason why the Mahayana Buddhists were able to develop and maintain the characteristics of a lay movement was that stupas, that is, the places they gathered for worship and practice, were managed by lay believers.

According to the monastic rules, the property and assets of monastic orders were strictly distinguished from those of stupas. If monks were to benefit from the land and assets of the stupas, or offerings made to the stupas, they would be accused of stealing-one of the four great prohibitions. Since stupas were strictly beyond the control of the monastic orders, the doctrines of lay Mahayana Buddhism were developed, spread widely and transmitted to younger generations without monastic influences. Since the stupas were not controlled by monks, people were free to perform music and dance there in honor of the Buddha. (Any form of entertainment was strictly prohibited in the monastic orders.) People also decorated the grounds of a stupa with various art works carved on gates, pillars and railings.

The Mahayana movement, in this sense, was also a great cultural and artistic movement based on Buddhist ideals. As stupa worship grew more popular, however, the members of monastic orders became hostile toward the Mahayana movement. According to some later Buddhist texts, some monks claimed that contributions for the monastic orders produced much more benefit than those made to stupas. The growing popularity of stupa worship also attracted the envy of the adherents of Brahmanism, who called a stupa "eduka," which meant a structure of rubbish.

THE MAHAYANA PRIESTHOOD AND ESOTERICISM

Only in its later stage did Mahayana Buddhism become a religion in which priesthood played a central role. Since the stupas included land and structures, people had to manage them. The caretaker of the stupa gradually came to be viewed as a sort of religious specialist who was neither a lay believer nor a priest. He would tell stories of the Buddha's life or past lives to the pilgrims who visited the stupa and *manag*e lodgings for them. But eventually a priestly order began to emerge from among those people. Meanwhile, by the beginning of the Common Era, stupas were being built on the grounds of monasteries and temples. Because of its continued popularity, stupa worship was gradually incorporated into monastic Buddhism as well. The absorption of the stupa worship into monastic orders, despite their initial hostility, undoubtedly had the effect of increasing their income from pilgrims' offerings.

Since Mahayana Buddhism emphasized believers' devotion to the Buddha, the concept of the Buddha became highly idealized and mystified over time. While the Mahayana practitioners taught the cultivation of wisdom and encouraged people to realize their own potential of Buddhahood, they also started to emphasize the saving powers of imagined Buddhas and *bodhisattvas.* In one sense, the essential Buddhist ideal of self-reliance began to be obscured by people's dependency on external deities. Many Mahayana scriptures expounded the blessings to be derived from magical incantations called dharani. Over the centuries, more magical elements were incorporated into Mahayana Buddhism. Furthermore, with the emergence of priesthood from within, Mahayana Buddhism eventually leaned toward esotericism.

Esoteric Buddhism emphasized rituals over doctrine. It thus became indistinguishable from Hinduism and was finally assimilated into Hinduism. With the assimilation of esoteric Buddhism into Hinduism and the Muslim invasion of India, Buddhism in India virtually disappeared by the end of the twelfth century. (Usually the end of Indian Buddhism is marked by the destruction of the Vikramasila Monastery by Muslim troops at the end of the twelfth century.) However, the fact that Hinduism remained strong even after the Muslim invasion suggests that the decline of Buddhism in India could be attributed more too internal causes than to a foreign enemy.

The decline of Buddhism in India is instructive precisely because it was mainly self caused. When Shakyamuni came to be deified and other imaginary Buddhas and *bodhisattvas* were invented, Buddhist practitioners began to depend more on priests as intermediaries to enjoy their supposed powers of salvation. Rituals conducted by priests became more central than their own efforts to practice for themselves and others. On one hand, Mahayana Buddhism revived the original spirit of Buddhism by emphasizing compassion for others. Its practitioners, however, eventually succumbed to their yearning for a transcendent deity while ignoring the greatness of the human Shakyamuni. They sought to commune with this transcendent Buddha-deity through priests as intermediaries.

The disappearance of Buddhism in India was caused in no small part by believers? Lack of self-reliant practice-as the Buddha, on his deathbed, had admonished them to develop. It was not hostile "Hinayana" monks or invading Muslims who brought about the decline of Mahayana and eventually all of Indian Buddhism. Ironically it was Mahayana priests who sapped the vigor of the popular Buddhist movement by inserting themselves between believers and a Buddha who had turned from a living example into an inaccessible god. Ultimately, however, it was the laity who came to yearn for external saviors and invited priests to bridge the gap between them. They had completely forgotten Shakyamuni's admonition of self-reliance: "Only a man himself can be the master of himself: who else from outside could be his master?"

In the "Preface" of the first edition of Leaves of Grass published in 1855, Walt Whitman (1819-1892) speaks to the future of priesthood:

There will soon be no more priests. Their work is done. They may wait awhile.. perhaps a generation or two.. dropping off by degree. A superior breed shall take their place.... The gangs of kosmos and prophets en masse shall take their place. A new order shall arise and they shall be the priests of man, and every man shall be his own priest.... They shall arise in America and be responded to from the remainder of the earth.

With the publication of Leaves of Grass, Whitman attempted to break a new ground in American literature. He challenged the traditions of the New England literary establishment with his new poetic form, subject and vision. Whitman saw himself as a poet of democracy who inspires people to seek their own communion with the universe and the divine. In this sense, he refused to be a poet who, as an intermediary, interprets the message of Mother Nature for the people. His theology was aptly expressed in such lines from "Song of Myself" as: "Divine am I inside and out, and I make holy whatever I touch or am touched from" or "In the faces of men and women I see God, and in my own face in the glass."

What he stood for in his poetry echoes important Mahayana ideals such as the universality of Buddhahood. And his rejection of priests as intermediaries between people and their own inherent divinity accords with the original Buddhist ideal of self-reliance. In this sense, Whitman's remarks about priests contain an invaluable insight. So do priests play a necessary role in Buddhism? I believe the answer depends on what we mean by the word priest. Whitman replaced one kind of priest with another, more universal kind of role that any of us can fulfill. I think we can conclude that Buddhist priests who do not fulfill their originally intended function - to protect and spread the teachings of Buddhism - are not really priests.

Nor are priests who are concerned with their own status - who deify the Buddha and insert themselves between the Buddha and the people to elevate that status - of use to anyone but themselves. On the other hand, I can find no reason to reject a priest who, in accord with the original role of the *samgha*, dedicates him or herself to protecting and spreading Buddhism, and to serving its believers. As we observed in the historical development of the *samgha*, the form of a Buddhist movement changes according to the circumstances while the essential teaching of Buddhism should not change. What Shakyamuni thought of as priests in his day is virtually an extinct species today. Particularly in Japan, Buddhist priests marry, own homes and live in relative comfort; they accumulate wealth, and conduct funerals and memorial services as a source of income. They are not Buddhist priests in any sense of the original meaning. They simply, over the centuries, invented themselves. As the form of priesthood changes, it would be foolish to be *Digha Nikaya* to a preconceived notion of priesthood. Rather than being preoccupied with the form of priesthood, we must look at the original spirit and functions of priesthood in Buddhism and try to fulfill those functions in a manner best suited to the time and place. What priesthood must do is protect and spread Buddhism. As I think of how best we as a community of Buddhists fulfill those functions in contemporary American society, I cannot help but think that shaved heads and robes would hamper rather than help us in our endeavor.

"Protecting" Buddhism means to correct any misconception or distortion of Buddhism and proclaim its truth among practitioners or in society at large. "Spreading" Buddhism means to communicate the joy and benefit of Buddhist practice to those unaware. Both functions of the *samgha* require a considerable degree of commitment in terms of social engagement. I do not think that priests who would lock themselves up in a temple or monastery are suited to fulfill those functions today. Early Mahayana Buddhists proudly called themselves the "*bodhisattva-samgha*," that is, a group of ordinary people who saw their innate Buddhahood and strove to manifest it while helping others do the same. Free from the influences of monks, they inspired people's lives with art and culture rooted in the rich spirituality of Buddhism. Centuries after Shakyamuni's death, they revived the original Buddhist spirit of compassion in the lives of ordinary people. I believe that this is exactly what the SGI is doing. Like Walt Whitman, we have become our own priests.

GRECO-BUDDHISM

Greco-Buddhism, sometimes spelled Græco-Buddhism, is the cultural syncretism between the culture of Classical Greece and Buddhism, which developed over a period of close to 800 years in Central Asia in the area corresponding to modern-day Afghanistan and Pakistan, between the 4th century BC and the 5th century AD. Greco-Buddhism influenced the artistic (and, possibly, conceptual) development of Buddhism, and in particular Mahayana Buddhism, before it was adopted by Central and Northeastern Asia from the 1st century AD, ultimately spreading to China, Korea and Japan.

General area of Greco-Buddhism and boundaries of the Kushan Empire at its greatest extent around 150 AD and the interaction between Hellenistic Greece and Buddhism started when Alexander the Great conquered Asia Minor and Central Asia in 334 BC, going as far as the Indus, thus establishing direct contact with India, the birthplace of Buddhism.

Alexander founded several cities in his new territories in the areas of the Oxus and Bactria, and Greek settlements further extended to the Khyber Pass, Gandhara and the Punjab. These regions correspond to a unique geographical passageway between the Himalayas and the Hindu Kush mountains, through which most of the interaction between India and Central Asia took place, generating intense cultural exchange and trade.

Following Alexander's death on June 10, 323 BC, his Diadochi (generals) founded their own kingdoms in Asia Minor and Central Asia. General Seleucus set up the Seleucid Kingdom, which extended as far as India. Later, the Eastern part of the Seleucid Kingdom broke away to form the Greco-Bactrian Kingdom (3rd–2nd century BC), followed by the Indo-Greek Kingdom (2nd–1st century BC), and later still by the Kushan Empire (1st–3rd century AD). The interaction of Greek and Buddhist cultures operated over several centuries until it ended in the 5th century AD with the invasions of the White Huns, and later the expansion of Islam.

ARTISTIC INFLUENCES

Numerous works of Greco-Buddhist art display the intermixing of Greek and Buddhist influences, around such creation centers as Gandhara. The subject matter of Gandharan art was definitely Buddhist, while most motifs were of Western Asiatic or Hellenistic origin.

THE ANTHROPOMORPHIC REPRESENTATION OF THE BUDDHA

Although there is still some debate, the first anthropomorphic representations of the Buddha himself are often considered a result of the Greco-Buddhist interaction. Before this innovation, Buddhist art was "aniconic": the Buddha was only represented through his symbols (an empty throne, the Bodhi tree, the Buddha's footprints, and the prayer wheel). This reluctance towards anthropomorphic representations of the Buddha, and the sophisticated development of aniconic symbols to avoid it (even in narrative scenes where other human figures would appear), seem to be connected to one of the Buddha's sayings, reported in the *Digha Nikaya*, that discouraged representations of himself after the extinction of his body.

Probably not feeling bound by these restrictions, and because of "their cult of form, the Greeks was the first to attempt a sculptural representation of the Buddha" (Linssen, "Zen Living"). In many parts of the Ancient World, the Greeks did develop syncretic divinities that could become a common religious focus for populations with different traditions: a well-known example is the syncretic God Sarapis, introduced by Ptolemy I in Egypt, which combined aspects of Greek and Egyptian Gods. In India as well, it was only natural for the Greeks to create a single common divinity by combining the image of a Greek God-King (The Sun-God Apollo, or possibly the deified founder of the Indo-Greek Kingdom, Demetrius), with the traditional attributes of the Buddha.

Many of the stylistic elements in the representations of the Buddha point to Greek influence: the Greco-Roman toga-like wavy robe covering both shoulders (more exactly, its lighter version, the Greek himation), the contrapposto stance of the upright figures. Greek artists were most probably the authors of these early representations of the Buddha, in particular the standing statues, which display "a realistic treatment of the folds and on some even a hint of modelled volume that characterizes the best Greek work. This is Classical or Hellenistic Greek, not archaizing Greek transmitted by Persia or Bactria, nor distinctively Roman" (Boardman).

The Greek stylistic influence on the representation of the Buddha, through its idealistic realism, also permitted a very accessible, understandable and attractive visualization of the ultimate state of enlightenment described by Buddhism, allowing it reach a wider audience: "One of the distinguishing features of the Gandharan school of art that emerged in north-west India is that it has been clearly influenced by the naturalism of the Classical Greek style. Thus, while these images still convey the inner peace that results from putting the Buddha's doctrine into practice, they also give us an impression of people who walked and talked, etc. and slept much as we do. I feel this is very important.

These figures are inspiring because they do not only depict the goal, but also the sense that people like us can achieve it if we try". During the following centuries, this anthropomorphic representation of the Buddha defined the canon of Buddhist art, but progressively evolved to incorporate more Indian and Asian elements.

A HELLENIZED BUDDHIST PANTHEON

Several other Buddhist deities may have been influenced by Greek gods. For example, Heracles with a lion-skin (who also happens to be the protector deity of Demetrius I) "served as an artistic model for Vajrapani, a protector of the Buddha". In Japan, this expression further translated into the wrath-filled and muscular Niô guardian gods of the Buddha, standing today at the entrance of many Buddhist temples.

According to Katsumi Tanabe, professor at Chuo University, Japan (in "Alexander the Great, East-West cultural contact from Greece to Japan"), besides Vajrapani, Greek influence also appears in several other gods of the Mahayana pantheon, such as the Japanese Wind God Fujin inspired from the Greek Boreas through the Greco-Buddhist Wardo, or the mother deity Hariti (Kariteimo and Kishibojin in Japan) inspired by Tyche. In addition, forms such as garland-bearing cherubs, vine scrolls, and such semi-human creatures as the centaur and triton, are part of the repertory of Hellenistic art introduced by Greco-Roman artists in the service of the Kushan court.

Religious interactions

The length of the Greek presence in Central Asia and

northern India provided opportunities for interaction, not only on the artistic, but also on the religious plane.

The Greek presence in Bactria (332 to 125 BC)

When Alexander conquered the Bactrian and Gandharan regions, these areas may already have been under Buddhist influence. According to a legend preserved in Pali, the language of the Theravada canon, two merchant brothers from Bactria, named Tapassu and Bhallika, visited the Buddha and became his disciples. They then returned to Bactria and built temples to the Buddha.

Alexander established in this same area several cities (Ai-Khanoum, Begram) and an administration that were to last more than two centuries under the Seleucids and the Greco-Bactrians, all the time in direct contact with Indian Territory. From 180 BC, the Greco-Bactrians were further to expand into India, where they established the Indo-Greek kingdom. In 125 BC, the northern Indo-European Yuezhi nomads (the future Kushans, promoters of the Mahayana faith) took control of the Bactrian territory, and displaced the remaining Greco-Bactrians to the northwestern part of the Indian subcontinent. The Yuezhi underwent a process of Hellenization for more than a century, as exemplified by their coins and their adoption of the Greek alphabet.

The Mauryan empire (322--183 BC)

The Indian emperor Chandragupta, founder of the Mauryan dynasty, re-conquered around 322 BC the northwest Indian Territory that had been lost to Alexander the Great. However, contacts were kept with his Greek neighbours in the Seleucid Empire, Chandragupta received the daughter of the Seleucid king Seleucus I after a peace treaty, and several Greeks, such as the historian Megasthenes, resided at the Mauryan court. Chandragupta's son Bindusara also had a Greek ambassador at his court, named Deimachus, and is known in Greek records for having requested a philosopher (a sophist) to the Seleucid king Antiochus I Soter (Athenaeus, "Deipnosophistae"). Chandragupta's grandson Asoka converted to the Buddhist faith and became a great proselytizer in the line of the traditional Pali canon of Theravada Buddhism, insisting on non-violence to humans and animals (ahimsa), and general precepts regulating the life of lay people. According to the Edicts of Ashoka, set in stone, some of them written in Greek, he sent Buddhist emissaries to the Greek lands in Asia and as far as the Mediterranean. The edicts name each of the rulers of the Hellenic world at the time.

Ashoka also claims he converted to Buddhism Greek populations within his realm: "Here in the king's domain among the Greeks, the Kambojas, the Nabhakas, the Nabhapamkits, the Bhojas, the Pitinikas, the Andhras and the Palidas, everywhere people are following Beloved-of-the-Gods' instructions in *Dhamma*." Rock Edict Nb13 (S. Dhammika) Finally, some of the emissaries of Ashoka, such as the famous Dharmaraksita, are described in Pali sources (the *Mahavamsa*, XII) as leading Greek Buddhist monks, active in Buddhist proselytism.

The Indo-Greek kingdom and Buddhism (180--1 BC)

The Greco-Bactrians conquered northern India from 180 BC, whence they are known as the Indo-Greeks. They controlled various areas of the northern Indian Territory until 1 BC. Buddhism flourished under the Indo-Greek kings, and it has been suggested that their invasion of India was intended to protect the Buddhist faith from the religious persecutions of the new Indian dynasty of the Sungas (185–73 BC) which had overthrown the Mauryans.

Coinage

The coins of the Indo-Greek king M enander (reigned 160 to 135 BC), found from Afghanistan to central India, and bear the inscription "Saviour King Menander" in Greek on the front. Several Indo-Greek kings after Menander, such as Zoilos I, Strato I, Heliokles II, Theophilos, Peukolaos, Menander II and Archebios display on their coins the title of "Maharajasa Dharmika" (lit. "King of the Dharma") in the Prakrit language and Kharoshthi script. Some of the coins of Menander I and Menander II incorporate the Buddhist symbol of the eight-spoked wheel, associated with the Greek symbols of victory, either the palm of victory, or the victory wreath handed over by the goddess Nike.

The ubiquitous symbol of the elephant in Indo-Greek coinage may also have been associated with Buddhism, as suggested by the parallel between coins of Antialcidas and Menander II, where the elephant in the coins of Antialcidas holds the same relationship to Zeus and Nike as the Buddhist wheel on the coins of Menander II. When the zoroastrian Indo-Parthians invaded northern India in the 1st century AD, they adopted a large part of the symbolism of Indo-Greek coinage, but refrained from ever using the elephant, suggesting that its meaning was not merely geographical.

Finally, after the reign of Menander I, several Indo-Greek rulers, such as Amyntas, King Nicias, Peukolaos, Hermaeus, Hippostratos and Menander II, depicted themselves or their Greek deities forming with the right hand a benediction gesture identical to the Buddhist vitarka mudra (thumb and index joined together, with other fingers extended), which in Buddhism signifies the transmission of Buddha's teaching.

Cities

According to Ptolemy, Greek cities were founded by the Greco-Bactrians in northern Pakistan. Menander established his capital in Sagala, today's Sialkot in Punjab, one of the centers of the blossoming Buddhist culture. A large Greek city built by Demetrius and rebuilt by Menander has been excavated at the archeological site of Sirkap near Taxila, where Buddhist stupas were standing side-by-side with Hindu and Greek temples, indicating religious tolerance and syncretism.

Scriptures

Evidence of direct religious interaction between Greek and Buddhist thought during the period include the Milinda Panha, a Buddhist discourse in the platonic style, held between

King Menander and the Buddhist monk Nagasena. Also the *Mahavamsa* records that during Menander's reign, "a Greek Buddhist head monk" named Mahadharmaraksita led 30,000 Buddhist monks from "the Greek city of Alexander-of-the-Caucasus" (around 150km north of today's Kabul in Afghanistan), to Sri Lanka for the dedication of a stupa, indicating that Buddhism flourished in Menander's territory and that Greeks took a very active part in it. Several Buddhist dedications by Greeks in India are recorded, such as that of the Greek meridarch (civil governor of a province) Theodorus, describing in Kharoshthi how he enshrined relics of the Buddha during the reign of Menander or his successor. Finally, Buddhist tradition recognizes Menander as one of the great benefactors of the faith, together with Asoka and Kanishka. Buddhist manuscripts in cursive Greek have been found in Afghanistan, praising various Buddhas and including mentions of the Mahayana Lokesvara-raja Buddha. These manuscripts have been dated later than the 2nd century AD. (Nicholas Sims-Williams, "A Bactrian Buddhist Manuscript").

The Mahayana movement probably began around the 1st century BC in northwestern India, at the time and place of these interactions. According to most scholars, the main sutras of Mahayana were written after 100 BC, when sectarian conflicts arose among Nikaya Buddhist sects regarding the humanity or super-humanity of the Buddha and questions of metaphysical essentialism, on which Greek thought may have had some influence: "It may have been a Greek-influenced and Greek-carried form of Buddhism that passed north and east along the Silk Road" (McEvilly, "The shape of ancient thought").

The Kushan Empire (1st–3rd century AD)

The Kushans, one of the five tribes of the Yuezhi confederation settled in Bactria since around 125 BC, invaded the northern parts of Pakistan and India from around 1 AD. By that time they had already been in contact with Greek culture and the Indo-Greek kingdoms for more than a century. They used the Greek script to write their language. The absorption of Greek historical and mythological culture is suggested by Kushan sculptures representing Dyonisiac scenes or even the story of the Trojan horse, and it is probable that Greek communities remained under Kushan rule.

The Kushan king Kanishka, who honored Zoroastrian, Greek and Brahmanic deities as well as the Buddha and was famous for his religious syncretism, convened the Fourth Buddhist Council around 100 AD in Kashmir, which marked the official recognition of the pantheistic Mahayana Buddhism and its scission with Nikaya Buddhism. Some of Kanishka's coins bear the earliest representations of the Buddha on a coin (around 120 AD), in Hellenistic style and with the word "Boddo" in Greek script. Kanishka also had the original Gandhari vernacular, or Prakrit, Mahayana Buddhist texts translated into the high literary language of Sanskrit, "a turning point in the evolution of the Buddhist literary canon".

The "Kanishka casket", dated to the first year of Kanishka's reign in 127 AD, was signed by a Greek artist named Age*silas*, who oversaw work at Kanishka's stupas (caitya), confirming the direct involvement of Greeks with Buddhist realizations at such a late date. The new syncretic form of Buddhism expanded fully into Eastern Asia soon after these events. The Kushan monk Lokaksema visited the Han Chinese court at Loyang in 178 AD, and worked there for ten years to make the first known translations of Mahayana texts into Chinese. The new faith later spread into Korea and Japan, and was itself at the origin of Zen.

GRECO-BUDDHISM AND THE RISE OF THE MAHAYANA

The geographical, cultural and historical context of the rise of Mahayana Buddhism during the 1st century BC in northwestern India, all point to intense multi-cultural influences: "Key formative influences on the early development of the Mahayana and Pure Land movements, which became so much part of East Asian civilization, are to be sought in Buddhism's earlier encounters along the Silk Road" (Foltz, Religions on the Silk Road).

Conceptual influences

Mahayana is an inclusive faith characterized by the adoption of new texts, in addition to the traditional Pali canon, and a shift in the understanding of Buddhism. It goes beyond the traditional Theravada ideal of the release from suffering (*Dukkha*) and personal enlightenment of the *Arhats,* to elevate the Buddha to a God-like status, and to create a pantheon of quasi-divine *Bodhisattvas* devoting themselves to personal excellence, ultimate knowledge and the salvation of humanity. These concepts, together with the sophisticated philosophical system of the Mahayana faith, may have been influenced by the interaction of Greek and Buddhist thought.

The Buddha as an idealized man-god

The Buddha was elevated to a man-god status, represented in idealized human form: "One might regard the classical influence as including the general idea of representing a man-god in this purely human form, which was of course well familiar in the West, and it is very likely that the example of westerners' treatment of their gods was indeed an important factor in the innovation... The Buddha, the man-god, is in many ways far more like a Greek god than any other eastern deity, no less for the narrative cycle of his story and appearance of his standing figure than for his humanity" (Boardman, "The Diffusion of Classical Art in Antiquity").

The supra-mundane understanding of the Buddha and *Bodhisattvas* may have been a consequence of the Greek's tendency to deify their rulers in the wake of Alexander's reign: "The god- king concept brought by Alexander (...) may have fed into the developing *bodhisattva* concept, which involved the portrayal of the Buddha in Gandharan art with the face of the sun god, Apollo" (McEvilly, "The Shape of Ancient Thought").

The Bodhisattva as a Universal ideal of excellence

Greek influence has been suggested (Etienne Lamotte, cited in Williams) in the definition of the *Bodhisattva* ideal in the oldest Mahayana text, the "Perfection of Wisdom" or *prajnâ* pâramitâ literature, between the 1st century BC and the 1st century AD in Northwestern India. These texts in particular redefine Buddhism around the universal *Bodhisattva* ideal, and its six central virtues of generosity, morality, patience, effort, meditation and, first and foremost, wisdom.

These qualities are reminiscent the Greek Stoicist philosophy, which may also have influenced the understanding of each individual as having the potential to reach excellence (Concept of Universal Buddha nature) and as being equally worthy of compassion (Compassion for all or "Karuna", related to the Greek Universal loving kindness, "Philanthropia"). The Stoics had a "conviction in the essential equality of all humankind (...), which did not provide for superior or inferior, dominant and subordinate relations between states. From the ideal of equality there followed the Stoics' emphasis on virtue, conscience, duty, and absolute personal integrity" (Bentley, "Old World Encounters").

Philosophical influences

The close association between Greeks and Buddhism probably led to exchanges on the philosophical plane as well. Many of the early Mahayana theories of reality and knowledge can be related to Greek philosophical schools of thought. Mahayana Buddhism has been described as the "form of Buddhism which (regardless of how Hinduized its later forms became) seems to have originated in the Greco-Buddhist communities of India, through a conflation of the Greek Democritean-Sophistic-Skeptical tradition with the rudimentary and unformalized empirical and skeptical elements already present in early Buddhism" (McEvilly, "The Shape of Ancient Thought"). In the Prajnaparamita, the rejection of the reality of passing phenomena as "empty, false and fleeting" can also be found in Greek Pyrrhonism. The distinction between conditioned and unconditioned being, and the denial of the reality of everyday experience in favour of an "unchanging and absolute ground of Being" is at the center of Platonism as well as Nagarjuna's Madhyamika thought. The perception of ultimate reality was, for the Cynics as well as for the Madyamikas and Zen teachers after them, only accessible through a non-conceptual and non-verbal approach (Greek "Phronesis"), which alone allowed to get rid of ordinary conceptions. The mental attitude of equanimity and dispassionate outlook in front of events was also characteristic of the Cynics and Stoics, who called it "Apatheia".

Greco-Persian cosmological influences

One of the most popular themes of Greco-Buddhist art, the future Buddha Maitreya, has often been linked to the Iranian saviour figure Mitra, itself adopted as a Greek syncretic cult under the name Mithras. Maitreya pertains to the traditions of the "Second coming" of a Messiah and "echoes the qualities of the Zoroastrian Saoshyant and the Christian Messiah" (Foltz). The Buddha Amitabha (literally meaning "Infinite radiance") with his Western paradisiacal "Pure Land" "seems to be understood as the Iranian god of light equated with the sun" (Foltz). The very notion of paradise is a Persian invention (Old Persian: "Para Daisa"), which was probably relayed by the Greeks. However, Mitra was also a solar diety of the Hindu Vedic Pantheon and Hindus have the notion of swarg, or the heavens.

Gandharan proselytism

Buddhist monks from the region of Gandhara, where Greco-Buddhism was most influential, played a key role in the development and the transmission of Buddhist ideas in the direction of northern Asia. Kushan monks, such as Lokaksema (c. 178 AD), travelled to the Chinese capital of Loyang, where they became the first translators of Mahayana Buddhist scriptures into Chinese. Central Asian and East Asian Buddhist monks appear to have maintained strong exchanges until around the 10th century, as indicated by frescos from the Tarim Basin.

Two half-brothers from Gandhara, Asanga and Vasubandhu (4th century), created the Yogacara or "Mind-only" school of Mahayana Buddhism, which through one of its major texts, the Lankavatara Sutra, became a founding block of Mahayana, and particularly Zen, philosophy. In 485 AD, according to the Chinese historic treatise Liang Shu, five monks from Gandhara travelled to the country of Fusang ("The country of the extreme East" beyond the sea, probably eastern Japan, although some historians suggest the American Continent), where they introduced Buddhism:

"Fusang is located to the east of China, 20,000 li (1,500 kilometers) east of the state of Da Han (itself east of the state of Wa in modern Kyushu, Japan). In former times, the people of Fusang knew nothing of the Buddhist religion, but in the second year of Da Ming of the Song dynasty (485 AD), five monks from Kipin (Kabul region of Gandhara) travelled by ship to Fusang. They propagated Buddhist doctrine, circulated scriptures and drawings, and advised the people to relinquish worldly attachments. As results the customs of Fusang changed".

Bodhidharma, the founder of Zen, is described as a Central Asian Buddhist monk in the first Chinese references to him (Yan Xuan-Zhi, 547 AD), although later traditions describe him as coming from South India.

INTELLECTUAL INFLUENCES IN ASIA

Through art and religion, the influence of Greco-Buddhism on the cultural make-up of Northern Asian countries, especially Korea and Japan, may have extended further into the intellectual area.

At the same time as Greco-Buddhist art and Mahayana schools of thought such as Zen were transmitted to northern Asia, central concepts of Hellenic culture such as virtue, excellence or quality may have been adopted by the cultures of Korea and Japan after a long diffusion among the Hellenized cities of Central Asia, to become a key part of their warrior and work ethics.

Greco-Buddhism and the West

In the direction of the West, the Greco-Buddhist syncretism may also have had some formative influence on the religions of the Mediterranean Basin.

Exchanges

Intense westward physical exchange at that time along the Silk Road is confirmed by the Roman craze for silk from the 1st century BC to the point that the Senate issued, in vain, several edicts to prohibit the wearing of silk, on economic and moral grounds. This is attested by at least three significant authors:

Strabo (64/ 63 BC–c. 24 AD).

Seneca the Younger (c. 3 BC–65 AD).

Pliny the Elder (23--79 AD).

The aforementioned Strabo and Plutarch (c. 45--125 AD) wrote about King Menander, confirming that information was circulating throughout the Hellenistic world.

Religious influences

Although the philosophical systems of Buddhism and Christianity have evolved in rather different ways, the moral precepts advocated by Buddhism from the time of Ashoka through his edicts do have a very strong similarity with the Christian moral precepts developed more than two centuries later: respect for life, respect for the weak, rejection of violence, and pardon to sinners, tolerance.

These similarities may indicate the propagation of Buddhist ideals into the Western World, the Greeks acting as intermediaries and religious syncretists: "Scholars have often considered the possibility that Buddhism influenced the early development of Christianity. They have drawn attention to many parallels concerning the births, lives, doctrines, and deaths of the Buddha and Jesus" (Bentley, "Old World Encounters"). The story of the birth of the Buddha was well known in the West, and possibly influenced the story of the birth of Jesus: Saint Jerome (4th century AD) mentions the birth of the Buddha, who he says "was born from the side of a virgin". Also a fragment of Archelaos of Carrha (278 AD) mentions the Buddha's virgin-birth.

The main Greek cities of the Middle-East happen to have

played a key role in the development of Christianity, such as Antioch and especially Alexandria, and "it was later in this very place that some of the most active centers of Christianity were established" (Robert Linssen, "Zen living").

4

Abhidharma Literature

One of the functions of the Abhidharma is definition. Definition is important because, to successfully communicate about a rather technical subject, we must know precisely what our terms mean. Thus I would like to look at a number of terms used frequently and popularly in speaking about Buddhist thought. I would like to arrive at an understanding of the definitions of these terms and then relate them to the nature of the teachings of the Buddha. Buddhism has often been called a religion, a philosophy, and, in recent years, a psychology. 'Religion' refers to belief in, or recognition of, a higher, unseen power that controls the course of the universe.

Moreover, religion has an emotional and moral component and has to do with rituals and worship. Because Buddhism does not recognize the existence of such a power and does not universally emphasize rituals and worship, it is difficult to categorize Buddhism in general - and particularly the Abhidharma - as a religion. In its original sense, 'philosophy' means the 'love of wisdom and knowledge.' More generally, it means investigation of the nature of the laws or causes of all being. This definition might apply to Buddhism except that it remains somewhat vague, due to the various meanings of the words 'nature' and 'being.'

This has led to two approaches in philosophical thinking, called metaphysics and phenomenology. Metaphysics is the study of absolute or first principles. It is also sometimes called the science of ontology, which means the study of essences or, in simple terms, the study of things in them. Phenomenology, in contrast, is the description of things as they are experienced by the individual; it is the science of epistemology, the study of things as they are known, as they appear to us. Insofar as Buddhism is philosophical, it is concerned primarily with phenomenology.

'Psychology' is the study of the mind and mental states. Like philosophy, it has two aspects - pure psychology, which is the general study of mental phenomena, and psychotherapy, or applied psychology, which is the application of the study of mental phenomena to the problem of disease and cure, disturbance and adjustment.

We might explain the difference between pure and applied psychology by means of an analogy. Imagine that a man climbs to the top of a hill and surveys the countryside without any particular purpose in mind. His survey will take in every detail - the hills, the woods, the rivers and streams - without discrimination. But if he has a purpose in mind - for instance, if he intends to reach another hilltop in the distance- then his survey will focus on the particular features that will help or hinder him in his progress toward that goal. When we speak of applied psychology or psychotherapy, we mean a study of the mind and mental states that focuses on those phenomena that will help or hinder one's progress toward mental well-being.

Having looked briefly at the definitions of religion, philosophy, and psychology, we can begin to see that the phenomenological aspect of philosophy and the therapeutic aspect of psychology relate best to an understanding of the Buddha's teaching. The Abhidharma, like Buddhist thought in general, is highly rational and logical. If we look closely at the methods of exposition and argument in the Abhidharma, we find the beginning of dialectics, which is the science of debate, and also the beginning of logical argument and analysis. This is particularly evident in the fourfold classification of the nature of questions.

It is said that familiarity with and ability to use this classification is indispensable for anyone who wants to engage fruitfully in discussion and debate about the Dharma, because to answer a question correctly, one has to understand the nature of the question. The first class of questions is the most direct and refers to those that can be answered directly and categorically, such as 'Do all living beings die?' To this the answer is 'Yes, all living beings die.' The second class can only be answered with qualifications, for instance, 'Will all living beings be reborn?' This kind of question cannot be answered directly and categorically because it has two possible interpretations.

Thus it must be analyzed and answered individually, taking into account each of the possible meanings: 'Living beings who are not free from the afflictions will be reborn, but those who are free from the afflictions, like the *Arhats*, will not be reborn.'

The third class of questions must be answered with counter-questions, as, for instance, 'Is man powerful?' Here the reference point of the question must be determined before the question can be answered: in other words, is man powerful with reference to the gods or to animals? If the former, then man is not powerful; if the latter, then man is powerful. The aim of the counter-question is to determine the reference point that the questioner has in mind. The fourth class of questions are those in which we are particularly interested here. These are questions that do not deserve an answer; the famous inexpressible propositions to which the Buddha remained silent fall into this category. Traditionally, there are fourteen unanswerable questions. We find them, for instance, in the Chulamalunkya Sutta.

These fourteen questions are grouped into three categories:

The first category contains eight questions that concern the absolute or final nature of the world: Is the world eternal or not eternal, or both or neither; finite or not finite, or both or neither? You can see that this category includes two sets of questions, and that both sets refer to the world. The first set refers to the existence of the world in time, and the second to the existence of the world in space.

The second category contains four questions: Does the *Tathagata* exist after death or not, or both or neither? These questions refer to the nature of nirvana, or ultimate reality. The third category contains two questions: Is the self identical with or different from the body? While the first category of questions refers to the world and the second to what is beyond the world, this last refers to personal experience. Do we die with our bodies, or are our personalities altogether different from and independent of our bodies?

The Buddha remained silent when asked these fourteen questions. He described them as a net and refused to be drawn into such a net of theories, speculations, and dogmas. He said that it was because he was free of the bondage of all theories and dogmas that he had attained liberation. Such speculations, he said, are attended by fever, unease, bewilderment, and suffering, and it is by freeing oneself of them that one achieves liberation. Let us look at the fourteen questions in general to see whether we can understand why the Buddha took this stand. Generally, the fourteen questions imply two basic attitudes toward the world.

The Buddha spoke of these two attitudes in his dialogue with Maha Kachchayana, when he said that there are two basic views, the view of existence and the view of nonexistence. He said that people are accustomed to think in these terms, and that as long as they remain entangled in these two views they will not attain liberation. The propositions that the world is eternal, that the world is infinite, that the Tathagatha exists after death, and that the self is independent of the body reflect the view of existence. The propositions that the world is not eternal, that the world is finite, that the *Tathagata* does not exist after death, and that the self is identical with the body reflect the view of nonexistence.

These two views were professed by teachers of other schools during the time of the Buddha. The view of existence is generally the view of the Brahmins; that of nonexistence is generally the view of the materialists and hedonists. When the Buddha refused to be drawn into the net of these dogmatic views of existence and nonexistence, I think he had two things in mind: (1) the ethical consequences of these two views, and, more importantly, (2) the fact that the views of absolute existence and nonexistence do not correspond to the way things really are.

For example, the eternalists view this self as permanent and unchanging. When the body dies, this self will not die because the self is by nature unchanging. If that is the case, it does not matter what this body does: actions of the body will not affect the destiny of the self. This view is incompatible with moral responsibility because if the self is eternal and unchanging, it will not be affected by wholesome and unwholesome actions. Similarly, if the self were identical with the body and the self dies along with the body, then it does not matter what the body does. If you believe that existence ends at death, there will be no constraint upon action. But in a situation where things exist through interdependent origination, absolute existence and nonexistence are impossible.

Another example drawn from the fourteen unanswerable questions also shows that the propositions do not correspond to the way things really are. Take the example of the world. The world does not exist absolutely or not exist absolutely in time. The world exists dependent on causes and conditions - ignorance, craving, and clinging. When ignorance, craving, and clinging are present, the world exists; when they are not present, the world ceases to exist. Hence the question of the absolute existence or nonexistence of the world is unanswerable. The same may be said of the other categories of questions that make up the fourteen unanswerables. Existence and nonexistence, taken as absolute ideas, do not apply to things as they really are.

This is why the Buddha refused to agree to absolute statements about the nature of things. He saw that the absolute categories of metaphysics do not apply to things as they really are. As for the Buddha's attitude toward psychology, there is no doubt that he placed a great deal of emphasis on the role of the mind. We are familiar with the famous verses in the *Dhammapada* where the Buddha speaks of the mind as the forerunner of all mental states. The text says that happiness and suffering result from acting with a pure mind and an impure mind, respectively. We need only look at the canonical texts to recognize the importance of mind in Buddhist teachings. There we find the five aggregates, four out of five of which are mental, and the thirty-seven factors of enlightenment, the majority of which are mental.

No matter where we look, we will be struck by the importance of mind in the teachings of the Buddha. Various religions and philosophies have their particular starting points. The theistic religions begin with God. Ethical teachings like Confucianism begin with man as a social entity. Buddhism begins with the mind. It is therefore not surprising that we often choose to describe the Buddha's teaching as a psychological one, and that we also describe it as psychotherapy, since the symbolism of disease and cure is prominent in the teaching of the Buddha.

The Four Noble Truths are a reflection of the ancient scheme of disease, diagnosis, cure, and treatment used in early medical science, and we might also recall that the Buddha was called the king of physicians. The Buddha was interested in cure, not in metaphysical categories. We find his use of various techniques of cure throughout the discourses in the Sutra Pitaka. For instance, take the Buddha's teaching about the self. In the *Dhammapada* the Buddha taught that the wise man can attain happiness by disciplining himself, and yet in other places in the discourses, we find the Buddha expounding the doctrine of not-self, the idea that nowhere in the psycho-physical components of experience is the permanent self to be found.

For the explanation of this apparent contradiction, we need to look at the Buddha's dialogue with Vachchhagotta, who asked the Buddha whether or not the self existed. The

Buddha remained silent, and after a time Vachchhagotta left. Ananda, who happened to be nearby, asked the Buddha why he had not replied. The Buddha explained that if he had said that the self existed, he would have been siding with those Brahmins who believed in the absolute existence of the self, but if he had told Vachchhagotta that the self did not exist, it would have been confusing for Vachchhagotta, who would have thought, 'Previously I had a self, but now I no longer have one.'

The Buddha chose to remain silent because he knew Vachchhagotta's predicament. Similarly, when confronted by those who did not believe in rebirth, he taught the existence of the self, whereas to those who believed in the reality of karma, in the fruit of good and bad actions, he taught the doctrine of not-self. This is the Buddha's skill in the means of instruction. We can see how this ties in with the Buddha's rejection of absolute categories when we look at his use of the symbol of the water-snake. Here we find the Buddha saying that the factors of experience are similar to a water-snake. When a person capable of handling a water-snake and knowledgeable in the method of capturing one attempts to catch one, he will do so successfully.

But when a person unaccustomed to handling a water-snake and ignorant of how to capture one attempts it, his attempt will end in lamentation and pain. Similarly, phenomena - the factors of experience - are nothing in themselves. They are not absolutely existent or absolutely nonexistent, neither absolutely good nor absolutely bad; rather, are they relative. Whether they result in happiness or pain, in progress along the path or in retrogression, depends not on the phenomena themselves but on how we handle them. If things are handled in the right way, through a conscious and deliberate adjustment of the mind, phenomena can be used for one's progress along the path.

A knife, for instance, is neither true nor false, yet someone who grasps it by the blade is surely in error. When we relate to phenomena in terms of craving, ill-will, and ignorance, this results in suffering. When we take them otherwise, this results in happiness. To summarize, we can use terms like 'philosophy' and 'psychology' in relation to the Buddhist tradition as long as we remember that we are interested in philosophy not as it concerns essences and absolute categories but as a description of phenomena, and that we are interested in psychology insofar as it concerns psychotherapy. These qualities of the philosophy and psychology of the Abhidharma are unique in the history of human thought.

Nowhere else, in the ancient or modern world, in Asia or the West, has such a phenomenology and psychotherapy evolved. What is unique about Buddhist phenomenology and psychotherapy is its rejection of the idea of a permanent self and its affirmation of the possibility of liberation. In all other systems, even those of western philosophical phenomenology and psychotherapy, we find an inability to reject the idea of a permanent self - the very rejection so characteristic of the teaching of the Buddha and of the Abhidharma. And nowhere within modern psychology do we find that possibility of ultimate and absolute freedom so central to the teachings of Buddhism.

There are two ways to depict a given person and his relation to the world around him: deductively and inductively. The rational or deductive method begins with an abstract idea and applies that idea to one's experience. The empirical or inductive method begins with the facts we encounter in experience; through observing and analyzing, interpreting and understanding these facts, we build up a picture of ourselves and the world around us. In short, the rational method begins with the abstract and tries to apply it to the concrete, whereas the inductive method begins with the concrete and builds up a picture of reality gradually and progressively. The inductive method, which is the one used in the Abhidharmic system, is quite close to the method of science, except that in science the focus of the inductive process is outward and in the Abhidharmic system the focus is inward, on the mind.

This is why the Abhidharmic method is sometimes called introspection or, to use a traditional term, meditation. When we say that the Abhidharmic method is empirical and inductive, we mean that it has to do primarily with mental experience. Sometimes we say that meditation is like internal or mental microscopy: it is a way of investigating very closely the facts of experience. The Abhidharmic method of introspection yields results because it *manag*es, through meditation, to slow down mental processes to a point where we can see and understand them. In this respect there is a remarkable parallel between the Abhidharmic method and the scientific method. In science, when we want to find out how a certain transformation actually takes place, we slow down the process or speed it up.

In Abhidharmic meditation, too, we can slow down mental processes so that we can see what is actually happening, or we can speed things up. If we could see our human life, from birth to death, within the space of five minutes, it would give us great insight into the nature of life. However, because this is usually not possible, we slow things down. This is the basis of Abhidharmic meditation. The lists of mental factors and the like in the books of the Abhidharma may appear tedious and speculative at first glance, but in fact they are just the written form of the data we find in this very careful investigation of experience. Far from being speculative, the Abhidharma is the result of careful and close introspective analysis of experience.

That said, you may question the use of studying the Abhidharma at all, thinking that it is surely more useful to sit in meditation and reproduce the Abhidharmic experience of reality in one's own meditation. This is true to the extent that, as in all aspects of Buddhist teaching, direct as well as indirect acquaintance is required. With the Abhidharmic view of the elements, the picture we get when we analyze experience is certainly much more effective if it is a direct picture achieved through our own meditation.

But even if it is an indirect picture gained through study, it is still of use to us, because when we sit down to meditate we will already have some intellectual acquaintance with the general outline of the picture we are trying to bring into focus. In this sense studying the Abhidharma can be useful in bringing about an indirect understanding of ourselves and the world around us in Abhidharmic terms.

There are two ways Abhidharmic investigation works: (1) through analysis, and (2) through synthesis, or relation. The basic structure of these two methods is given in the first and last books of the Abhidharma Pitaka, the *Dhammasangani* (Classification of Factors) and the *Patthana* (Book of Causal Relations), respectively. These are the two most important books of the Abhidharma. It is through the analytical method and the synthetic or relational method that the Abhidharma arrives at a basic understanding of not-self and emptiness. Let us look first at the analytical method and then at the relational method; finally, we will combine the two, as, indeed, we must to reap the full benefit of the Abhidharmic method of investigation.

In *The Questions of King Milinda* (Milinda Panha), it is said that the Buddha has accomplished a very difficult task: 'If a man,' Nagasena says in reply to King Milinda, 'were to take a boat out to the sea, and if he were to take a handful of sea water and were then able to tell you that in it this much water is from the Ganges, this much from the Yamuna, and this much from the other great rivers of India, this would certainly be a very difficult thing to accomplish. In the same way, the Buddha has analyzed a single conscious moment of experience- for instance, the experience of seeing a form - into its various component parts: matter, feeling, perception, volition, and consciousness.' Analysis is the dissection of an apparently unitary, homogeneous whole into its component parts. This analysis can be applied not only to the self, as we find in the analysis of personal experience, but also to external objects: just as we can break down the personality into the five aggregates, so we can break down external phenomena into their component parts.

For example, we can break down a table into its legs; it's top, and so forth, and, even further, into the molecules and atoms of various elements that compose the table. The purpose of dissecting an apparent whole is to uproot attachment to internal and external phenomena. Once we recognize that this apparently homogeneous self is really just a collection of components, our attachment to the notion of the self is weakened; similarly, once we realize that external phenomena are just collections of individual smaller components; our attachment to external objects is weakened. What do we have as a result of our analytical process? Internally, we are left with moments of consciousness; externally, we are left with atoms. If we consider the two together, we are left with elements, or factors of experience.

The mental and material elements of experience do not in themselves bring us to the ultimate understanding of reality because we are left with moments of consciousness and atoms of matter - elements of experience. These elements remain irreducible no matter how long and how far we go in our process of dissection.

Although we come up with smaller and smaller parts, we are left with a picture of reality that is broken up into little bits and pieces as a result of dissection. This in itself is not an accurate and complete picture of reality. To arrive at the ultimate picture of reality, we need to couple the analytical approach with the synthetic or relational approach. That is why a great Buddhist scholar and saint, Nagarjuna, once expressed his reverence for the Buddha as 'the teacher of interdependent origination.' The truth of interdependent origination pacifies and calms the agitation of thought-construction.

This is an indication of the importance of relation, interdependence, or conditionality in understanding the real nature of things. It is also why scholars have focused on the Book of Causal Relations, which supplies the other half of the Abhidharmic method of investigation. Just as, through analysis, we arrive at the insubstantiality of personality and phenomena (because we see that they are made up of component parts), so, through the process of relational investigation, we arrive at the emptiness of personality and phenomena (because we see that the component parts which constitute them are all conditioned by and relative to each other). We arrive at this insubstantiality and emptiness by focusing on the teaching of interdependent origination.

We can see how, within a given thing - be it the personality or an external object - the component parts depend on one another for their existence. For instance, within a single phenomenon, such as an apparently unitary table, there are several component parts (the legs, the top, and so forth) that depend on each other for their existence as part of a table. Similarly, the table depends on its antecedent causes (the wood, the iron, and action of the craftsman who put it together) and also on proximate conditions (like the floor on which it stands). We can also explore the idea of interdependence in relation to three dimensions: time, space, and karma. For instance, the table is dependent in terms of time in the sense that, prior to the table existing, a series of events occurred - the cutting of lumber, the construction of the table, and so forth. This sequence of events led to the arising of the table. Similarly, the table is dependent in terms of space in the sense that it stands on the floor, and so forth.

The third dimension of conditionality operates beyond time and space. This dimension is explained by karma, because karma has its effects depending on time and space, yet it is not directly apparent in time and space. Because of karma, an action done at a very distant point in time and space can have its effects here and now. Conditionality is therefore not only temporal and spatial, but also has a karmic dimension. Let us take two examples to establish more firmly what we mean by the analytical approach and the relational approach. Take a chariot, which is a phenomenon, an identifiable entity.

We apply the analytical approach to the chariot by breaking it down into its component parts: the wheels, axle, body, shaft, and so forth. Application of the synthetic method looks at the same chariot in terms of the lumber that goes to it, the action of the builders who put it together, and so forth. Alternatively, we can take the classical examples of the flame in an oil lamp, which exists dependent on the oil and the wick, and the sprout, which depends on a seed, soil, sunlight, and so forth.

The analytical and the relational methods together yield the ultimate picture of things as they really are. They yield this ultimate picture through careful investigation. We use the analytical method to break things up into the component parts of an apparent whole; then we use the relational method to show that these component parts do not exist independently and separately but depend on other factors for their existence. There are many places in the Buddha's teaching where methods of investigation are used singly and then in combination. For example, we apply mindfulness first to internal phenomena, then to external phenomena, and finally both to internal and external phenomena. By using analysis and relation together, we overcome many problems. Not only do we overcome the idea of self, substance, and personality, we also overcome the problems that result if we believe in the independent existence of separate factors and ideas like existence and nonexistence, identity and difference.

The analytical and the synthetic approaches are actually reflected in the chemistry of the brain. Neurologists have discovered that the brain is divided into two hemispheres, one whose function is analytical and one whose function is synthetic. If these two functions are not in harmony, not in balance, personality disturbances result. Someone who is too analytical tends to overlook the more intuitive, dynamic, fluid aspects of life, while someone who is too relational tends to lack precision, clarity, and focus. Thus even in our personal lives we need to combine analytical and relational thinking.

The psychological and neurological dimensions of these two approaches are also clear in the development of western philosophy and science. Philosophies in which the analytical approach is predominant have left us with realistic, pluralistic, and atomistic systems like the philosophy of Bertrand Russell.

By the same token, in the latest developments of science, such as quantum theory, we find a more relational view of reality gaining ground. When we look at the history of philosophy and science in the West, we can see that each of these two approaches to investigation has been dominant at one time or another. Perhaps we are reaching a point where we can combine the two even in western science and philosophy. Perhaps we can arrive at a view of reality not too different from the one that the Abhidharma arrives at through the experience of introspective meditation- a view of reality that is both analytical (in that it rejects the idea of a homogeneous whole) and relational (in that it rejects the idea of independent, separately existing bits and pieces of reality). We would then have a very fluid and open view of reality in which experience saturated by suffering could be dynamically transformed into experience free from all suffering.

To understand why we begin our Abhidharmic analysis of experience with consciousness, it is important to remember the therapeutic concern of Buddhist philosophy in general and the Abhidharma in particular. The starting point of Buddhist thought is the truth of suffering. Suffering is a problem of consciousness; only that which is conscious can suffer. Consciousness is subject to suffering because of ignorance, or fundamental not-knowing, which divides consciousness into subject and object, into a self and other-than-self (i.e., the objects and people around the self). In Buddhism, ignorance is defined as the notion of a permanent, independent self and its object. Once we have this division of consciousness into a self and other-than-self, we have suffering, because tension is created between the two. We also have craving and aversion, because we want those things that support the self and are averse to those things that are not conducive to the self.

This division or discrimination between the self (or subject) and the other-than-the-self (or object) is the fundamental cause of suffering. Such a division is possible because of ignorance- the belief in a real self existing independently and in opposition to the other-than-self. Thus it is not surprising that the Abhidharma should turn first to an analysis of subjectivity and objectivity. Indeed, when we examine the teaching of the five aggregates, we see that form (*rupa*) is the objective component, while name (*nama*), consciousness, and the mental aggregates of volition, perception, and feeling are the subjective component.

Before looking at how this division affects the Abhidharmic analysis of consciousness, we must be clear about what it means. In Buddhism, this division does not mean that we have an essential, irreducible duality of mind and matter. Buddhism is not concerned with mind and matter as ultimate metaphysical facts but with mind and matter as they are experienced. Mind and matter are forms of experience, not essences. This is why Buddhism is a phenomenological, not an ontological, philosophy, and why the division of mind and matter in Buddhism is a phenomenological division. There are two systems for classifying consciousness in the Abhidharma: objective and subjective. Objective classification refers to the objects of consciousness, while subjective classification refers to the nature of consciousness. Objective classification primarily takes into account the direction in which consciousness is oriented. Within this objective scheme, there is a division into four classes of consciousness: (1) the sense-sphere consciousness or consciousness directed toward the world of sense desire (*kamavachara*); (2) the consciousness directed toward the sphere of form (*rupavachara*); (3) the consciousness directed toward the formless sphere (*arupavachara*); and (4) the consciousness directed toward nirvana (*lokuttara*).

The first three classes of consciousness are worldly (lokiya) and are concerned with the world of conditioned things. The fourth class, also known as supramundane consciousness (alokiya chitta), refers to the transcendental direction of consciousness (*lokuttara*) and is the consciousness of the four types of noble ones - the stream-winner, once-returner, non-returner, and liberated one. The object of the *kamavachara* is material and limited; the object of the *rupavachara* is not material but is still limited; and the object of the *arupavachara* is not material and is unlimited. If we look at these three in order, we find (a) a material and limited object, (b) an immaterial but still limited object, and (c) an immaterial and unlimited object of consciousness.

All three types of consciousness are directed toward mundane objects. There is a progressive unification and homogenization in the object of each consciousness. The object of the consciousness of the sphere of sense desire is the most proliferated and differentiated; those of the form and formless types of consciousness are increasingly less proliferated. The fourth type of consciousness is directed toward a transcendental type of object. Let us now look at the subjective classification of consciousness. This consciousness has to do with the nature of the subjective consciousness itself and is also divided into four classes: the wholesome consciousness (*kusala*), the unwholesome consciousness (*akusala*), the resultant consciousness (*Vipaka*), and the ineffective or functional consciousness (*kiriya*).

The wholesome and unwholesome classes are karmically active classes of consciousness; in other words, they have karmic potential. The resultant and functional types of consciousness are not karmically active and do not have karmic potential. The resultant class cannot bring about results because it is itself the result, while the functional class cannot do so because its potentiality is exhausted in the action itself. We can thus place the wholesome and unwholesome categories in the more general category of karmically active consciousnesses, and the resultant and functional types into the category of passive consciousnesses that do not have karmic potential.

It might be useful to look for a moment at the meaning of the terms 'wholesome' (*kusala*) and 'unwholesome' (*akusala*), and then at the definition of the wholesome and unwholesome categories of subjective consciousness. Wholesome means 'what tends toward cure' or 'what tends toward desirable results.' Here we are again reminded of the therapeutic concern of Buddhist philosophy.

Unwholesome means 'what tends toward undesirable results' or 'what tends toward perpetuation of suffering.' The terms 'wholesome' and 'unwholesome' are also related to skillful and unskillful, or intelligent and unintelligent, moments of consciousness. However, for convenience, people still sometimes refer to wholesome and unwholesome consciousness as good and bad, moral and immoral. 'Wholesome' and 'unwholesome' can also be defined with reference to the three wholesome and unwholesome root causes (non-greed, non ill-will, and non-delusion, and greed, ill-will, and delusion, respectively).

Greed, ill-will, and delusion are the derivative forms of fundamental ignorance, which is the mistaken notion of a self as opposed to what is other-than-self. Ignorance in its fundamental sense might be likened to the root of a tree, and greed, ill-will, and delusion to its branches. The karmic potential of a moment of consciousness conditioned by any of the three unwholesome causes is unwholesome, while the potential of a moment conditioned by any of the three wholesome causes is wholesome. These wholesome and unwholesome classes of consciousness are karmically active, and they are followed by a resultant class - in other words, by the ripened results of those wholesome and unwholesome actions.

The inactive or functional class refers to actions that are not productive of further karma, and that also do not result from wholesome and unwholesome karma, such as the actions of enlightened ones - the Buddhas and *Arhats* - and deeds of indifferent or neutral karmic content. In addition to these two general systems for classifying consciousness- the objective, which classifies consciousness according to its object and direction, and the subjective, which classifies consciousness according to its nature- we have a third system in which consciousness is distinguished according to feeling, knowledge, and volition.

In the classification according to feeling, every conscious factor partakes of an emotional quality: agreeable, disagreeable, or indifferent. These three can be expanded into five by dividing the agreeable category into mentally agreeable and physically agreeable, and the disagreeable category into mentally disagreeable and physically disagreeable. There is no category of physically indifferent consciousness because indifference is primarily a mental quality. In the classification in terms of knowledge, again we have a threefold division: conscious factors accompanied by knowledge of the nature of the object, conscious factors unaccompanied by knowledge of the nature of the object, and conscious factors accompanied by definite wrong views about the nature of the object. These can also be called the presence of correct knowledge, the absence of correct knowledge, and the presence of erroneous knowledge.

Finally, in the classification according to volition, there is a twofold division into automatic and volitional consciousness - in other words, moments of consciousness that are automatic in nature, and moments that have an intentional element. Let us now look at the sense-sphere consciousness (*kamavachara*). There are fifty-four types of consciousness in this category, which divide into three groups:

The first group consists of twelve factors that are karmically active and that have unwholesome karmic potential. The twelve can be subdivided into factors conditioned by one of the three unwholesome conditions of greed, ill-will, and delusion.

The second group consists of eighteen reactive or passive factors of consciousness, which can be further broken down into those that are resultant and those that are functional. Fifteen of the eighteen are resultant, and refer in general terms to experiences that are agreeable or disagreeable, the result of wholesome or unwholesome factors experienced through the five physical senses and the sixth mental sense. The remaining three are functional, having no karmic potential and not being the consequence of karmically active wholesome or unwholesome factors. The third category consists of twenty-four wholesome factors of consciousness that are karmically active and thus have karmic potential conditioned by non-greed, non-ill-will, and non-delusion.

Within the class of sense-sphere consciousness, therefore, we have fifty-four types of consciousness that can be analyzed in terms of active and passive, wholesome and unwholesome, resultant and functional, and even in terms of feeling, knowledge, and volition and to conclude by spending a few moments on the multivalent nature of terms in the Abhidharma in particular and in Buddhism in general. The factors of consciousness listed in the Abhidharma, and the terms used to describe them, have different values and meanings according to the functions they perform. Failure to understand this leads to confusion about Abhidharmic classifications. Even in the early years of the Abhidharma, there were critics who failed to understand that the factors in it are classified functionally, not ontologically.

What this means is that if you survey the factors of consciousness listed in the Abhidharma literature, you find the same factor occurring in different categories. Your initial conclusion may be that there is a great deal of repetition in Abhidharmic material, but this is not the point. The presence of the same factor in different categories is due to its functioning differently in each one. The commentary to the *Dhammasangani* (Classification of Factors) records the objection of repetition raised by an opponent. It replies with the analogy that when a king collects taxes from people, he does so not on the basis of their existence as identifiable individuals, but of their functions as earning entities. (This is also the case today, when one pays taxes on the basis of being a property owner, a salaried worker, on the earnings of one's stocks and bonds, and so forth.)

In the same way, the factors enumerated in the Abhidharma occur in different categories because in each case it is the factor's function that counts, not its essence. This is also the case with terms. We need to understand terms in context - by the way they are used - rather than imposing rigid, essentialistic, and naturalistic definitions. Take, for instance, 'suffering' (*Dukkha*) and 'happiness' (*sukha*). In the analysis of the factors of consciousness, these terms mean physical suffering and physical happiness. Yet when we talk about *Dukkha* in the context of the first noble truth, it includes not only four physical sufferings but also four mental sufferings. Similarly, *sankhara* means simply 'volition' in one context but 'all compounded things' in another. Thus when we study the Abhidharma, we need to understand the words in context. If we keep this in mind, we will be adopting the phenomenological spirit of Buddhist philosophy and will find it easier to approach the significance of what is being said. Otherwise, we will find ourselves trapped into rigid, unworkable definitions of terms and rigid, unhelpful ideas about factors of experience. First, to acquire understanding, one needs to cultivate (1) study, (2) consideration, and (3) meditation. It is not enough just to hear or read about the classifications of consciousness: one needs to consider exactly how they function, exactly what their meaning is. From my own experience, these schemes of classification will not begin to make sense until one spends some time running them back and forth in one's mind. Finally, after study and consideration, one can use them in one's meditation.

Second, to understand these classifications, it helps to consider a more concrete and accessible model. Suppose you want to know how many people are likely to watch daytime television in Singapore. You might classify the population into employed and unemployed; again, you might divide the unemployed group into English-speaking and Chinese-speaking, so you know how many are likely to watch English programs compared to Chinese ones. You might divide the population into male and female, or into school-going and non-school-going, and the school-going group into those who attend English schools and those who attend Chinese schools. Given a certain group of factors- in this case, the individual people who make up a population- there are many ways to classify them depending on what you want to find out.

It is the same way with the Abhịdharmic classification of consciousness: we have a set of types of consciousness, and we classify them in different ways according to what we want to find out. If we remember this general rule about why and how we classify factors of consciousness, and then run the schemes back and forth in our minds, they will begin to make more sense. In this chapter we will look at the form-sphere consciousness (*rupavachara*) and the formless-sphere consciousness. Here we are primarily concerned with the analysis of types of consciousness that arise from meditation, concentration, or absorption (*jhana*). As in the genesis of the Abhidharma itself, Sariputta played a vital role in the beginnings of Abhidharmic analysis of consciousness. In the Anupada Sutta it is mentioned that, after achieving the various states of meditation, Sariputta applied an Abhidharmic type of analysis by enumerating, classifying, and identifying the types of consciousness he had experienced.

Much emphasis was placed on analysis even in the early period of Buddhist history, because the experience of extraordinary states of meditation can be easily misinterpreted. In non-Buddhist traditions, such states are consistently misinterpreted as evidence of a transcendental, supranatural being or of an eternal soul. By pointing out that states of meditation, like experience in general, are characterized by impermanence, transience, and insubstantiality, analysis wards off the three defilements of: (a) craving or attachment to the supernatural and extraordinary states of consciousness achieved through meditation; (b) false views, that is, the misinterpretation of these states of meditation as evidence of the existence of a transcendental being or eternal soul; and (c) conceit, which arises from the notion that one has achieved extraordinary states of meditation.

The cultivation of states of meditation and the attainment of the absorptions is a very important part of Buddhist practice because it is the aim of mental development, which is one of the three major divisions of the Buddhist path (i.e., morality, mental development, and wisdom). To achieve these states of meditation, one needs to create the foundation of morality and withdraw to some extent from involvement in worldly activities. Having achieved these preliminary conditions, one then proceeds to cultivate the states of meditation through various methods. Briefly, one proceeds by means of some forty traditional objects of meditation, which include ten supports (*kasina*). These objects are coordinated to the temperament of the meditator. In other words, particular objects of meditation are prescribed for certain kinds of temperament. In general, one begins with an external support, gradually that external support is internalized and conceptualized, and finally that support is discarded and one enters the state of meditation proper.

Five factors of absorption (*jhananga*) are crucial to developing the states of meditation that result in the type of consciousness belonging to the form and formless spheres: (i) initial application (*Vitakka*), (ii) sustained application (*vichara*), (iii) interest, enthusiasm, or rapture (*piti*), (iv) happiness or bliss (*sukha*), and (v) one-pointedness (*ekaggata*). These five factors are also evident in most types of consciousness, including the sense-sphere consciousness and even the consciousness of some of the more developed animals. Take, for instance, one-pointedness. Every conscious moment participates in one-pointedness to some degree. This one-pointedness enables us to focus on a particular object in our conscious experience. If it were not for one-pointedness, we would not be able to pick out an object of consciousness from the stream of objects of consciousness.

The five factors of absorption play a particular role in the development of meditative consciousness in that they raise our consciousness from the sense sphere to the form sphere, and thence to the formless sphere, through intensification. Intensification implies the enhancement and development of the power of particular functions of consciousness. Intensification of the first two factors, initial application and sustained application, leads to the development of the intellect, which can then serve to develop insight. Similarly, intensification of the fifth factor, one-pointedness, leads to the development of fully concentrated or absorbed consciousness. Intensification of all five factors leads progressively to the attainment of supernormal powers. The five factors also help elevate one's consciousness from the sense sphere to the form and formless spheres by removing the five hindrances (nivarana): initial application corrects sloth and torpor; sustained application corrects doubt; enthusiasm corrects ill-will; happiness corrects restlessness and worry; and one-pointedness corrects sensual desire.

Let us look more closely at the five factors of absorption to see how they produce concentrated consciousness. To do this, we need to look in greater detail at their meaning. In the context of developing meditative consciousness, initial application (*Vitakka*) is better termed 'applied thought,' since it means 'hitting upon,' 'striking,' or 'mounting.' *Vitakka* mounts the mind, placing it on the object of meditation; vichara (sustained application) then keeps the mind firmly on that object, maintaining the placement of the mind. The third factor of absorption - enthusiasm, interest, or rapture (*piti*) - motivates one to pursue the activity of meditation diligently. It may be helpful to contrast interest (*piti*) and happiness (*sukha*) to understand the relationship between the two. Interest and happiness belong to two different classes of experience: interest to the volitional class (*sankhara*), and happiness to the feeling class (*vedana*).

On the one hand, interest is active anticipation and enthusiasm; on the other hand, happiness is a feeling of contentment or bliss. The commentaries have given the following example to illustrate the relation between the terms. Suppose a man in a desert is told that there is a pond of fresh water at the edge of a village nearby. Upon hearing the news, he experiences a keen sense of interest (*piti*) and is motivated and encouraged by the information. But when he actually reaches the pond and quenches his thirst, he experiences happiness (*sukha*). Thus it is interest or enthusiasm that encourages us to proceed toward concentrated consciousness, whereas happiness or bliss is the actual experience of mental happiness that results from concentrated consciousness. One-pointedness (*ekaggata*) is collection, non-distraction of the mind, focusing the mind without wavering on the object of meditation. It is like the flame of a lamp which remains steadfast in a room free of drafts.

When all five factors of absorption are present, we have the first form-sphere consciousness, or absorption. As factors of absorption are eliminated one by one, we progress step by step to the fifth form-sphere consciousness. In other words, when we eliminate initial application, we have the second form-sphere absorption; when sustained application is removed, we have the third form-sphere absorption; when interest is removed, we have the fourth form-sphere absorption; and when happiness is removed, we have the fifth form-sphere absorption. These five types of consciousness are karmically active, wholesome types of consciousness. In addition, there are five reactive, resultant and five inactive or functional types of consciousness. The first five are karmically active and are present in this life.

The second five are the result of the first five; in other words, cultivation of form-sphere absorption results in rebirth in the form sphere. The third five are the five form-sphere absorptions as practiced by the liberated ones (*Arhats*), who have broken the bonds of action and reaction; hence the five form-sphere absorptions are regarded as inactive when practiced by them. Thus there are fifteen types of form-sphere consciousness: five wholesome-active, five resultant, and five inactive. When one has attained the fifth form-sphere consciousness, one experiences dissatisfaction with the limited nature of the form-sphere absorptions. One then progresses to formless-sphere meditation, again by means of an object of meditation, commonly one of the ten supports (*kasina*). One achieves this transition by extending the support until it covers the infinity of space, then discarding the support and meditating on the infinity of space, thereby achieving the first of the formless-sphere absorptions.

When this is achieved, one progresses to the second formless-sphere absorption, which dwells on the infinity of consciousness. At this stage, rather than focusing on the object of the meditating consciousness (i.e., the infinity of space), one focuses on the subject of the meditative consciousness (i.e., the consciousness that pervades infinite space, or infinite consciousness). The third formless-sphere absorption dwells on the present nonexistence of the preceding infinite consciousness that pervaded infinity. In other words, the third formless-sphere absorption dwells on nothing at all, nothingness, or voidness. Finally, the fourth formless-sphere absorption dwells on the realm of neither perception nor non-perception, a condition where consciousness is so subtle that it cannot be described as existent or nonexistent.

As with the form-sphere absorptions, there are three sets of formless-sphere consciousness (but with four instead of five types each). Four formless-sphere types of consciousness belong to the wholesome-active category; four belong to the resultant-reactive category, that is, rebirth in the formless sphere; and four belong to the inactive or functional category, the formless-sphere absorptions as practiced by the *Arhats*. In sum, there twelve types of formless-sphere consciousness: four wholesome-active, four resultant, and four inactive. If we look at the progression in the formless-sphere absorptions, we see a gradual unification and rarefaction of consciousness-an absorption in the infinity of the object (space), then an absorption in the infinity of the subject (consciousness), followed by an absorption in nothingness, and, finally, an absorption in neither perception nor non-perception. You will remember that, when we talked about consciousness and its object as the fundamental, germinal structure of experience, we had in the sense-sphere consciousness the most fragmented type of experience, where consciousness and its object are broken down into many factors.

As we progress through the form and formless spheres, gradually we have a unification of the subject and a unification of the object, so that when we arrive at the fourth formless-sphere absorption, we have reached the summit of mundane experience. It is interesting that the form-sphere and formless-sphere absorptions were known to yogis before the time of the Buddha and were practiced by the Buddha's contemp-oraries. We have reason to believe that the two teachers with whom Gotama studied before his enlightenment were practitioners of these meditations. The formless-sphere absorptions were the highest level of spiritual development to which man could aspire before the Buddha, on the night of his enlightenment, demonstrated that absorption has to be combined with wisdom to become truly supramundane.

This is why it is said that, although one can achieve the highest development possible in meditation and be reborn at the pinnacle of the formless sphere, when the power of that meditative absorption- which is, after all, impermanent- wanes, one will be reborn in a lower sphere. For this reason, one must go beyond even these very rarefied and highly developed levels of meditative consciousness. One has to couple the concentrated and unified consciousness of the absorptions with wisdom; only then can one progress beyond the mundane to the supramundane types of consciousness. There are two ways of distinguishing the supramundane types of consciousness from the mundane types (the consciousness of the sense sphere, form sphere, and formless sphere). The first distinction is in terms of determination and direction.

The mundane consciousness is determined, undirected, and subject to karma and conditions, whereas the supramundane consciousness is determining, directed toward a goal, and no longer subject to forces beyond its control. Supramundane consciousness is determining because of the predominance not of karma but of wisdom. The second distinction is that the mundane types of consciousness have as their object conditioned phenomena, whereas the supramundane types have as their object the unconditioned - namely, nirvana. The Buddha spoke of nirvana as an unborn and uncreated state. Such a state is necessary in order that there be a way out of the conditioned world of suffering. In this sense the object of the supramundane type of consciousness is uncreated and unconditioned.

We can generally divide the supramundane types of consciousness into four active and four passive types of consciousness. Normally, types of consciousness can be active or passive, and the passive types can be reactive (resultant) or inactive (functional). However, there are no functional or inactive types of consciousness in this category because here the types of consciousness are determining, not determined. These eight basic types of supramundane consciousness, four active and four passive, each correspond to the path and the fruit of the four types of noble ones- the stream-winner (*sotapanna*), the once-returner (*sakadagami*), the non-returner (*anagami*), and the *Arhat*. Here I ought to point out another distinction between supramundane and mundane consciousness. In the mundane types of consciousness, active and resultant types of consciousness can be separated by relatively long periods of time: in other words, an active, conscious factor may not produce its resultant factor until much later in the present life or even until a future life. For example, in the case of the consciousness of the form and formless spheres, the resultant consciousness does not occur until a subsequent life. In the supramundane types of consciousness, however, the resultant (or fruit) consciousness follows the active (or path) consciousness immediately.

The eight types of supramundane consciousness can be expanded to forty by combining each of the eight with each of the five form-sphere absorptions. The four types of active supramundane consciousness (the path consciousness of the stream-winner and so forth) combine with the consciousness belonging to the first absorption and so forth, so that there are twenty types of active supramundane consciousness associated with the four types of noble persons and five form-sphere absorptions. Similarly, the four types of resultant supramundane consciousness (the fruit consciousness of the stream-winner and so forth) combine with the consciousness belonging to the first absorption and so forth, so that there are twenty types of resultant supramundane consciousness, and forty in all.

This occurs in the following way. Based on the first form-sphere absorption, the path and fruit consciousness of the stream-winner arise. Similarly, based on the second third, fourth, and fifth form-sphere absorptions, the path and the fruit consciousness of the once-returner, the non-returner, and the *Arhat* arise. The consciousness belonging to the supramundane consciousness is therefore developed based on the various absorptions. Let us go on to define the four stages of enlightenment: stream-winner (*sotapanna*), once-returner (*sakadagami*), non-returner (*anagami*), and *Arhat*. The progress of a noble one through the four stages of enlightenment is marked by his or her ability to overcome certain fetters at each stage. There is a progressive elimination of the ten fetters (*samyojana*) that bind us to the conditioned universe until such time as we are able to achieve liberation.

Entry into the stream is marked by the elimination of three fetters. The first is the belief in the independent and permanent existence of an individual person (*sakkaya ditthi*) - namely, taking the mental and physical factors of the personality (form, feeling, volition, perception, and consciousness) to be the self. It is therefore not coincidental that we say that the mundane types of consciousness are conditioned by the aggregates, whereas the supramundane types of consciousness are undetermined by the aggregates. Overcoming the first fetter marks one's passage from the status of an ordinary worldling to the status of a noble person. The second fetter overcome by the stream-winner is doubt (*vichikichchha*). This is primarily doubt about the Buddha, Dharma, and *Sangha*, but also about the rules of discipline and interdependent origination.

The third fetter is belief in rules and rituals (*silabbataparamasa*). This fetter has often been misunderstood, but refers to the practices of non-Buddhists who believe that adhering to codes of moral discipline and ascetic rituals alone can lead them to liberation. When these three fetters are overcome, one enters the stream and will achieve liberation within no more than seven lifetimes. One will not be reborn in states of woe (the realms of the hell beings, hungry ghosts, and animals), and one is guaranteed implicit faith in the Buddha, Dharma, and *Sangha*. Having achieved this first stage of enlightenment, the noble person goes on to weaken two additional fetters, sensual desire and ill-will, thus attaining the status of a once-returner.

These fetters are particularly strong, which is why, even on this stage, they are only weakened, not removed. Sensual desire and ill-will may still occasionally arise, although not arise in the gross form familiar to worldly persons. When these two fetters are finally eliminated, one attains the stage of the non-returner. At this third stage one is no longer reborn in the cycle of birth and death but only in the pure abodes reserved for non-returners and *Arhats*. When the five remaining fetters are eliminated-attachment to the sphere of form (*rupa raga*), attachment to the formless sphere (*arupa raga*), conceit (*mana*), agitation (*uddhachcha*), and ignorance (*avijja*) - one achieves the pinnacle of the supramundane types of consciousness, the fruit consciousness of the *Arhat*. These four stages may be divided into two groups: the first three, which are called stages of one in training, and the fourth, the stage of one who is no longer in training.

For this reason, it may be useful to think of progress to Arhatship as a process of graduation, as in a program of academic studies. On each stage one overcomes certain barriers of ignorance and thereby graduates to a higher stage of training. At this point, a qualitative change occurs, from an undirected and determined condition to a directed and determining one. How does one make nirvana the object of one's consciousness, thereby transforming a mundane consciousness whose object is conditioned into a supramundane consciousness whose object is unconditioned? How does one realize nirvana? This is done through developing insight, or wisdom (*panna*).

To develop insight, we apply the two Abhidharmic methods of analysis and synthesis. We apply the analytical method in our examination of consciousness and its object - in other words, mind and matter. Through this analysis we arrive at the realization that what we previously took to be a homogeneous, unitary, and substantial phenomenon is in fact composed of individual elements, all of which are impermanent and in a constant state of flux. This is true of both mind and matter. Similarly, we apply the synthetic method by considering the causes and the conditions of our personal existence. In relation to what factors do we exist as a psycho-physical entity? This examination reveals that the personality existence is dependent on five factors- ignorance, craving, clinging, karma, and the material sustenance of life (namely, nourishment).

Insight in general is developed through applying the two Abhidharmic methods by dissecting internal and external, mental and physical phenomena and examining them in relation to their causes and conditions. These analytical and relational investigations reveal three interrelated, universal characteristics of existence: (1) impermanence, (2) suffering, and (3) not-self. Whatever is impermanence is suffering, because when we see the factors of experience disintegrate, their disintegration and their impermanence are an occasion for suffering. Moreover, whatever is impermanent and suffering cannot be the self, because self can neither be transient nor can it be painful. Penetrating these three characteristics leads to renunciation, to freedom from the conditioned universe.

Through understanding these three, one realizes that the three mundane spheres are like a banana tree - without essence. This realization leads to renunciation, to a disengagement from the conditioned sphere, and enables the consciousness to direct itself toward an unconditioned object, nirvana. Any one of the three characteristics can serve as a key to this new orientation. Any one of the three can be taken as an object of contemplation to develop one's insight. We can see this in the biographical accounts of the foremost disciples of the Buddha. Khema, for instance, achieved liberation through the contemplation of impermanence.

Once one has developed insight into one of the three universal characteristics, one can experience briefly a vision of nirvana. One's first acquaintance with nirvana may be likened to a flash of lightning that illuminates one's way in the darkness of night. The clarity of that flash remains for a long time impressed upon one's mind, and enables one to continue on one's way knowing that one is proceeding in the right direction. The first glimpse of nirvana achieved by the stream-winner serves as the orientation by which he directs his progress toward nirvana. One might almost liken this gradual development of insight to the acquisition of a skill. After first managing to bicycle a few yards without falling, it may be some time before one becomes an expert cyclist. But having successfully ridden those first few yards, one never forgets that experience and can confidently progress toward one's goal.

It is in this sense that contemplation of the three characteristics leads to the three doors of liberation: the door of signlessness, the door of wishlessness, and the door of emptiness. Contemplating the characteristic of impermanence leads to the door of signlessness; contemplating suffering leads to the door of wishlessness, or freedom from desire; and contemplating not-self leads to the door of emptiness. These three doors of liberation are the culmination of meditation on the three universal characteristics. Thus one gradually progresses through the four stages of enlightenment and eventually achieves Arhatship, that stage of victory over the afflictions in which the unwholesome roots of greed, ill-will, and delusion are totally removed. Having uprooted the afflictions, the *Arhat* is free from the cycle of birth and death and is no longer reborn.

Despite some attempts to tarnish it with the charge of selfishness, the goal of Arhatship is a beneficial and compassionate mode of being. One need only look at the Buddha's instructions to his eminent *Arhat* disciples, and also at the careers of these disciples, to see that in the time of the Buddha Arhatship was not a passive or selfish state of being. Sariputta, Moggallana, and others were actively engaged in teaching both the laity and other members of the Buddhist Order. The Buddha himself exhorted his *Arhat* disciples to go forth for the benefit of the many. The goal of Arhatship is a glorious and worthy one that ought not to be depreciated in any way by the fact that the Buddhist tradition also acknowledges the goal of the private or individual Buddha (Pachcheka Buddha) and the goal of Buddhahood.

In the Abhidharma, mental states are defined as 'those factor which are associated with consciousness, which arise and perish with consciousness, and which have the same object and bases as consciousness.' This immediately indicates the very close relationship between consciousness (*citta*) and mental states (*cetasika*). One of the best analogies to describe their relationship is that of the framework of a building and the building materials, or a skeleton and the flesh that covers it. Here the types of consciousness are the skeleton, while the mental states are the flesh that goes to build up a body of conscious experience. With this in mind, it is helpful to consider the types of consciousness enumerated in the Abhidharmic analysis of consciousness in terms of the mental states with which they are likely to be associated.

One's own analysis will not necessarily correspond exactly to the analysis in the texts. But insofar as certain mental states naturally appear to follow from particular types of consciousness, we will arrive at an understanding of how certain mental states and types of consciousness go together. This is far more important than memorizing the list of mental states. There are three general categories of mental states: wholesome, unwholesome, and unspecified. Unspecified mental states are neither wholesome nor unwholesome, but take on the nature of the other mental states with which they are associated. These unspecified mental states play a central role in the construction of conscious experience, much like the cement without which the building of experience cannot hold together.

There are two groups of unspecified mental states: universal (or primary), and particular (or secondary). The universal mental states are present in all types of consciousness without exception, whereas the particular mental states only occur in certain types of consciousness. There are seven universal unspecified mental states: (1) contact, (2) feeling, (3) perception, (4) volition, (5) one-pointedness, (6) attention, and (7) vitality.

1. Contact is the conjunction of consciousness with an object. It is the coexistence of subject and object which is the foundation of all conscious experience.
2. Feeling is the emotional quality of an experience- pleasant, unpleasant, or indifferent.
3. Perception implies recognition of the sense-sphere of the faculty to which a given sense impression pertains, that is, to the sphere of eye consciousness, ear consciousness, and so on.
4. Volition, in this context, does not mean free will but an instinctive volitional response.
5. One-pointedness occurs not in the sense of a factor of absorption but in the sense of the limitation of consciousness

to a particular object. One-pointedness occurs even in ordinary, non-meditative types of consciousness. One-pointedness is a necessary mental state in all types of consciousness because it is one-pointedness that isolates a given object from the undifferentiated stream of objects.

6. Attention can be seen in relation to one-pointedness. One-pointedness and attention are the negative and positive aspects of the same function. One-pointedness limits one's experience to a particular object whereas attention directs one's awareness to a particular object. One-pointedness and attention function together to isolate and make one conscious of a particular object.
7. Vitality refers to the force which binds together the other six states of consciousness.

There are six particular unspecified mental states: (1) initial application, (2) sustained application, (3) decision, (4) envy, (5) interest, and (6) desire. We have already encountered some of these in the context of the factors of absorption. The third particular mental state, usually translated as 'decision' (*adhimokkha*), is a very important one that indicates a particular decisive function of consciousness. The literal meaning of the original term is 'liberation,' in the sense here of 'liberation from doubt.' The sixth particular mental state, 'desire' (*chanda*), may be so translated as long as we remember that desire for sensual pleasure (*kamachhanda*) is negative and destructive, whereas desire for liberation (*Dhammachhanda*) is positive and constructive. Desire, therefore, has both a wholesome and an unwholesome function, depending both on the object of desire and on the other mental states with which desire is associated.

Let us go on to look at the unwholesome mental states. There are fourteen of them, and they are associated with the twelve unwholesome types of consciousness in five ways, which differentiates them into five groups. The first three groups take their character from the three unwholesome roots: delusion (*moha*), greed (*lobha*), and ill-will (*dosa*). The fourth group consists of sloth and torpor (*thina* and *middha*); the fifth consists of doubt (*vichikichchha*). Let us look at the group headed by delusion. This group is universally present in all types of unwholesome consciousness and it includes four factors: delusion, shamelessness, unscrupulousness, or fearlessness, and restlessness. Both shamelessness and fearlessness have moral and ethical connotations, which function internally and externally.

When we speak here of shamelessness, what we mean is an internal inability to restrain oneself from unwholesome actions due to the inability to apply one's personal standards to one's actions. And when we speak of fearlessness, or lack of dread, what we mean is the inability to recognize the application of social standards of morality to one's actions. With these two terms, we have an indication that standards of morality are arrived at both inwardly, in relation to oneself, and outwardly, in relation to others. Particularly in cases of deluded consciousness, we find a peculiar pattern of behaviour. When a person's consciousness is dominated by delusion and he is unable to apply internal standards of morality, he acts in an unwholesome way. Similarly, when he is unable to apply social standards of morality, he is careless about his actions.

This inability to apply internal and external standards of morality to one's actions creates restlessness, the fourth factor in this delusion-dominated group. The second of the five groups of unwholesome mental states is the greed-dominated group: here greed is accompanied by mistaken belief and conceit. The personal and practical extension of a greed-dominated consciousness is a tendency toward self-aggrandizement, the accumulation and exhibition of knowledge, and the occurrence of pride, egoism, and conceit. The third group of unwholesome mental states is that dominated by ill-will. This ill-will is accompanied by envy, avarice, and worry. The fourth group includes sloth and torpor, which are particularly relevant in the context of volitionally induced categories of consciousness.

The fifth group consists of doubt, which applies in all cases where decision is not present - namely, the decision (or 'liberation from doubt') that is one of the six particular unspecified mental states. There are nineteen mental states common to all wholesome types of consciousness. A number of these are factors conducive to enlightenment (*Bodhipakkhiya Dhamma*), and thus play an important role in the cultivation and development of one's spiritual potential. The list begins with faith and includes mindfulness, shame, dread, non-greed, non-hatred, balance of mind, tranquillity, lightness, elasticity, adaptability, and proficiency and rectitude of psychic elements and of mind. Notice the presence of shame and dread, the direct opposites of the unwholesome mental states of shamelessness and fearlessness.

The nineteen wholesome mental states are occasionally accompanied by six additional ones: the three abstinences (right speech, right action, and right livelihood); the two illimitables or immeasurables (compassion and appreciative joy); and reason or wisdom. When these six are included, there are twenty-five wholesome mental states in all. Wisdom occupies a position within the wholesome mental states similar to the position of desire within the unspecified ones. Just as desire can be unwholesome or wholesome depending on its object, so wisdom can be mundane or supramundane depending on whether its object is ordinary knowledge or ultimate reality. To reinforce what have said about the close relationship between the types of consciousness and the mental states, refer to the subjective classification of consciousness. There we spoke of the types of consciousness according to their karmic value - wholesome, unwholesome, resultant, and functional. Particularly within the sphere of sense desire, we spoke of a further classification of consciousness in terms of feeling, knowledge, and volition.

Combining these, we have within the sphere of sense desire a fourfold subjective classification of consciousness according to its karmic, emotional, intellectual, and volitional value - in other words, (1) in terms of wholesome, unwholesome, or neutral; (2) in terms of pleasant, unpleasant, or indifferent; (3) in terms of being associated with knowledge, disassociated with knowledge, or associated with wrong beliefs; and (4) in terms of being prompted or unprompted. With this fourfold scheme, we can see how the types of consciousness are determined by the presence of mental states. For example, within the karmic value category, wholesome types of consciousness are determined by wholesome mental states. Within the emotional value category, the types of consciousness are determined by the presence of states that belong to the feeling group (mental pleasure, mental pain, physical pleasure, physical pain, and indifference). Within the intellectual value category, the presence or absence of delusion determines whether a particular type of consciousness is associated with knowledge, disassociated with knowledge, or associated with wrong belief.

And within the volitional value category, the presence or absence of doubt and decision determines whether a particular type of consciousness is prompted or unprompted, non-spontaneous or spontaneous. Thus the four subjective classifications of consciousness clarify just how the various types of consciousness are determined by the presence of appropriate mental states- wholesome, unwholesome, associated with knowledge, and so forth. Finally, I would like to examine how the mental states operate in counteracting each type of consciousness. This is interesting because the Abhidharmic analysis of consciousness has sometimes been likened to the Periodic Table's analysis of elements by their respective atomic values. One cannot help but be struck by the almost chemical properties of the mental states: just as, in chemistry, a base neutralizes an acid, and vice versa, so in the analysis of consciousness, one mental state counteracts certain other mental states, and vice versa.

For example, within the factors of absorption, the five mental states counteract the five hindrances (initial application counteracts sloth and torpor; sustained application counteracts doubt; interest counteracts ill-will; happiness counteracts restlessness and worry; and one-pointedness counteracts sensual desire). Where there isn't a one-to-one relationship, groups of wholesome factors counteract a single unwholesome factor or group of unwholesome factors (faith counteracts doubt and delusion; mental balance and tranquillity counteract doubt and worry; lightness, elasticity, adaptability, and proficiency of the mind and the psychic elements counteract sloth and torpor; and so forth). Again, when decision is present, doubt is not.

In this way, the various wholesome mental states counter and oppose various unwholesome ones. The presence of certain mental states eliminates states opposed to them and thus makes room for states in accord with them. Through understanding the relationship between consciousness and mental states, and through cultivating the wholesome mental states, we can gradually change and improve the character of our conscious experience. Why analyze the processes of thought or the processes of perception? To answer this, we need to remind ourselves of the general purpose of the Abhidharma- namely, to facilitate our understanding of the ultimate nature of things, which share the three universal characteristics of impermanence, suffering, and not-self. In the analysis of thought-processes, we can see impermanence and not-self clearly revealed, as two analogies from the discourses of the Buddha show.

The Buddha likened the life span of a living being to a single point on the wheel of a chariot. He said that, strictly speaking, a living being only endures for the time it takes one thought to arise and perish, just as the chariot wheel, whether rolling or at rest, makes contact with the ground at only a single point. In this context, the past moment existed but it does not exist now, nor will it exist in the future; the present moment exists now but did not exist in the past, nor will it exist in the future; and the future moment, although it will exist in the future, does not exist now, nor did it exist in the past. The Buddha also referred to the case of a king who had never heard the sound of a lute. When he did hear one, the king asked his ministers what it was that was so enchanting and enthralling. His ministers replied that it was the sound of a lute.

The king asked for the lute; when his ministers brought one, he asked them where the sound was. When the ministers explained that the sound was produced by a combination of diverse factors, the king said that the lute was a poor thing indeed, broke it up with his own hands, and had the pieces burned and their ashes scattered. What the ministers called the sound of a lute, the king said, was nowhere to be found. Similarly, nowhere among the physical and mental factors of experience- among factors of form, feeling, perception, volition, and consciousness- is there a self to be found. Thought-processes are, like the sound of a lute, also devoid of self. The analysis of thought-processes also has a very specific application in the area of mental development, in the mastery and control of objects of the senses. You may recall that we spoke earlier about the sensitivity of the mind to the objects of the senses, and said that the mind is constantly subject to distractions that arise because of contact with sights, sounds, smells, tastes, and tactile sensations.

The Buddha himself declared that one is either conquered by sense objects or conquers them: in other words, one is either controlled by and subject to sense stimuli or manages and dominates sense stimuli. This is why Nagarjuna once said that even an animal can be victorious in battle, whereas he who is able to conquer the momentary, ever-changing objects of the senses is the true hero. When someone subdues, masters, and controls the objects of the senses, we call him heedful. Heedfulness is akin to mindfulness, which the Buddha said is the one way to freedom. Heedlessness is the source of death and of bondage in *samsara,* while heedfulness is the source of the deathless, or Nirvana. Those who were formerly heedless and later become heedful, like Nanda and Angulimala, are able to achieve the goal of freedom. By analyzing and understanding how the objects of the senses are perceived and assimilated by consciousness, we can pave the way toward right understanding in terms of impermanence and not-self, and toward control over the momentary objects of the senses.

Finally, we can achieve heedfulness, which is the key to changing our existence from one dominated by the afflictions to one that is purified and noble. We can begin our analysis of thought-processes by examining their place in our experience. Take the comparison of life to a river, with a source and an outlet. Between birth and death, between the source of the river and its mouth, there is a continuum but not an identity. In Abhidharmic terms, birth or rebirth is the 'uniting' or 'connecting' factor (*patisandhi*), the life continuum is the 'subconscious' factor (*bhavanga*), and death is the 'falling away' factor (*cuti*). These three factors have one thing in common: their object is the last conscious factor of the preceding life. This object determines them as wholesome or unwholesome resultant factors of consciousness. In this context, it is important to remember that *bhavanga* runs concurrent with the reproductive karma that gives a particular life its general characteristics and sustains it until it is either interrupted or exhausted. Thus the past, present, and future of an individual life are united not only consciously, by the continuum of *patisandhi, bhavanga,* and *cuti,* but also subconsciously, by *bhavanga* alone.

This subconscious factor of life continuum preserves continuity and sustains life even in the absence of conscious thought-processes, as in dreamless sleep and moments of unconsciousness like coma. In between the various conscious thought-processes, *bhavanga* reasserts itself and preserves the continuity of life. To summarize, our life begins with the uniting or connecting conscious factor (*patisandhi*) that joins the previous life to this life. It is sustained throughout the course of this life by the subconscious factor of life continuum (*bhavanga*), and it ends with the falling away (*cuti*) that again precedes union (in the form of *patisandhi*) with the subsequent life. Consciousness, as opposed to subconsciousness (*bhavanga*), arises as a phenomenon of resistance and vibration.

In other words, *bhavanga* remains subconscious until it is interrupted or obstructed by an object, as when we place a dam across a river and find that the course of the river is interrupted, or subject an electrical current to resistance and find that the phenomenon of light arises. This contact between *bhavanga* and an object results in resistance, and this resistance results in vibration, which in turn results in a conscious thought-process. The thought-processes that arise as a result of this interruption are either (1) physical thought-processes that operate through the five sense doors (eyes, ears, nose, tongue, and body), or (2) mental thought-processes that operate through the mind, the sixth sense organ.

Physical thought-processes are determined by the intensity, or impact, of the object that brings about the interruption of the stream of life continuum. In this sense, the largest obstruction will cause the longest thought-process, and the smallest obstruction will cause the shortest thought-process. There are four types of physical thought-processes, from one that runs for seventeen thought-moments to one that fails even to reach the point of determination or identification of the object. There are two types of mental thought-processes: (1) one termed 'clear,' which runs through to retention, the final stage of thought-processes, and (2) one termed 'obscure,' which ends before the stage of retention. Depending on the intensity of the obstruction in the subconscious stream of life continuum, we have a more intensive and lengthier thought-process or a less intensive and briefer one.

Let us look at the seventeen thought-moments that make up the longest of any of the thought-processes, physical or mental. Remember that each of these thought-moments is said to last less than one billionth the time it takes to wink an eye. Thus when the Buddha said that a living being endures only as long as a single thought-moment, he was talking about an extremely brief period of time. The first of these seventeen thought-moments is termed 'entry' and refers to an object impinging upon the stream of life continuum, or the placing of an object of obstruction in the river of life. The second moment is termed 'vibrating' because the entry of the object into the stream of life continuum sets up a vibration. The third is the 'arresting' moment because at this point the obstruction interrupts or arrests, the stream of life continuum. Here we might ask how is it that the stream of life continuum (*bhavanga*), which has its own object that forms the basis of the factor of unification (*patisandhi*) and the factor of decay (*cuti*), comes to have a secondary object in the form of a material object of the senses. This is explained by means of an analogy. Buddhaghosa said that, just as tapping one grain of sugar among many scattered on the surface of a drum causes a vibration that affects a fly sitting on another grain of sugar on the drum, so material objects of the five physical senses impinge upon and set up vibrations that affect *bhavanga*. Once these three moments- entry, vibration, and interruption or arresting- have taken place, the object enters the conscious sphere. It does this through the fourth thought-moment, which is the moment of the 'adverting consciousness.' In the case of the physical thought-processes, the adverting consciousness can be of five types - eye, ear, nose, tongue, and body.

This is succeeded by the fifth moment, the 'perceiving consciousness,' which can be of the five types - eye consciousness, ear consciousness, and so forth. This is followed by the sixth moment, the 'receiving consciousness'; the seventh moment, the 'investigating consciousness'; and the eighth moment, the 'determining consciousness.' It is the determining consciousness that identifies and recognizes the object of perception. This determining consciousness is followed by seven moments of 'impulse consciousness' (*javana*), which have the function of running through the object, thereby assimilating the object wholly into consciousness. These ninth through fifteenth thought-moments are followed by two moments of resultant, retentive consciousness, for seventeen thought-moments in all. The seven moments of impulse consciousness are karmically active and can be wholesome or unwholesome.

The moments of resultant, retentive consciousness, too, are either wholesome or unwholesome. For the purpose of practice of the path, it is important to know at which point in these seventeen thought-moments one is able to act freely, for better or for worse. The three moments of *bhavanga* are resultant. The adverting consciousness and the determining consciousness are functional. The perceiving consciousness is resultant. Thus the seven moments of impulse consciousness (*javana*) are the first karmically active thought-moments. The first of these seven moments determines the next six, so if it is wholesome, the rest are wholesome, and if it is unwholesome, the rest are unwholesome, too. It is at the point when determining consciousness is followed by the seven impulse moments that resultant or functional states give way to active states.

This is the all-important point in thought-processes, because one cannot alter the character of resultant or functional states but can alter the character of active states, which have a wholesome or unwholesome karmic potential. At the moment when the *javana* moments commence, the presence or absence of wise attention is therefore very important. If wise attention is present, the probability of wholesome impulses is greater; if absent, unwholesome impulses are more likely to predominate. The actual object of the seventeen thought-moments is of little importance here because the object in itself, no matter how desirable or undesirable does not determine whether the seven impulse moments are wholesome or unwholesome. You may recall the case of the Elder Tissa.

It happened that the daughter-in-law of a certain family, having quarreled with her husband, dressed in her best garments and jewelry and set out to return to her father's house. When she came upon the Elder Tissa, being of an irreverent nature, she let out a loud laugh. Seeing her teeth, Tissa reacted in terms of the perception of the foulness of the body, and by the strength of that perception won through to Arhatship on the spot. When the woman's husband came along and asked whether Tissa had seen a woman going that way, the *Arhat* replied that he was not aware whether it had been a man or woman but knew that he had seen a heap of bones walking along the road. This story indicates that no matter what the nature of the determining consciousness, the seven moments of impulse consciousness can be an occasion for either winning through to the stage of Arhatship or for the further accumulation of moments of consciousness that have an unwholesome karmic value.

To a man other than Tissa, the sight of the woman laughing might have given rise to impulses rooted in lust rather than ones leading to the realization of Arhatship. Since wise attention or the lack of it determines the karmic value of the impulse moments that follow, we need to apply wise attention to decrease the chances of unwholesome impulses arising and increase the chances of wholesome moments of impulse consciousness and to conclude by referring to a simile popularized by Buddhaghosa in his Path of Purification (*Visuddhi Magga*) to illustrate the seventeen moments of consciousness in a thought-process. Suppose a man has gone to sleep at the foot of a mango tree full of ripened fruit. A ripened mango is loosened from a branch and falls to the ground. The sound of the mango falling to the ground stimulates the ears of the sleeping man, who awakes, opens his eyes, and sees the fruit lying not far from where he is. He stretches out his arm and takes the mango in his hand. He squeezes the mango, smells it, and then eats it.

This whole process illustrates the seventeen moments of perceiving a physical object. The sound of the falling mango impinging upon the man's ears is analogous to the three moments of *bhavanga* - entry, vibration, and interruption. When the man uses his eyes and spots the mango, this is analogous to the moments of adverting and perception; when he stretches out his hand to take the fruit, to the moment of receiving; when he squeezes the mango, to the moment of investigating; when he smells it, to the moment of determining; when he eats it and enjoys it, to the seven moments of impulse consciousness; and (although apparently Buddhaghosa did not do this) one might add that when he digests it, this is analogous to the two resultant moments of retention.

If we analyze our thought-processes carefully, and if through heedfulness we master them, this can result in a deepened understanding of the ultimate nature of things as impermanent and not-self. This analysis can also lead to mastery over the objects of the senses, the result of which is dispassion, joy, and freedom. We should therefore apply the knowledge we gain about the momentary, conditioned, and transient nature of the processes of thought and perception to our daily experience, in order to seek out that understanding and wise attention which will enable us to multiply our moments of wholesome karmic potential and minimize our moments of unwholesome karmic potential.

If we can do this, we will have taken a very important step in extending our study of the Abhidharma from the merely intellectual sphere to the practical and experiential sphere. The Abhidharma is supposed to deal with four ultimate realities- consciousness (*citta*), mental states (*cetasika*), matter (*rupa*), and nirvana. Matter shares with consciousness and mental states the character of being a conditioned reality, whereas nirvana is an unconditioned reality. In considering the three conditioned realities, we can simultaneously treat the five aggregates of psycho-physical existence. This harks back to what we said about the relationship between subject and object, mind and matter. Both these schemes can be reduced to two elements: the subjective or mental element, and the objective or material element.

On the one hand we have mind and the mental states- consciousness, volition, perception, and feeling- and on the other hand we have the object- form, or matter. In the context of the Abhidharma, it is important to remember that matter is not something separate from consciousness. In fact, mind and matter can be simply called the subjective and objective forms of experience. We will see more precisely why this is true when we consider the four essentials of matter (earth, water, fire, and air) as qualities of matter rather than as the substance of matter. Because Buddhism has a phenomenological approach to existence, matter is only important insofar as it is an object of experience that affects our psychological being. Whereas certain other systems assert a radical and absolute dualism, a dichotomy between mind and body, in Buddhism we simply have subjective and objective forms of experience.

In the classification and enumeration of matter in the Abhidharma, matter is divided into twenty-eight elements. The four primary elements, or four essentials of matter, are simply called earth, water, fire, and air. However, earth might better be called 'the principle of extension or resistance'; water, 'the principle of cohesion'; fire, 'the principle of heat'; and air, 'the principle of motion or oscillation.' These are the four primary building-blocks of matter. From them are derived the five physical sense organs and their objects. In this context, as well as in the context of the five aggregates, matter refers not only to our bodies but also to the physical objects of experience that belong to the external world. Beyond organs and their objects, matter is also present in masculinity and femininity, in the heart, or the principle of vitality, and in nourishment.

There are also six further elements of matter, which are: the principle of limitation or space, the two principles of communication (bodily communication and verbal communication), lightness, softness and adaptability. Finally, there are four elements that are termed 'characteristics': production, duration, destruction, and impermanence. There are thus twenty-eight components of matter or, to be more precise, of material experience, in all: the four essentials, the five sense organs and their corresponding objects, the two dimensions of sexuality, vitality, nourishment, space, the two forms of communication, lightness, softness and adaptability and the four characteristics. Let us look more closely at the four essentials in terms of their reality as sensory qualities. It is important to remember that when we speak of the four primary elements of matter, we are concerned not with earth, water, fire, and air in themselves but with the sensory qualities of these elements- the qualities that we can feel and that give rise to the experience of matter. Thus we are concerned with sensory qualities like hardness and softness, which belong to the principle of extension, and warmth and cold, which belong to the principle of heat.

We are not dealing with essences. Rather, we are dealing with qualities that are experienced. This means, in turn, that we are dealing with a purely phenomenological treatment of matter, in which sensory qualities function as the definitive characteristics of matter. It is the sensory qualities that constitute ultimate realities. In other words, it is neither the table nor my body, but the sensory qualities of hardness and softness that belong to both the table and my body, that give rise to the experience of matter. In this context, the objects of my experience (such as the table and my body) are conventional realities, whereas the sensory qualities of hardness, softness, and so forth that give rise to the experience of matter are ultimate realities.

This is what is called in philosophy a 'modal view,' a view that concentrates on the qualities of experience rather than on the essence of experience. To seek the essence of matter is to enter the world of speculation, to go beyond our empirical experience; to deal with the qualities of matter is to confine ourselves to phenomena, to experience. It is interesting to note that this modal view of matter is shared by some modern philosophers, Bertrand Russell perhaps being the best known among them. It is this modal view of reality which also informs much contemporary thought about matter. Scientists have come to recognize matter as a phenomenon, to recognize that it is impossible to arrive at the essence of matter, and this has been substantiated by the discovery of the infinite divisibility of the atom.

This model view of reality has another important implication: Insofar as we take a purely phenomenological and experiential view of reality, of existence, the question of the external world - in the sense of a reality existing somewhere 'out there,' beyond the limit of our experience - does not arise. Insofar as the external world gives rise to the experience of matter, it is just the objective or material dimension of our experience, not an independent reality that exists in it.

On a personal level, we find that our psycho-physical existence is made up of two components: the mental component, or the mind, and the physical component, or the body. The mind and the body differ somewhat in their nature - primarily in that the mind is more pliant and changeable than the body. The Buddha once said that we might be more justified in regarding the body as the self than the mind, because the body at least maintains recognizable features for a longer period of time.

We can verify this through our own experience. Our minds change much more quickly than our bodies. For example, I can make a mental resolution to refrain from eating starchy foods and fats, but it will take a considerable amount of time for that mental change to reflect itself in the shape of my body. The body is more resistant to change than the mind, and this is in keeping with the characteristic of earth, as represented in the principle of resistance. The body is the product of past karma, past consciousness, and is at the same time the basis of present consciousness. This lies at the heart of the uneasiness many intellectuals have felt about the body. A famous philosopher, Plotinus, once remarked that he felt like a prisoner in his own body, which he considered to be like a tomb.

Sometimes we would like to sit longer in meditation were it not for the physical discomfort we experience as a result of the body. Sometimes we want to work longer (or to stay awake to watch a particular television programme) but cannot do so because of the weariness that accompanies the body. There is a tension between mind and body due to the fact that the body is the materialized form of past karma, and because of the body's characteristic of resistance, it responds much more slowly to volitional actions than does the mind. Thus the body is, in a sense, an impediment that hinders mental development. We can see this clearly in the case of liberated beings. In *The Questions of King Milinda*, the king asks Nagasena whether *Arhats* can experience pain. Nagasena replies that although *Arhats* no longer experience mental pain, they can still experience physical pain.

Arhats no longer experience mental pain because the bases for mental pain (aversion, ill-will, and hatred) are no longer present, but they can experience physical pain as long as the basis for physical pain (the body) remains. Until an *Arhat* enters final nirvana- 'nirvana without residue,' without the psycho-physical personality- the possibility of physical pain remains. This is why, in the accounts of the Buddha's life and the lives of his prominent disciples, there are occasions when they experienced physical pain. The body has a peculiar, intermediate position, in that it is the product of past consciousness and the basis of present consciousness. This intermediate position is also reflected in the fact that some bodily functions are conscious and can be controlled by an act of will, while others are unconscious and proceed automatically. I can decide to eat another plate of food, but it is an unconscious bodily function that digests or fails to digest the meal; I cannot will my body to digest it.

Breathing, too, is representative of this intermediate position of the body; because breathing can be either an unconscious function or it can be raised to a volitional and conscious function for the purpose of concentrating and calming the body and mind. In coping with our existence as a composite of mind and body, we need to remember that the mind represents the dynamic, fluid, and volitional principle, while the body represents the principle of resistance. Because of this, it is not possible for the body to change as quickly as the mind in the process of development and liberation. The analysis of relations, or conditionality, is as important as the analysis of consciousness and the other aspects of psychophysical experience we have considered. This analysis has often been neglected in studies of the Abhidharma, which is paradoxical if you remember that, of the seven books of the Abhidharma Pitaka, the Book of Causal Relations (*Patthana*), which deals with conditionality, is one of the largest.

It is only by devoting sufficient attention to the analysis of conditionality that we can avoid some of the pitfalls of an overly analytical view of reality. I alluded to this, when I devoted some time to examination and comparison of the analytical and the relational methods of investigation, which together make up the comprehensive approach of Abhidharma philosophy. Perhaps because the analytical approach of the Abhidharma has received more attention than the relational, we find Abhidharma philosophy categorized as 'realistic pluralism' by some scholars. This kind of categorization awakens all kinds of associations with movements of modern western philosophy, such as positivism and the work of Bertrand Russell. It implies that the result of Buddhist analysis is a universe in which numerous individual, separate, and self-existing entities exist in own right and ultimately.

While this may have been the view of some early schools of Buddhism in India, it is certainly not the view of mainstream Buddhism, whether Theravada or Mahayana. The only way we can avoid this pluralistic, fragmentary view of reality is by taking due account of the relational approach outlined in the Patthana and also developed in the Compendium of Relations (*Abhidhamma ttha Sangaha*). By doing so, we will achieve a correct and balanced view of Buddhist philosophy, a view that takes into account the static and analytical aspect of experience as well as the dynamic and relational aspect. The importance of understanding relations, or conditionality, is clearly indicated in the Buddha's own words.

On a number of occasions the Buddha specifically associated the understanding of conditionality, or interdependent origination, with the attainment of liberation. He said that it is because of the failure to understand interdependent origination that we have so long wandered in this round of repeated rebirth. The Buddha's enlightenment is frequently described as consisting of his penetrating the knowledge of interdependent origination. This very close connection between the knowledge of interdependent origination and enlightenment is further illustrated by the fact that ignorance is most frequently defined, both in the sutras and in the Abhidharma, as either ignorance of the Four Noble Truths or ignorance of interdependent origination. Now, the theme underlying both the Four Noble Truths and interdependent origination is conditionality or causality, the relation between cause and effect. Thus the knowledge of conditionality is equivalent to the destruction of ignorance and the attainment of enlightenment.

The analysis of conditionality in the Abhidharma tradition is treated under two headings: (1) the analysis of interdependent origination, and (2) the analysis of the twenty-four conditions. We will look at them separately and then together, to see how they interact, support, and inform each other. I will not explain each of the twelve components of interdependent origination here, since they are described elsewhere. I would, however, like to briefly mention the three fundamental schemes of interpretation of the twelve components: (a) the scheme that divides and distributes the twelve components over the course of three lifetimes - past, present, and future; (b) the scheme that divides the components into afflictions, actions, and sufferings; and (c) the scheme that divides the components into active (or causal) and reactive (or resultant) categories.

In this third scheme, ignorance, mental formation or volition, craving, clinging, and becoming belong to the causal category and can belong to either the past life or the present life, while consciousness, name and form, the six senses, contact, feeling, birth and old age and death belong to the effect category and can belong to either the present life or the future life. Thus there is an analysis of cause and effect, or conditionality, in the formula of interdependent origination. The twenty-four conditions are not mutually exclusive. Many of them are partly or entirely identifiable with one another. The only explanation for several instances of almost (if not completely) identical factors is the desire of the authors' to be absolutely comprehensive, so as to avoid the slightest possibility of neglecting a mode of conditionality.

Let us look at each of the twenty-four conditions in turn: (1) cause, (2) objective condition, (3) predominance, (4) contiguity, (5) immediacy, (6) simultaneous origination, (7) reciprocity, (8) support, (9) decisive support, (10) preexistence, (11) post-existence, (12) repetition, (13) karma, (14) effect, (15) nutriment, (16) control, (17) absorption, (18) path, (19) association, (20) disassociation, (21) presence, (22) absence, (23) separation, and (24) non-separation.

A distinction must be made between cause, or root cause, and condition. We need to look at the Abhidharma literature if we want to distinguish cause from condition, because in the Sutra literature the two terms seem to be used interchangeably. Generally, we can understand the distinction by recourse to an analogy taken from the physical world: while the seed is the cause of the sprout, factors like water, earth, and sunlight are the conditions of the sprout. In the Abhidharmic treatment of conditionality, cause operates in the mental sphere and refers to the six wholesome or unwholesome roots - non-greed, non-hatred, and non-delusion and their opposites, greed, hatred, and delusion. Objective condition refers generally to the object which conditions experience. For example, a visual object is the objective condition of visual consciousness. Predominance refers to four categories of mental or volitional activities- wish, thought, effort, and reason- which have an overriding influence on factors of experience.

Contiguity and immediacy are virtually synonymous and refer to the conditioning of a thought-moment by the immediately preceding thought-moment. Contiguity and immediacy also refer to the conditioning of a given state of mind or matter by the immediately preceding state of mind or matter. We can perhaps understand this better if we think of contiguity and immediacy in the sense of immediate proximity in time and space, respectively. Simultaneous origination can be seen in the case of the mental aggregates of consciousness, volition, perception, and feeling, and also in the case of the four essentials of matter (earth, water, fire, and air). Reciprocity or mutuality refers to the mutual dependence and support of factors, as in the case of the legs of a tripod that depends on and supports one another.

Support means the basis of any particular factor, in the way that the earth is the support of trees or canvas is the support of a painting. But when simple support becomes decisive support, it should be understood in the sense of inducement in a particular direction. This will become clearer when we examine how the twenty-four modes of conditionality function in relation to the twelve components of interdependent origination. Preexistence or antecedence refers to the preexistence of factors that continue to exist after subsequent factors come into being. This is illustrated by the preexistence of the sense organs and objects of the senses, which continue to exist and thereby condition subsequent physical and mental experience. Post-existence complements preexistence and refers to the existence of subsequent factors such as mental and physical experience that condition preexisting factors like the sense organs and objects.

Repetition is important in the sphere of mental life and leads to skill or familiarity. This is exemplified in the seven moments of impulse consciousness. Repetition is particularly important in the sphere of wholesome and unwholesome action because it increases the force of wholesome or unwholesome thought-moments. Karma is volitional action of a wholesome or unwholesome variety. Effect or result indicates that the reactive aspect of previous karma has an influence and serves to condition coexisting phenomena. It is interesting to note that even effects do, to a limited extent, function as conditions or as causes. This will become clear if we remember that we are considering the functional rather than the essentialistic definitions of such factors.

Nutriment refers to not only physical food, which is one of the conditions of the physical body, but also to mental food, such as impressions, which are the mental food of the aggregate of feeling. Control refers to confidence, mindfulness, and so forth, which master or control their opposites. Absorption refers not only to meditative absorption but also to absorption in a more general sense, which encompasses both wholesome and unwholesome absorptions. You may remember that the factors of absorption (*jhananga*) are not necessarily wholesome and pertain not only to the states of meditative absorption but also to a general condition of intensification of consciousness, whether wholesome or unwholesome. Path refers to the path leading to unhappy states encompassing wrong views, wrong effort, and so forth, and also to the Noble Eightfold Path. Association refers to the conditioning of a factor by a similar factor, whereas disassociation is the conditioning by a dissimilar factor, such as the way sweetness and bitterness, light and darkness condition each other. Thus conditionality is not only positive but also negative. In other words, a particular factor of experience is conditioned not only by factors that are similar but also by factors that are dissimilar. Presence refers to the necessary existence of certain conditions in order that other phenomena occur. For instance, light must be present for the experience of a visible form to arise. Absence is, like disassociation, a negative form of conditionality.

For example, the disappearance of light is a condition for the arising of darkness. Separation and non-separation are identical to disassociation and association, respectively. The twenty-four modes of conditionality operate in conjunction with the twelve components of interdependent origination. For example, ignorance, the first of the twelve components, conditions volition, the second component, by way of two modes of conditionality: objective condition and decisive support. This can be understood as follows: Volition can be meritorious or demeritorious, and ignorance functions as the decisive support of both. Ignorance functions as the decisive support conditioning meritorious volition if it is made the object of your meditation, in that the desire to free yourself from ignorance induces you to practice meditation and so forth. Conversely, if an unwholesome state of mind, such as greed (which is born of ignorance), becomes the object of your absorption, then ignorance functions as the decisive support of demeritorious volition.

If you then commit an unwholesome action (steal a cookie, say), it is because ignorance has functioned as a decisive supporting condition inducing you to create the unwholesome volition on which the unwholesome action was based. Ignorance can also condition volition by way of contiguity, repetition, and so forth. Volition (the second component of interdependent origination) conditions rebirth consciousness (the third component) by means of karma and decisive support, while consciousness conditions name and form (the fourth component) through reciprocity and also by means of support. Thus each of the twelve components conditions the subsequent component in a particular way identifiable in terms of the twenty-four conditions. We could cite more examples, but they would only reiterate how these twenty-four modes of conditionality condition the twelve components of interdependent origination.

The idea at the heart of the teaching of interdependent origination and the teaching of conditionality is the avoidance of the two extremes, the erroneous views of eternalism and nihilism. The Buddha said that seeing the doer of an action and the one who experiences the fruit of that action as identical is one extreme, while seeing them as different is another extreme. He taught the avoidance of these two extremes when he taught the Middle Way, which emerges from an understanding of interdependent origination and conditionality. If we examine the twelve factors of interdependent origination in the light of the twenty-four modes of conditionality, we find that in all twelve factors there is no self, but only processes conditioned by other processes- processes that are, in their actual nature, empty of self and substance. This understanding of the emptiness of self and substance is achieved through an understanding of conditionality.

It is in this sense that the consciousness belonging to this life and the consciousness belonging to the next life are neither identical nor different. When we understand the relationship between this life and the next- between the doer of an action and the experiencer of an action- as one that cannot be described in terms of either identity or difference, we arrive at an understanding of the Middle Way. The relationship between this life and the next is one of cause and effect, and the relation of cause and effect is one of neither identity nor difference. In this way we can successfully avoid both the extreme of belief in an eternal self and the extreme of rejection of the law of moral responsibility, or karma. We can perhaps make this conditioned relationship between cause and effect clearer by looking at examples from daily life. Take the case of the seed and the sprout.

The sprout originates dependent on the seed, but the sprout and the seed are neither identical nor different. They are obviously not identical, but by the same token, neither are they altogether different. Similarly, when a sound produces an echo, the two are not identical but neither are they altogether different. In the same way, this life and the next life are neither identical nor different; rather, the next life arises dependent on this life, volition, and ignorance. In this process of conditioned arising, there is no persistent, permanent, and identical self, but neither is there an annihilation of the continuity of the process of cause and effect. If we can understand the relation between cause (or condition) and effect (or result) as a relation that cannot be described in terms of identity and difference, permanence and annihilation, we will understand emptiness, the Middle

Way, and how not-self and insubstantiality are compatible with moral responsibility and rebirth.

THE FACTORS OF ENLIGHTENMENT

The thirty-seven factors conducive to enlightenment (*Bodhipakkhiya Dhamma*) are important for two reasons. First, according to tradition, they were recommended by the Buddha, shortly before his entry into final nirvana, as primary means of gaining enlightenment. Second, these factors form a fundamental part of the foundation of the Abhidharma, in that they belong to that category of teaching, like the teaching on the five aggregates that comprises the Abhidharmic contents of the Sutra Pitaka. Previously, we talked about the characteristics of the Abhidharma and the relation between Abhidharmic material and the contents of the discourses, or sutras. The factors conducive to enlightenment belong to this category of material, which is Abhidharmic in nature and yet found in the discourses. Thus they belong to the early period of Abhidharmic philosophy.

The thirty-seven factors of enlightenment are without doubt Abhidharmic in nature. All five characteristics of Abhidharmic material apply to them: (1) definition of factors, (2) relation of factors to other factors, (3) analysis of factors, (4) classification of factors, and (5) arrangement in numerical order. The thirty-seven factors are classified under seven groups: (a) the four stations of mindfulness (*satipatthana*), (b) the four right efforts (*sammappadana*), (c) the four roads to power (*iddhipada*), (d) the five controlling faculties (*indriya*), (e) the five powers (*bala*), (f) the seven limbs of enlightenment (*bojjhanga*), and (g) the Noble Eightfold Path (*atthangika magga*). The Buddha called mindfulness the one way to the elimination of the afflictions. The Buddha has also said that the mind is the root of all virtues. The most important practice, therefore, is to discipline the mind.

One can also understand the importance of mindfulness from the fact that mindfulness occurs in five of the seven groups that make up the thirty-seven factors conducive to enlightenment, and that the first of these groups is devoted exclusively to the four stations of mindfulness (*satipatthana*). Mindfulness is also taught in the *Satipatthana* Sutta (The Discourse on the Stations of Mindfulness), which occurs twice in the Buddhist canon. All this indicates the importance of mindfulness. In recent years there has been a great resurgence of interest in the four stations of mindfulness both within the Theravada tradition, particularly in Burma, and also in the Mahayana tradition, where the importance of the four stations of mindfulness as a part of the practice of meditation has now come to be appreciated.

One of the reasons these four stations have occupied such an important place in Buddhist meditation is that they lead to the realization of the three universal characteristics (impermanence, suffering, and not-self). Exactly how this works will become clearer once we enumerate the four stations: (i) mindfulness with regard to the body, (ii) mindfulness with regard to feeling, (iii) mindfulness with regard to consciousness, and (iv) mindfulness with regard to mental objects. Mindfulness with regard to the body is more inclusive here than it is in the context of the forty traditional supports of meditation, where it occurs as one of the ten recollections but is restricted only to the body. Here it applies not only to mindfulness with regard to the body but also to mindfulness regarding the process of inhalation and exhalation, the elements of matter, the decomposing body, and so forth.

Mindfulness with regard to feeling refers to the emotional contents of personal experience, to feelings that are pleasant, unpleasant, or indifferent. Mindfulness with regard to consciousness- or, to be more precise, mindfulness with regard to thought - implies observation of the arising and perishing of thoughts. Mindfulness with regard to mental objects refers to the contents of consciousness, particularly concepts such as impermanence and the like. With the first station of mindfulness, we exhaust the material dimension of personal experience, and with the three subsequent stations we exhaust the mental dimension of personal experience (i.e., the aggregates of consciousness, volition, perception, and feeling). The thorough application of mindfulness results in abandoning the three erroneous views (permanence, happiness, and self) and attaining insight into the three universal characteristics (impermanence, suffering, and not-self).

Interpretations of the objects of the four stations of mindfulness vary according to the various traditions of Buddhist meditation. In general, however, the explanation here should be acceptable to most of the traditions. Let us look at the four roads to power (*iddhipada*): (i) wish or desire, (ii) energy, (iii) mind or thought, and (iv) reasoning. These four factors are also found in the twenty-four modes of conditionality, where they are termed 'predominant conditions' (*adhipati*). Both the 'roads to power' and 'predominant conditions' clearly suggest the power of the mind to influence experience. A simple example is the power to control, up to a certain point, the movements of our bodies and the exercise of our speech. This is a case of the undeveloped power of the mind, desire, energy, and reason to control physical phenomena.

When these predominant factors are intensified by cultivation of the five factors of absorption (initial application, sustained application, interest, happiness, and one-pointedness)- particularly the intensification of one-pointedness, which occurs upon attaining the fifth stage of the form-sphere absorptions- they become roads to power. Through intensification, the predominant factors lead to what are called mundane types of super knowledge and the supramundane knowledge. There are five types of mundane super knowledge: the ability to fly through the sky cross-legged, to walk on water, to move through the earth, to read the thoughts of others, and to recollect one's former lives. The supramundane knowledge is knowledge of the destruction of the defilements (*asava*), ignorance, and so forth. This is perhaps why it is sometimes said that the four predominant conditions may be either mundane or supramundane.

If they are directed toward the mundane sphere, they result in the five types of mundane super knowledge, whereas if they are directed toward the supramundane sphere, or nirvana, they result in penetration of the Four Noble Truths and in the destruction of the defilements. Like the four roads to power, the five controlling faculties (*indriya*) - (i) faith, (ii) energy, (iii) mindfulness, (iv) concentration, and (v) wisdom- are also found in the twenty-four modes of conditionality. In the Book of Causal Relations (*Patthana*), the five controlling faculties are defined as dominating factors. There is a very close connection between the five controlling faculties and the four roads to power, as indicated by their mutual presence in the modes of conditionality and their similarity in the sense of controlling, dominating, or mastering.

The five faculties are called 'controlling' because they are said to control or master their opposites: faith (or confidence) controls lack of faith (or doubt); energy controls laziness; mindfulness controls heedlessness; concentration controls distraction; and wisdom controls ignorance. Like the four roads to power, the five controlling faculties can only really control their opposites when they are intensified by the factors of absorption. For instance, faith can only function as a controlling faculty when it is strengthened by the presence of the three factors of absorption of interest, happiness, and one-pointedness; and wisdom can only function effectively when it is strengthened by initial application, sustained application, and one-pointedness. These five factors of absorption strengthen and intensify the five controlling faculties so that the latter can function effectively to propel one toward enlightenment.

Similarly, the five controlling faculties strengthen the five factors of absorption. For instance, concentration strengthens interest and happiness. Thus the relationship between the two sets of factors is one of reciprocal support and intensification. Although the five controlling faculties are indispensable in bringing about the transformation from a doubtful, lethargic, heedless, distracted, and ignorant mode of being to an enlightened mode of being, they must be cultivated in a balanced way. What this means is that within the five controlling faculties there are factors that balance each other. For instance, faith and wisdom is a reciprocal pair: if faith is allowed to dominate wisdom, these results in a weakening of one's critical faculties, one's intellectual powers of analysis and investigation; and if wisdom is allowed to dominate faith, this diminishes confidence to the point of uncertainty and a lack of initial commitment to practice.

Similarly, if energy is allowed to dominate concentration, this leads to agitation, and if concentration is allowed to dominate energy, this leads to sloth and torpor. Thus faith, energy, concentration, and wisdom must be developed and maintained in a balanced manner, and the faculty that enables one to do this is mindfulness. Mindfulness is the watchdog that ensures the proper reciprocal, balanced relationship between faith and wisdom, and between energy and concentration. The next group of factors of enlightenment, the five powers (*bala*) - (i) faith, (ii) energy, (iii) mindfulness, (iv) concentration, and (v) wisdom- is numerically and terminologically identical to the five controlling faculties. These five factors are called powers because on this stage faith, energy, mindfulness, concentration, and wisdom become firm, steady, and powerful.

The Buddha indicated that the five controlling faculties and five powers are two aspects of the same thing, just as an island in the middle of a river can lead people to call one side of the river the eastern part and the other side the western part, even though the two parts of the river are one and the same. Similarly, the five controlling faculties and the five powers are one and the same. The five controlling faculties are potentialities that must be intensified and developed through their combination with the five factors of absorption. When they become firm and steady through this intensification, they can then be termed powers. We might add that the five powers become absolutely unshakable only in the case of the noble ones. On becoming a stream-winner, for example, faith becomes an unshakable power because the fetter of doubt is removed.

Although only the five controlling faculties and five powers are listed in the thirty-seven factors, in the expanded

Abhidharmic classification of the controlling faculties and powers, there are three more faculties added to the five already mentioned (mind, joy, and vitality), and two more powers (moral shame and moral dread, known collectively as 'the guardians of the world'). Moral shame and moral dread are explained as one's own sense of moral uprightness and fear of censure or blame. They are called guardians of the world because, when developed to the level of powers, they become guardians of wholesome actions. The last group we will consider here are the seven limbs of enlightenment (*bojjhanga*): (i) mindfulness, (ii) investigation, (iii) energy, (iv) interest, (v) tranquillity, (vi) concentration, and (vii) equanimity. Mindfulness again appears as one of the factors, and again it leads the group, because it is with mindfulness that the way to enlightenment begins.

Thus it is through awareness of one's situation that progress on the path begins. This progress is sustained through investigation- in this case, the investigation of factors. Energy occurs here, as it did in the four roads to power, the five controlling faculties, and the five powers. Energy is essential to sustain the progress one makes along one's spiritual path. All too often, our efforts are sporadic; we make a great effort for a short period of time and then relapse for a much longer time. If progress is to be sustained it must be steady, and energy contributes to steady, consistent progress along the path. The fourth factor, interest, which is also one of the five factors of absorption, is suffused with happiness, although it can best be understood more as interest than as joy or rapture per se. Tranquillity in this context is the tranquillity of mind that results from eliminating the afflictions of ignorance, ill-will, and attachment. Concentration is synonymous with one-pointedness, which is one of the five factors of absorption. Equanimity is the elimination of the mind's tendency to wander. Like so many Abhidharmic terms, equanimity functions on a number of levels. At the level of feeling, it can be indifference. At the level of the cultivation of the Four Immeasurable meditations (*brahmavihara*), equanimity is even-mindedness toward sentient beings- the absence of attachment to near and dear ones, and the absence of aversion to enemies. In the analysis of personal experience in the teaching on the five aggregates, equanimity is the neutralization of the eight worldly conditions (happiness and pain, gain and loss, praise and blame, and fame and infamy).

Here, in the context of the seven limbs of enlightenment, equanimity is that integrated and unshakable state of mind which is totally free of mind's habitual tendency to wander. These thirty-seven factors were codified, preserved, and taught by generations of masters for one reason only: they were found to be useful and beneficial in developing one's mind, and particularly in aiding progress toward enlightenment. Whether we choose to concentrate on the four stations of mindfulness, the four efforts, the four roads to power, the five controlling faculties, the five powers, the seven limbs of enlightenment, or the Noble Eightfold Path, familiarity with these factors of enlightenment can manifestly and immediately aid our progress toward that goal.

ABHIDHARMA IN DAILY LIFE

Although it may not be possible to make complete use of what we have learned, I hope it will remain in the corner of your mind, and that you will be able to return to it and use it as time goes by. I would like to begin by drawing your attention to the fundamental orientation of the Buddha and Buddhism toward the whole question of spiritual progress. You will recall that the majority of the thirty-seven factors conducive to enlightenment relate to effort and to the mind. The emphasis in Buddhism has always been on these two aspects, in marked contrast to other religious traditions, where the most frequent answers to the question of spiritual progress refer to fate or grace- in other words, to some power outside us (whether an impersonal, unseen power, like fate, or a personal power, like God) that determines our progress and destiny. Fate and grace were typical answers given by other traditions in the Buddha's time, and they remain so today. Such approaches have one thing in common: they rely on something outside us, over which we have little or no control.

The Buddha, however, taught that it is one's own mind and effort that determine one's progress and destiny. Mind and effort are the keys to self-development, as is clearly reflected in the thirty-seven factors of enlightenment. This is why it has often been said that the mind is the most valuable thing we have. The mind has sometimes been likened to a wish-fulfilling gem, in that it can grant rebirth in fortunate or unfortunate states. It is on the basis of mind that one crosses the threshold of conditioned existence and enters the supramundane states of the noble ones. It is the mind which determines this, and it does so through intentional action, or karma- the expressed will of the mind, which results in the particular conditions in which we find ourselves. We can also see the importance of the mind reflected in the four roads to power, which are mental factors that can affect and control matter. What we need to do is intensify, cultivate, and elevate the mind.

We can see this clearly when we look at the five factors of absorption or intensification (*jhananga*) and the five hindrances (nivarana), two aspects of our ordinary, mundane consciousness. The five hindrances are typical of very low levels of conscious development, such as the consciousness of animals, which is saturated with these factors. The presence of these hindrances means that one's mind is totally conditioned and manipulated by various stimuli. In opposition to these five hindrances are the five factors of absorption, which are also present even in the consciousness of animals. The five absorptions counter and eventually eliminate the five hindrances. Thus we can reduce the controlling power of the hindrances to whatever extent we can cultivate the absorptions.

In a sense, we are standing at a crossroads. All ten factors, hindrances and absorptions, are present in our minds, and it is a question of whether we allow the hindrances to dominate or develop the factors of intensification so that they begin to dominate our minds. This is a very important battle because as long as the hindrances predominate we are very likely to see the results in this life and in the next life, in the form of rebirth in unfavorable or miserable states. But if our minds are raised by cultivating the five factors of absorption, we reach a higher level of development in both this life and the next. Once we have intensified and elevated the power of our minds by developing the five factors of absorption, we can motivate and direct our minds in a particular direction. This is done through the five controlling faculties: faith, energy, mindfulness, concentration, and wisdom.

It has been said that, to practice the Dharma, two things are essential: (1) faith and (2) wisdom. Wisdom is the main thing, while faith is the prerequisite. In some non-Buddhist traditions, faith means blind adherence, but in the Buddhist tradition, faith means confidence in the possibility of success. In other words, if we do not believe we can succeed, there will be no chance of achieving success no matter what we try to do. In this sense spiritual practice without faith is like a burned seed that will never put forth the seedling of spiritual progress, no matter how rich the soil or how carefully we tend it. Faith and wisdom are the first and last of the five controlling faculties. Together with the remaining three faculties of energy, mindfulness, and concentration, they are present in the Noble Eightfold Path. Energy, mindfulness, and concentration correspond to the three factors of right effort, right mindfulness, and right concentration of the mental development group of the Eightfold Path. Faith is related to the morality group of the Eightfold Path because it is faith, after all, which compels us to observe the rules of good conduct and believe in the law of karma at the beginning of our practice. Unless and until we have achieved supernormal levels of consciousness (like the Buddha and his foremost disciples, who were able to directly perceive the effects of wholesome and unwholesome actions), we must rely on faith to create the foundation of our practice of morality. Wisdom corresponds exactly to the wisdom group of the Eightfold Path. In the five controlling faculties, therefore, we have in germinal form the eight steps of the Noble Eightfold Path.

To summarize, to progress toward our goal of enlightenment, we need to intensify, elevate, and motivate our minds. The way we can do this is (1) to cultivate the five factors of absorption to reduce the influence of the five hindrances, and then (2) to develop the five controlling faculties and connect them to our practice of the Noble Eightfold Path. When the five controlling faculties become unshakable, they develop into the five powers, which bring with them the supramundane states of the noble ones. Wisdom, which is the last group of practice in the Noble Eightfold Path, is particularly relevant to the Abhidharmic studies we have undertaken because wisdom is the understanding of ultimate reality, and the Abhidharma is concerned with the presentation of ultimate reality. When we speak of wisdom, we have two components principally in mind: (1) not-self and (2) emptiness.

We have discussed the analytical and relational approaches to the analysis of personal experience in the teaching of not-self and in the teaching of dependent origination, respectively. When we consider not-self, we need to think of the self in relation to the five aggregates. Just as the erroneous idea of a snake exists dependent on and in relation to the rope and darkness, so when we look for the self in relation to the aggregates, we find that it does not exist in any way. The self cannot be found in any of the aggregates of consciousness, feeling, perception, volition, and form. The self cannot possess the aggregates in the way we might own a car. The self does not control the aggregates. It does not control the mind, nor does it control the body. The self is not in any way ascertainable within or without the aggregates. Having arrived at this understanding of not-self, we might look for a moment at the aggregates. At this point, we move from an analysis of personal experience in terms of the five aggregates to an analysis of the five aggregates in terms of dependent origination. The five aggregates do not originate by chance, nor do they originate without any cause. They originate dependently- dependent on the afflictions (ignorance, craving, and clinging) and on karma, volition, and becoming. It has been said that interdependent origination is the greatest treasure of the Buddha's teaching. Understanding interdependent origination is the key to undoing the knot that has kept us bound for so long in *samsara*.

The Buddha himself said that he who sees interdependent origination sees the Dharma, and that he who sees the Dharma sees the Buddha. This is a very encouraging remark, for if we can begin to see our daily experience in terms of interdependent origination- in terms of the conditioned, relative, and empty nature of the factors of experience - then we will see the Dharma, and through seeing the Dharma, we will see the Buddha. It will then no longer be true to say that we cannot see the Buddha, that the Buddha is not present here and now. I hope that this study of the Abhidharma will not remain an intellectual exercise but will be applied to our daily lives, however slightly. Insofar as we have moved toward a new way of understanding reality in terms of factors and functions that are interdependent and relative, we have moved some way toward seeing the Dharma and the Buddha.

5

The Organization of the Dharmas in the Abhidharma

The Dharmakâya (lit. Truth Body or Reality Body) is a central concept in Mahayana Buddhism forming part of the Trikaya doctrine that was first expounded in the *Saddharma Pundarika Sutra* (The Lotus Sutra), composed in the first century BCE. It constitutes the unmanifested, 'inconceivable' (Sanskrit: *acintya*) aspect of a Buddha out of which Buddhas and indeed all 'phenomena' (Sanskrit: dharmas) arise and to which they return after their dissolution. Buddhas are manifestations of the *Dharmakaya* called *Nirmanakayas.*

Unlike ordinary unenlightened persons, Buddhas (and *Arhats*) do not die (though their physical bodies undergo the cessation of biological functions and subsequent disintegration). In the Lotus Sutra (sixth fascicle) Buddha explains that he has always and will always exist to lead beings to their salvation. This eternal aspect of Buddha is the *Dharmakaya*. The *Dharmakaya* may be considered the most sublime or truest reality in the Universe corresponding closely to the post-Vedic conception of Brahman and that of the Father in the Christian Trinity.

Tibetan: *chos sku* "Chos" (Tibetan) holds the semantic field of "dharma" (Sanskrit). "Sku" (Tibetan) holds the semantic field of: "body, form, image, bodily form, and figure". Thondup & Talbott render it as the "ultimate body". In a key scholarly collaborative Nyingmapa translation work published in 2005, furthermore notable as the first complete rendering of the *Bardo Thodol* into the English language from the Tibetan, this technical term was configured into English as "Buddha-body of Reality". Padmasambhava, Karma Lingpa, Gyurme Dorje, Graham Coleman and Thupten Jinpa define 'Buddha-body of Reality' which is a rendering of the Tibetan Wylie 'chos-sku' and the Sanskrit 'dharmakâya' as:

> ...the ultimate nature or essence of the enlightened mind [*byang-chub sems*], which is uncreated (*skye-med*), free from the limits of conceptual elaboration (*spros-pa'i mtha'-bral*), empty of inherent existence (*rang-bzhin-gyis stong-pa*), naturally radiant, beyond duality and spacious like the sky. The intermediate state of the time of death (*'chi-kha'i bar-do*) is considered to be an optimum time for the realisation of the Buddha-body of Reality.

QUALITIES

Though attributeless and unattributable, *Dharmakaya* is held to possesses three great qualities: 'great purity' (Wylie: *sPang Pa Chen Po*), 'great realization' (Wylie: *rTogs Pa Chen Po*) and 'great mind' (Wylie: *Sems Pa Chen Po*).

ICONOGRAPHY

Thondup & Talbott (1996, 2002: p.48) identify '*Dharmakaya*' with the 'naked' ("sky-clad"; Sanskrit: *Digâmbara*), unornamented, sky-blue 'Samantabhadra':

> In Nyingma icons, Dharmakâya is symbolized by a naked, sky-coloured (light blue) male and female Buddha in union [Kâmamudrâ], called Samantabhadra [and Samantabhadri].

Unlike the 'form bodies' (Sanskrit: *rûpakâya*) of *Sambhogakaya* and *Nirmanakaya*, the *Dharmakaya* does not possess any 'divine attributes' nor 'ornamentation' (Wylie: *phyag mtshan*) as it is not only 'without form' or 'formless' (Sanskrit: *arûpa*) but beyond any concept, form, ornament, attribute or quality of the 'three realms' (Wylie: *khams-gsum*; Sanskrit: *tridhatu*). In the early traditions of what has been given the nomenclature Buddhism, depictions of the

Shakyamuni Buddha were neither iconic nor aniconic but depictions of empty space and absence: petrosomatoglyphs and footprints, for example. This is a worthy visual device to draw attention to the 'absence' and 'emptiness' of "thus gone" (Sanskrit: *Tathâgata*) and the doctrine of Úûnyatâ and represent whilst not representing.

Later representations of the Buddha were introduced as "skillful means" (Sanskrit: *upâya*). In the Dzogchen tradition, the Five Pure Lights which are the uncreated origin of the Five Wisdoms (the Five Wisdoms are the fabric of that which constitutes the *Sambhogakaya*, and this is common to both the Dzogchen traditions of the Nyingmapa and Bonpo), the colour blue is an iconographic polysemic rendering of the Mahâbhûta (Sanskrit) element, the "pure light" of 'space' (Sanskrit: *Âkâúa*). Fremantle (2001: p.85) states:

> Space is simultaneously the first and the last of the great elements. It is the origin and precondition of the other four and it is also their culmination...The Sanskrit word for space is the same as for the sky: *akasa*, which means "shining and clear." What is it that we call the sky? It marks the boundary of our vision, the limit our sight can reach. If we could see more clearly, the sky would extend infinitely into outer space. The sky is an imaginary boundary set by the limitations of our senses, and also by the limitations of our mind, since we find it almost impossible to imagine a totally limitless [U]niverse. Space is the dimension in which everything exists. It is all-encompassing, all-pervading, and boundless. It is synonymous with emptiness: that emptiness which is simultaneously fullness.

The conceptually bridging and building poetic device of analogy, as an exemplar where *Dharmakaya* is evocatively likened to 'sky' and 'space', is a persistent and pervasive visual metaphor throughout the early Dzogchen and Nyingma literature and functions as a linkage and conduit between the 'conceptual' and 'conceivable' and the 'ineffable' and 'inconceivable' (Sanskrit: *acintya*). In particular refer the *Gongpa Zangtal* (Wylie: *kun tu bzang po'i dgongs pa zang thal du bstan pa*; English: *Direct Revelation of Samantabhadra's Mind*), a terma cycle revealed by Rigdzin Gödem (1337-1408) and part of the 'Northern Treasures' or 'Jangter' (*chang ter*; Wylie: *byang gter*).

Sawyer (1998: unpaginated) in an essay to accompany curatorial notes for an exhibition, conveys the importance of 'mirror' iconography to *Dharmakaya*:

The looking glass/mirror (T. me-long, Skt. adarsa), which represents the *Dharmakaya* or Truth Body, having the aspects of purity (a mirror is clear of pollution) and wisdom (a mirror reflects all phenomena without distinction).

In the Pali Canon The Buddha tells Vasettha that the *Tathagata* (the Buddha) is *Dhamma*-kaya, the 'Truth-body' or the 'Embodiment of Truth', as well as Dharmabhuta, 'Truth-become', that is, 'One who has become Truth' (*Digha Nikaya*). On another occasion, the Buddha told Vakkali:'He who sees the *Dhamma* (Truth) sees the *Tathagata*, he who sees the *Tathagata* sees the *Dhamma* (*Samyutta Nikaya*). That is to say, the Buddha is equal to Truth, and all Buddhas are one and the same, being no different from one another in the Dharma-kaya, because Truth is one.' During the Buddha's life great reverence and veneration was shown towards him by persons from the highest to the lowest social classes.

The Buddha understood that this veneration was sometimes misguided based on superficialities and appearances and he warned people against turning him into an object of worship. Thus he forbade carvings and sculptures that represented his physical form. Nonetheless, a mythology developed concerning the physical characteristics of Universal Buddhas. In the Pali scriptures it is claimed that all Buddhas have the 32 major marks, and the 80 minor marks of a superior being. These marks are not necessarily physical, but are talked about as bodily features. They include the 'ushinisha' or a bump on the top of the head; hair tightly curled; a white tuft of hair between the eyes, long arms that reach to their knees, long fingers and toes that are webbed; his penis is completely covered by his foreskin; images of an eight-spoked wheel on the soles of their feet, forty teeth, etc.

Clearly if these were physical marks the Buddha would have been a strange looking individual. But since not everyone was able to discern these marks on him, we can assume that they were either metaphorical, or a psychic phenomenon. After the Buddha's Parinirvana a distinction was made between the Buddhas physical body, *rupakaya;* and his *Dharmakaya* aspect. This was an understandable and necessary development. As the Buddha told Vakkali, he was a living example of the 'Truth' of the Dharma. Without that form to relate to, the Buddha's followers could only relate to the *Dharmakaya* aspect of him. Despite the growth of the stupa cult in which the remains, or relics, of enlightened beings were worshipped, Buddhism sees such things as symbols of the Truth, rather than the Truth itself.

TRIKAYA DOCTRINE

Later Mahayana Buddhists were concerned with the transcendent aspect of the Dharma. So therefore if the Dharma is transcendental, totally beyond space and time, then so is the *Dharmakaya.* One response to this was the development of the *Tathagatagarbha* Doctrine, wherein the *Tathagatagarbha* or Buddha Nature is on occasion equated with the *Dharmakaya.* Another was the introduction of the *Sambhogakaya* which conceptually fits between the *Nirmanakaya* (which is what the *Rupakaya* came to be called according in the Buddhist Canon) and the *Dharmakaya.* The Trikaya doctrine (Sanskrit, literally "Three bodies or personalities"; Chinese: *Sânshén,* Japanese: sanjin) is an important Buddhist teaching both on the nature of reality, and what a Buddha is. By the 4th century CE the Trikaya Doctrine had assumed the form that we now know.

Briefly the doctrine says that a Buddha has three 'bodies': the *Nirmana-ka*ya or created body which manifests in time and space; the sambhoga-kaya or body of mutual enjoyment which is an archetypal manifestation; and the Dharma-kaya or 'Reality body' which 'embodies' the very principle of enlightenment and is omnipresent and boundless. The *Sambhogakaya* is that aspect of the Buddha, or the Dharma, that one meets in visions and in deep meditation. It could be considered an interface with the *Dharmakaya*. What it does, and what the *Tathagatagarbha* doctrine also does, is to bring the transcendental within reach, it places the transcendental on the plane of immanence. Buddha dharma is essentially atheistic, in that it does not operate with a theistic transcendentalism, but rather eliminates such confusion. On the other hand it is erroneous to say that Buddha dharma rejects the existence of cosmic intelligence.

TIBETAN MAHAYANA TEACHINGS

According to Jamgon Kongtrul's 19th century commentary to the Lojong slogan, "To see confusion as the four kayas, the sunyata protection is unsurpassable" (as translated by Ken McLeod) when one meditates on ultimate *bodhicitta* and rests in a state where appearances simply appear but there is no clinging to them, the *Dharmakaya* aspect is that all appearances are empty in nature, the *sambhogakaya* is that they appear with clarity, the *nirmanakaya* is that this emptiness and clarity occur together, and the *svabhavikakaya* aspect is that these are inseparable.

BUDDHIST ORGANIZATION

Recently, *Dharmakaya* has also become the name for an organization founded by H. E. the 4th Trungram Gyaltrul Rinpoche, and is affiliated with his global organization the United Trungram Buddhist Fellowship (UTBF). Gyaltrul Rinpoche's *Dharmakaya* organization was founded for the specific purpose of bringing the teachings and meditation practices from the Trungram Tradition of the Karma Kagyu lineage to North America. Phakchok Rinpoche is the Supreme Head of the Taklung Kagyu lineage, the Abbot of a monastery in Chapagaon in the southern Kathmandu Valley, and the Head of Riwoche Monastery in Tibet's Dokham region. Born in 1981 to Chokling Rinpoche and his wife Dechen Paldron, Phakchok Rinpoche is grandson of Tulku Ugyen Rinpoche and the eldest brother of the Yangsi Dilgo Khyentse Rinpoche.

Recognized by the Kagyu regents and ordained by His

Holiness the Dalai Lama, he has studied with a number of great lamas, including Khyentse Rinpoche, Dudjom Rinpoche, Tulku Ugyen Rinpoche, Penor Rinpoche, Trulshik Rinpoche and Nyoshul Khen Rinpoche. An enthusiastic and vibrant young lama, his teachings are direct, accessible, and always fresh, opening up our minds in a playful and inspiring way.

Phakchok Rinpoche is currently Vajra Master of Ka-Nying Shedrub Ling Monastery in Boudhanath, Kathmandu, and Abbot of Do-ngak Nyida Zungdrel Sherab Raldri Ling Monastery (Nepal). He is directing the development of the Vajravarahi Free Clinic, to be completed in 2007, which will provide free allopathic, Tibetan, Chinese, and Ayurvedic health care to the disadvantaged in the local community, and the Vajravarahi Monk School, to be completed in 2008, which will provide secular and religious education, training, room & board to 100 novice monks.

Phakchok Rinpoche is also Abbot of Pal Kagyu Shedrub Tashi Dhargye Phuntsok Ling Monastery, and President of Rangjung Yeshe Shenpen Nepal, a volunteer-based, non-profit organization that serves the poor and disadvantaged in areas of health, education, vocational training, street children, the elderly, and animals. Phakchok Rinpoche received the mKhan po title (similar to a PhD) from H.H. 14th Dalai Lama and H.E. Dzongsar Khyentse Rinpoche. He completed in seven years the traditional nine-year curriculum of Buddhist philosophy at the Dzongsar Institute of Advanced Buddhist Studies, Bir, and Himachal Pradesh, India. He specialized in studies of the Sakya school of Tibetan Buddhism under the guidance of Khenchen Kunga Wangchuk Rinpoche and H.E. Dzongsar Khyentse Rinpoche.

An enthusiastic and vibrant young lama, Phakchok Rinpoche's lectures are direct and accessible. He serves as Professor of Buddhist Philosophy, Rangjung Yeshe Institute Shedra, Center of Buddhist Studies, and Kathmandu University, where he teaches General Buddhist philosophy with emphasis on the Middle Way. He has been guest-lecturer at various centers in Denmark, Germany, Austria, Switzerland,

Belgium, United States of America, and Canada, and he recently established several new Buddhist centers in Malaysia. Phakchok Rinpoche is an Advisory Board Member of the Chokling Tersar Foundation.

Following Shakyamuni Buddha's passing some 2500 years ago, his teachings about how to live a worthwhile human life and train one's mind through meditation practices spread widely. At one time or another, the Buddhist world encompassed countries from Japan and China in the east, Sri Lanka and Indonesia in the south, Afghanistan in the west, and Korea and Mongolia in the north. The traditions we have today stem from particular teachings given by the Buddha at various times and places, later influenced by the characteristics and temperaments of people in the different Buddhist countries.

In the past, if you were interested in meditation or learning about the Buddha's teachings (the dharma, in Sanskrit), you simply went to the monastery nearest your village. Nowadays, thanks to the internet, easy communications, and travel, we have many choices that can feel confusing or overwhelming at the beginning. So many lineages! So many foreign words! This simplified view of the different Buddhist traditions alive today - a roadmap of sorts - may help.

THE THERAVADA LINEAGE

Following his enlightenment at Bodhgaya in India, the Buddha first taught at Sarnath, near modern Varanasi. These teachings - covering topics such as suffering, its cause, its cessation, and the path to cessation (the Four Noble Truths); interdependence; self-liberation from suffering; and so on - comprise the First Turning of the Wheel of the Dharma. At one time, more than twenty different schools focused on these teachings, but today only the Theravada lineage (found in Sri Lanka, Burma, Thailand, Lao, Cambodia, and Vietnam) survives as an independent philosophical school. (Two other lineages survive as the monastic lineages practiced in Mahayana traditions, but not as independent schools.)

These are often called the 'Hinayana' schools. Literally the word means 'lesser' - understood in the sense that their teachings focus on individuals liberating themselves from the world of suffering (*samsara*), which can be contrasted with other schools that emphasize liberating others. The Theravada scriptures (the *Tripitaka*) are written in the Pali language, one of many Indian vernaculars of the time, and because Theravada practitioners naturally do not believe that they are doing anything 'lesser', recently scholars have introduced the term Pali Buddhism to distinguish this school from others called Sanskrit Buddhism because their *Tripitakas* were first written in Sanskrit before being translated into local languages. The *Dhammapada, Dhammasangani*, and the *Visuddhimagga (Path of Purification)* are widely known Pali texts.

MAHAYANA LINEAGES

In the Second Turning of the Wheel of Dharma, taught at Rajgir in India and elsewhere, the Buddha emphasized that both people and phenomena lack any solid, independent existence or self. These are the teachings on emptiness (shunyata) and form the philosophical basis for the Mahayana schools. Along with the view of emptiness, these schools emphasize cultivating an outlook of compassion for all beings and working for the benefit of others. The term 'Mahayana' means 'Great Vehicle' - again, 'great' in the sense that compassionate activity to benefit others is of larger scope than concern only with oneself.

Mahayana lineages spread in Afghanistan, Indonesia, and other countries, and today are found in Bhutan, China, Japan, Korea, Mongolia, Nepal, Tibet, and Vietnam. The Zen lineages (called Ch'an in China) of Soto and Rinzai are the most widely known Mahayana lineages in the West, but there are others as well. The *Lotus Sutra*, the *Lankavatara Sutra*, and the *Prajnaparamita Sutras* are widely known Mahayana texts.

VAJRAYANA LINEAGES

Describing reality as suffering - the Hinayana view - is true and accurate, but perhaps incomplete. Describing it as empty is more complete and profound because it is a more subtle description of how things really are - without independent existence. The teachings of the Third Turning of the Wheel of Dharma are still more subtle, examining the enlightened essence (buddha-nature, *Tathagatagarbha*) that is spontaneously present in all sentient beings. True, all beings lack a self, but they also spontaneously possess all the qualities of enlightened beings once their confusion is clarified.

Buddha-nature is discussed at length in Mahayana contexts, but assumes an even greater importance as the philosophical basis for the third broad group of Buddhist schools: the Vajrayana, or Tantrayana. Having flourished for hundreds of years in India, following the demise of the dharma there, Vajrayana lineages survived in Bhutan, China, Japan (the Shingon School), Mongolia, Nepal, Tibet, and parts of northern India. Vajrayana lineages often describe themselves as operating within the broader Mahayana context but employing additional skillful means. Because buddha-nature is inherent in all beings and in all experience, anything whatsoever could become a means towards experiencing a profound moment of awakening. This accounts for the colorful aspects of the Tibetan tradition - where music, dance, costumes, and food are used within the context of meditation practices - that seem so outlandish when contrasted with the simplicity of the Theravada. The *Uttaratantra (Highest Continuum)* is a widely known third-turning text.

Looking at Shakyamuni Buddha's teaching career through the perspective of the three turnings of the wheel of dharma is one way of making sense of the different lineages that have arisen since his passing. The different schools described above each have their own sets of scriptures, or *Tripitaka,* which they regard as complete and authentic. The *Tripitaka* in turn is divided into three sections: the Vinaya (the rules of behavior for monks and nuns), the Sutra (meditation advice), and the Abhidharma (how an enlightened person experiences the world). The Tibetan tradition also includes another class of literature, the Tantras, considered a fourth *pitaka.*

Each of these schools includes sub-schools and particular lineages within those. This is most clearly the case in Tibet, where the four best-known present-day schools (Nyingma, Kagyu, Sakya, and Geluk) quickly branch out into numerous sub-schools and lineages. But even within the Theravada lineage, it is not the case that every teacher communicates the dharma in the same way, and particular lineages of meditation certainly have their own styles and emphases.

Shakyamuni Buddha said clearly that his attainment, though from one point of view an extraordinary achievement, was possible for all human beings regardless of wealth, position, sex, or caste. Nevertheless, the path of meditation can be a subtle one, and it is difficult to judge one's progress for oneself. Therefore since the time of Shakyamuni himself, Buddhists have placed great value on lineage: that one fully realized master (a lineage holder) instructs students who then attain the same understanding, which the master is in a position to verify. Thus, the experience of the dharma always remains up-to-date but complete from one generation of practitioners to the next. All the schools described here trace their lineages back to the Buddha.

Traditionally one does not set oneself up as a teacher, but begins teaching only after being told to by one's own master. Such authorization by a lineage holder becomes a guarantee of sorts for students: as long as new teachers work within the limits of their understanding and the authorization given by their teachers, the unbroken lineage has been maintained and new students can trust the quality of their instruction. There is a growing consensus in Western thought and science that we may understand ourselves and our world more deeply if we think in terms of patterns of relationships rather than of reified essences or entities - if we think, in short, in terms of dependent arising.

This chapter explores such possibilities by focusing upon two core concepts, the dependent arising of our "world of experience," and the notion of *vijnana*, "discerning cognitive awareness" or simply "consciousness," ultimately arriving at its most important development in the Yogacara school of Indian Buddhism, the *alayavijnana*, a form of subliminal cognitive awareness or "unconscious structuring of the world."

We will draw upon ideas from such modern fields as general systems theory, evolutionary biology and cognitive science in order to elucidate these ancient Buddhist notions, resulting in provocatively different, yet to my mind more evocatively contemporary, interpretations of key Buddhist concepts. Rather than pursue a simple point-by-point comparison between these traditions, however, we seek to invoke their commonalities by engaging in an inductive, almost phenomenological inquiry into the possibilities of speaking about experience "without using the personal pronoun."

To anticipate both the argument and structure of this chapter, we will focus on a number of areas where Indian Buddhist thought constructively converges with current trends in scientific approaches to mind: They both focus on patterns of dependent relationships rather than on actions of independent entities; within which cognitive awareness (*vijnana*) is understood as a process which arises by depending upon conditions, rather than a faculty that acts by cognizing objects. It arises, moreover, as the awareness of differences within a circumscribed cognitive domain, rather than as the perception of objects within a pre-existing external world.

These cognitive domains have arisen through processes of circular causality (feed back systems) in large part brought about by those very discernments of difference. Such differences themselves mainly arise within a larger classificatory context, through unconscious processes pre-formed by linguistic categories, rather than through conscious processes performing rational procedures. This "linguistification" of human mental processes gives rise to a symbolic self, which is dependent upon the reflexive possibilities of language rather than reflecting the existence of substantive souls.

Finally, the notion of a "cognitive unconscious" epitomizes all of the above points: it develops through evolutionary processes of circular causality, which give rise to forms of awareness without an experiencing subject, by means of which our world of experience is continuously yet unconsciously constructed, classified, and mapped. This unconscious structuring of experience, both traditions submit, imparts the cogency of human experience, with its deep sense of subjective coherence, without relying upon essential or substantive causal agents, either external or internal. In this way, at least some Buddhist thinkers and some modern scientists have reached some accord in ways to think about "Thoughts without a Thinker."

6

Phenomenology of Experience

The Indian Buddhists observed that we can best understand complex causality - how things come to be - by understanding the systemic relations in which they are embedded and the patterns of dependence upon which they arise, that is, their "dependent arising." As we shall see, this formula subsequently became the basis for a model of circular causality in which certain specific patterns of conditions continuously feedback upon themselves, reinforcing their own evolutionary processes.

The classical Indian Buddhist conception of causality is singularly expressed in the simple formula of dependent arising: When this is, that comes to be; with the arising of this, that arises. When this is not, that does not come to be; with the cessation of this, that ceases.

One of its most important implications is that it dispenses with the notion of fixed entities or unchanging essences altogether. Instead of asking how independent entities act within or upon an objective world, the view of dependent arising asks "under what conditions does such and such a phenomenon arise?," or, more elaborately, "what various complex conditions interact in what recurrently patterned ways in order to routinely give rise to what kind of phenomena?"

In other words, our attention toward independent agents acting on independent objects, the entrenched grammatical syntax of conventional language, is changed into an investigation of the complex, processual and interactive arising of things. But this requires focusing upon patterns of arising rather than on actions of agents; and patterns are relational, not substantive, and arising is dynamic, not static. The Buddhist dismissal of selves, essences or unchanging entities, therefore, does not depend upon logical propositions derived from first principles, such as "all is change," as much as it logically follows from the nature of the questions being raised, "how do things come to be?"-A point which is more obvious by a similar disavowal of essences, entities or substantive selves in modern science.

This is the conceptual framework, the causal syntax if you will, within which earlier Buddhist analyses of mind took place. It is an approach to describing and understanding experience as it arises. It is, in a word, a phenomenology of consciousness.

THE DEPENDENT ARISING OF COGNITIVE AWARENESS

This is well exemplified in the concept of *vijnana* (P. *vinnana*), "cognitive awareness" or "consciousness," the central most concepts in Buddhist understanding of mind. Although the Buddha generally declared that "Apart from conditions, there is no arising of cognitive awareness", each form of cognitive awareness arises in conjunction with particular factors: "Visual cognitive awareness arises dependent on the eye and (visual) form." That is, when an object appears in a sense-field, impinging upon its respective sense-organ, a moment of cognitive awareness (*vijnana*) arises.

Sense-object and sense-organ (or faculties) are thus correlatively defined: a visual object, by definition, is that kind of stimulus which can impinge upon an eye. Although it is common to speak of cognitive awareness as if it actively cognizes objects, in the syntax of dependent arising cognitive awareness does not actually cognize anything - it simply is the awareness which arises when the requisite conditions come together. Vasubandhu, author of the fifth-century *Abhidharmakos'a,* makes precisely this point:

> The sutra teaches: "By reason of the organ of sight and of visible matter there arises the visual consciousness": there is not there either an organ that sees, or visible matter that is seen; there is not there any action of seeing, nor any agent that sees; this is only a play of cause and effect.
>
> In the light of [common] practice, one speaks, metaphorically, of this process: "The eye sees, and the consciousness discerns." But one should not cling to these metaphors. In other words, to interpret vijna-na as an act of cognition rather than an occurrence of cognitive awareness is to ignore the syntax of dependent arising, which takes no active subject. Once again, the traditional Buddhist denial of a substantive, unchanging entity may be seen as less a metaphysical position than a function of its mode of analysis.

Cognition, in these terms, is thus neither purely subjective nor wholly objective. Like a transaction that takes place between individuals, cognitive awareness occurs at the interface, the concomitance of a sense-organ and its correlative stimulus. Cognitive awareness is thus also neither an exact "mirror of nature" which reflects things "as they are" - since what constitutes an "object" is necessarily defined by the capacities of a particular sense organ; nor is it a unilateral projection of a priori categories - since the cognitive capacities of a sense organ are also correlatively defined by the kinds of stimuli that may impinge upon them. This entails a number of important implications, for discerning cognitive awareness is not only an event that occurs temporally, but one which equally depends upon relational distinctions - and relational distinctions are hardly substances.

THE DEPENDENT ARISING OF AWARENESS OF DIFFERENCE

Perception operates only on difference. All receipt of information is necessarily the receipt of news of difference. G. Bateson. In his popular book, Mind and Nature, Bateson (1979,

121) analyzes cognitive processes by comparing them to a simple electric switch:

> The switch, considered as a part of an electric circuit, does not exist when it is in the on position. From the point of view of the circuit, it is not different from the conducting wire which leads to it and the wire which leads away from it. It is merely "more conductor." Conversely, but similarly, when the switch is off, it does not exist from the point of view of the circuit. It is nothing, a gap between two conductors which themselves exist only as conductors when the switch is on. In other words, the switch is not except at the moments of its change of setting, and the concept "switch" has thus a special relation to time. It is related to the notion "change" rather than to the notion "object."

The switch exists, as a switch, only at the moment of switching; otherwise it remains indistinguishable from the rest of the circuit. Our sense organs function similarly, Bateson avers: they only operate relative to, that is, are only triggered by, and changes in stimuli, by events. Bateson is not simply parroting the ancient platitude that "everything changes." Rather, he is suggesting the more fundamental notion that change is constitutive of perception itself. Hence, to even speak of perception is necessarily to speak of events - and this is to speak in terms of dependent arising. Just as the switch does not exist, for the circuit, except while the switch is switching, so too distinct stimuli do not exist, for a cognitive system, except insofar as they involve contextual differences.

This is not to say that, "differences are perceived" (which would abandon the syntax of dependent arising), but rather that an awareness of difference is constitutive of perception in the same way change is. To even speak of perception is to necessarily to speak of awareness of differences. Awareness of differences, however, cannot arise outside of a context, since differences occur between phenomena. An absolutely isolated object would be imperceptible. Contextual differences, however, have no singular location. As Bateson avers: "Difference of being in the nature of relationship is not located in time or in space." Since awareness of differences arises contextually rather than independently, and is episodic rather than enduring, it has no substantive existence. Not being a substance, it neither comes nor goes anywhere.

These ideas suggest an interesting approach to the elusive notion of dharma in Abhidharma. Abhidharma represents a systematic attempt to analyze mental processes in terms of experiential events - and it is these momentary14 and distinctive events that are called dharmas. A dharma refers, in other words, to each momentary and distinct aspect of experience insofar as it is causally involved in the arising of cognitive awareness. Thus, it logically follows from our mode of analysis that dharmas arise from nowhere and go nowhere. That is, dharmas have neither any actual substance nor any singular location; they are neither a "something" nor a "nothing," ontologically speaking. (These are, of course, the same conclusions we drew above with our analysis of perception, except that they may now also be reflexively applied to the systemic differentiation between the terms of analysis themselves.

Abhidharma, in other words, is a "metapsychology," which self-consciously "deals with the various concepts and categories of consciousness as the primary objects of investigation." While dharmas may ultimately refer to experiential phenomena, what counts as a dharma in any system of description must always be distinguished from other dharmas. Dharmas cannot therefore refer to independent, self-sufficient entities. Or rather, and more precisely, we cannot speak about the "true nature" of a dharma outside of a given system of analysis.) The arising of cognitive awareness is, moreover, not just correlative to our sense organs or faculties, but to the implicit schemas enstructured in those organs and faculties themselves.

We cannot help but see something as red rather than blue, hearing pitches as high or low, feeling distinct textures or temperatures, or smelling odors odious or enticing. Since such distinctions are constitutive of cognitive awareness, the classifications they depend upon are also indispensable for any arising of discerning cognitive awareness (vij*n*a-na). As cognitive scientists Lakoff and Johnson point out, Categorization is... a consequence of how we are embodied.... We categorize as we do because we have the brains and bodies we have and because we interact in the world the way we do... What that means is that the categories we form are part of our experience. Our cognitions and distinctions, and the implicit schemas that inform them, thus constitute our experienced "world."

CIRCULAR CAUSALITY BRINGS FORTH A WORLD

Our capacities for such awareness of distinctions did not arise uncaused, nor are they without their own consequences. They developed in dependence upon previous kinds of experience and in turn condition the kinds of experience, the kinds of cognitive awareness, which may arise in the future. The momentary arising of the discernment of differences is thus part of a larger feedback cycle in which "the effects of differences are to be regarded as transforms of the difference which preceded them." These two notions - circular causality, in the form of recursive feedback processes, and epigenesis, wherein the results of previous events serve as the basis for succeeding ones - in another area where Buddhist philosophy has much in common with scientific models of causality, particularly those of cognitive science and evolutionary biology.

Stimuli are always impinging upon the sense organs, giving rise to forms of cognitive awareness; and these processes continuously but subtly modulate the structures of these organs, which in turn influence their receptivity to subsequent stimuli. These two notions - that living entails continuous cognition and cognition entails continuous modification of living structure - introduces an important causal reciprocity between the structure of sense organs and the arising of cognitive awareness. These reciprocal processes take place not only at the micro level of cognition, but also at the macro level of evolution.

Both evolutionary biology and the view of dependent arising articulate models of circular causality to describe how things come into being over the long term through recursive processes of feedback causality. This means that the very minds and bodies we embody today reflect the gradually accumulated results of reproductively successful interactions between our forebears and their natural and social environments. As with our analysis of cognitive awareness, evolutionary theory thus shifts attention from the arising of entities to the patterns of interaction.

"What evolves," Maturana and Varela observe "is always a unit of interactions", neither the organism by itself, and certainly not the environment alone, but the organism-in-environment. In other words, it is patterns of interaction that evolve, representing "the evolution of the cognitive domains." And, similarly and reciprocally, the evolution of its cognitive domain is the evolution of the "world" - for that specific kind of organism, a process Maturana and Varela call a "structural coupling with the world."

What constitutes the "world" or "environment" for any given organism, therefore, depends upon these evolved cognitive structures. We cannot speak of an independent, objective world that organisms have access to, because "the domains of classes of interactions into which an organism can enter constitute its entire cognitive reality." To even speak of a "world" therefore is necessarily to speak of a cognizing, that is, an interacting organism. In this sense, and consonant with the view of dependent arising, "world and perceiver specify each other."

We may now better appreciate some of the implications of the formula of dependent arising, whose cyclic nature warranted the appellation "*samsara*," literally "the going around." The series of dependent arising depicts a recursively cyclic process between the constructed complexes (*samskara*), cognitive awareness (*vijnana*), and the constructing afflicted actions these both enable and elicit: for as long as the cognitive processes give rise to sensation and feeling, then craving and grasping will tend to arise, which in turn tend to elicit the intentional afflicted activities, the karma, that ultimately create and sustain the structures (*samskara*) that support further existence and the "arising of the world."

And for as long as these structures persist, they provide the conditions that both enable and conduce to further cognitive and afflictive processes, and so on. This model of circular causality - enabling structures that give rise to cognitive awareness, which in turn elicit the afflictions that instigate actions which reinforce those very structures, etc. and the core of the pre-Mahayana Buddhist world view. Evolutionary biology and Buddhist thought thus both analyze the causal relations underlying momentary cognitive processes and long-term evolutionary processes in a similar fashion: the "arising of the world" for an individual, its phylogeny, as well as for a species, its ontogeny, can be equally well understood as the "arising of the world, the "bringing forth" of specific cognitive domains, out of the dynamic vortex of cyclic causality.

Since the interaction between cognitive awareness and its enabling structures, which entails continuous modification of these structures, is also causally effective at a developmental or evolutionary scale, this means that the particular implicit and innate classificatory systems that condition cognitive awareness themselves become important factors in the further development of living structures (*samskara*), that is, they impart causal influences on human evolution in their own right. Living forms have, in effect, "enstructured" their cognitive maps, their capacities for cognitive discernment, through the extended epigenetic processes of circular causality. This is true at the individual level, in our neural pathways, for example, as well as at the level of the species, as in evolutionary theory.

But classifications, we remember, refer to patterns of relationships, not properties of substances, to maps not territory. That is to say, that the distinctions that constitute our cognitive maps - which have no spatial location and come from nowhere and go nowhere - were indispensable conditions for the dependent arising of our minds and bodies. In Buddhist terms, the dharmas that are discerned are constitutive conditions for "the arising of the world," not just epistemologically, which is obvious, but ontologically as well. In short, there would be no distinctively human embodiment without the classifications and categorizations constitutive of the arising of cognitive awareness itself.

And what is the greatest source of human categorization and classification, whose differences have no spatial location either inside or outside of our brains, and is, furthermore, one of the most salient features of the physical and mental structures of human life? Language. It appears that we are not only the results of what we have thought, felt and done, but above all, of what we heard and said. We are, in short, the word become flesh.

ARISING FROM CONSENSUAL COMMUNICATION

Our linguistic capabilities did not, of course, spring fully formed from the head of Zeus. They too are part of the accumulative, constructive and interactive processes of evolution whereby cognitive processes condition living structures, which in turn condition further processes and so on. As symbolic communication "dependently arose" in early hominid species it became a powerful evolutionary force in its own right, radically and irrevocably changing the structures and processes of the human brain. This momentous change centered on an increasingly enlarged prefrontal cortex, where such symbolizing processes apparently occur.

As language use and this "prefrontalization" mutually reinforced each other, the symbolic-linguistic mode of cognition that is dependent upon them came to dominate other, originally nonlinguistic, processes. Human cognitive processes, even simple sensory ones, in other words, unavoidably arise in dependence upon our linguistified brain. Language, then, along with the systemic distinctions upon which it depends, is not something added on to human cognitive processes. Systemic symbolic thinking is constitutive of normal human cognitive processes.

This prefrontalization of human cognition, however, is fraught with unintended consequences, consequences that follow from the very nature of linguistic symbolification. Language gives rise to its own feedback cycles: "[S]ymbolically mediated models of things..," Deacon notes, "exhibit complicated nonlinearity and recursive structure as well as nearly infinite flexibility and capacity for novelty due to their combinatorial nature." "We cannot help but see the world in symbolic categorical terms," Deacon declares, "dividing it up according to opposed features, and organizing our lives according to themes and narratives."

This linguistification of human cognitive processes thus represents a physiologically enstructured, dominating cognitive strategy characterized by compulsive yet creative recursivity, based upon words that are defined mutually and systemically, not independently or substantively, and whose ultimate meanings are conventional determined. No wonder Deacon ambivalently observes: "we are not just a species that uses symbols. The symbolic universe has ensnared us in an inescapable web."

Buddhist analysis of mind also connects reflexivity, and the linguistic categorizations it gives rise to, with cognitive processes (*vijnana*) that have been built up through the accumulating, epigenetic cycles of dependent arising. Its reflexivity and recursivity also depend upon the reciprocal relationships between sensory cognitive awareness, non-sensory (symbolic) "objects" such as thoughts or ideas, and the ensnaring web of conceptual proliferation entailed by language use:

Dependent on the eye and forms, eye-consciousness arises. The meeting of the three is contact. With contact as condition there is feeling. What one feels, that one apperceives. What one apperceives, that one thinks about. What one thinks about, that one mentally proliferates? With what one has mentally proliferated as the source, apperceptions and notions tinged by mental proliferation [*papancasannasankhara*] beset a man with respect to past, future, and present forms cognizable through the eye.... mind-objects cognizable through the mind.

The most deeply entrenched source of these recursive possibilities, which also doubles back to generate its own linguistically generated recursivity, is no doubt our sense of self as an enduring, experiencing agent. As one text declares, the notion "I am" is a proliferation; "I am this" is a proliferation; "I shall be" is a proliferation." The very thought "I am" is, according to the *Suttanipata,* the root (*mula*) of proliferation itself. In other words, as long as the thought "I am" persists, so long will endless cycles of apperceptions, conceptual proliferation and further apperceptions, etc. keep spinning.

This sense of self, however, derives its compelling cogency, it's enduring and endearing allure, from the same social and linguistic matrix other words and symbols do: symbolic representation. Like language, this symbolic self is a product of massive interdependency; like other relational phenomenon, it has no substantive existence in time or space. "It is a final irony," Deacon concludes, that it is the virtual, not actual, reference that symbols provide, which gives rise to this experience of self... it is the symbolic realm of consciousness that we most identify with and from which our sense of agency and self-control originate.

EMBODIED STRUCTURING OF EXPERIENCE

Language and the symbolic self that language enables are also both complex results of interdependent processes which have, over time, become enstructured into enduring physiological and psychological structures. "It is the goal of most cognitive processes," Deacon declares, "to make information processing unconscious and automatic - as quick, easy, and efficient as possible." We must distinguish, therefore, between those immediate but intermittent processes of discerning cognitive awareness accompanied by attention, from the underlying but continuous processes operating automatically. This distinction was intimated in the two distinct formulas for the arising of cognitive awareness in

Indian Buddhism thought:

Depending on eye and forms visual cognitive awareness arises.

Depending on sankhkara (*samskara*) cognitive awareness arises.

It was not until the Yogacara school (circa 2-7th century CE), however, that the forms of supraliminal cognitive awareness (*pravrttivijnana*), which arise in conjunction with present stimuli accompanied by attention, was explicitly distinguished from the subliminal forms of cognitive awareness, which are subsumed under the term "*alayavijnana*" (roughly "store-house" consciousness), that arise in conjunction with more enduring structures (*samskara*).

This Buddhist "cognitive unconscious," however, is no more an experiencer, agent or enduring subject than was cognitive awareness in the earlier model. It still has all the qualities and qualifications mentioned above: "it is related to the notion "change" rather than to the notion "object"... admit[ing] only news of difference", it comes into being through the accumulating, epigenetic processes of cyclic causality, and it specifies cognitive domains that constitute a particular cognitive reality, a dependently arisen "world of experience".

According to the Samdhinirmocana-sutra, this form of subliminal cognitive awareness, the mind with all the seeds matures, congeals, grows, develops, and increases based upon the two-fold substratum (or: appropriation, upadana ; that is, (1) the substratum of the material sense-faculties along with their supports (*sadhisthanarupa-indriyaupadana*), (2) and the substratum which consists of the predispositions toward conceptual proliferation in terms of conventional usage of images, names, and conceptualizations.

That is, subliminal cognitive awareness (*alayavijnana*) continuously arises in conjunction with (1) the living sense-faculties and (2) the predispositions instilled by past linguistic experience, conceptualization, naming, etc., bringing forth as its cognitive domain an "external world" outside of immediate awareness. We live, that is, in a "world" whose predominant structuring influences - linguistic and physiological structures built up over time through extended organism-environment interaction - we cannot fully discern. And this is, if I am not mistaken, nearly exactly the current notion of the "cognitive unconscious."

There is also a continuous and simultaneously reinforcing relationship between sub- and supra-liminal cognitive processes in order for even ordinary human activities such as conversations to occur. That is, on the one hand, all supraliminal cognitive processes are said to simultaneously arise based on subliminal cognitive awareness (*alayavijnana*), continuously and simultaneously informed by the classifications these predispositions (vasana) toward conceptual proliferation. On the other hand, the arising of supraliminal cognitive awareness also continuously entails modulations or transformations of the forms of unconscious cognitive awareness themselves, implanting "seeds" (*bija*) or impressions (*vasana*) as the texts say.

These reciprocally reinforcing and gradually accumulating processes, however, take place not only simultaneously, ceaselessly and mostly automatically, but also, in large part, unconsciously. Since linguistic categories and classifications underlie all forms of cognitive awareness, subliminal as well as supraliminal, then we are susceptible to the same conceptual prolixity, the ensnaring recursivity that language entails, at unconscious levels as well. Concomitantly, our sense of self - enabled by and arising out of the reflexivity of linguistic representation - has also become enstructured so that it too occurs "unconsciously and automatically" in nearly every moment of mind.

Therefore, it follows that, since the systemic classifications underlying our cognitive processes have informed and instigated intentional activities that, in the long term, have been instrumental in shaping the contours of human evolution, our linguistically-based symbolic self, unconsciously embedded and virtually real, has played a leading a role in the coming to be of our entire "world of experience."

The symbolic self, in other words, although generated out of the vortex of the linguistic recursivity underlying all cognitive processes, from the unconscious level up, has compelling causal efficacy in its own right. And this is true both within a single lifetime, that is, ontogenetically, as well as in the traditional Buddhist conception of multiple lifetimes, that is, (after a fashion) phylogenetically.

GENERATIVE MATRIX OF OUR COMMON WORLD

We live our lives in this shared virtual world... The doorway into this virtual world was opened to us alone by the evolution of language. How is it that we collectively "bring forth" our shared world of human experience? We live in this "shared virtual world," as Deacon puts it, in large part because "the evolution of symbolic communication... created a mode of extrabiological inheritance... [that] is intrinsically social," one that evolved "neither inside nor outside brains, but at the interface where cultural evolutionary processes affect biological evolutionary processes".

That is, we have similar kinds of cognitive processes because they developed historically through continuous interaction with other human beings, giving rise to our common bodily forms, with our species-specific propensities toward cultural and social conditioning, and the dominating influences of linguistic classification, conceptualization, nominalization, etc., through which we collectively yet unconsciously bring forth a shared world of experience.

With allowances for the issue of rebirth, this is largely compatible with mainstream views of causality in the Yogacara tradition. As the commentary to MSg I.60, explains:

[The statement:] "The common [characteristic of the *alayavijnana*] is the seed of the receptacle-world" means that it is the cause (karanahetu) of perceptions (*vijnapti*) which appear as the receptacle world. It is common because these perceptions appear similarly to all who experience them through the force of maturation (*Vipaka*) that is in accordance with their own similar karma.

Our "world" appears to us in similar ways because we have similar karma to experience it similarly. It is language that provides the means through which the "common aspects" of the *alayavijnana* give rise to a "common" receptacle world. And it is just because our cognitive structures are constituted by linguistic predispositions that cognitive awareness is subject to language's endless recursivity (prapanca).

The "predispositions or impressions of speech" (*abhilapavasana*), which have the "special power" (*s'aktivis'esa*) of the predispositions of conventional expressions (*vyavahara*) to give rise to manifest cognitive awareness (*vijnana*) in regard to expressions of selves (*Atman*), dharmas, and actions, etc. (ad MSg I.58) are never fully "used up" (*anupabhukta*), MSg I.61.2 explains, because "the seeds of the impressions of language give rise to conceptual proliferation since beginningless time."

In other words, this linguistic recursivity is the generative matrix from which endlessly springs forth our symbolic world, one that virtually supercedes the physical world we apparently inhabit. The reciprocal feedback processes that language invites thus operate at a variety of levels, not only synchronically - between the *alayavijnana* and supraliminal forms of cognitive awareness - but also diachronically, between our previous linguistic experience and our present proclivities conditioned by the "impressions" of language.

These operate both within a single lifetime, and, in traditional Buddhist terms, over multiple lifetimes. There is also a third, unconscious yet thoroughly intersubjective, feedback system, which, like the other two, continuously proliferates and perpetuates samsaric existence, but which, unlike them, bridges the individual and collective experience of the "world," connecting our similar karmic activities with the similar "worlds" these activities bring about. Our commonality of worlds, then, dependent upon our common species-specific cognitive structures, is ultimately inseparable from our commonality of cognitive awareness, dependent upon our

> common linguistic, symbolic structures. As Deacon declares, a person's symbolic experience of consciousness... is not within the head... This [symbolic] self is indeed not bounded within a mind or body... [it] is intersubjective in the most thoroughgoing sense of the term.

It is our unconscious habits of body, speech, and mind to which we are habituated that give rise, in the long term and in the aggregate, to the habitats we inhabit. And, this, we suggest, is as true for some twentieth century biologists and neuroscientists, as it was for fifth-century Yogacarin Buddhists.

7

Buddhist Cosmology and the Theory of Karma

Karma is the law of moral causation. The theory of Karma is a fundamental doctrine in Buddhism. This belief was prevalent in India before the advent of the Buddha. Nevertheless, it was the Buddha who explained and formulated this doctrine in the complete form in which we have it today. What is the cause of the inequality that exists among mankind? Why should one person be brought up in the lap of luxury, endowed with fine mental, moral and physical qualities, and another in absolute poverty, steeped in misery? Why should one person be a mental prodigy, and another an idiot? Why should one person be born with saintly characteristics and another with criminal tendencies? Why should some be linguistic, artistic, mathematically inclined, or musical from the very cradle? Why should others be congenitally blind, deaf, or deformed? Why should some be blessed, and others cursed from their births?

Either this inequality of mankind has a cause, or it is purely accidental. No sensible person would think of attributing this unevenness, this inequality, and this diversity to blind chance or pure accident. In this world nothing happens to a person that he does not for some reason or other deserve. Usually, men of ordinary intellect cannot comprehend the actual reason or reasons. The definite invisible cause or causes of the visible effect is not necessarily confined to the present life, they may be traced to a proximate or remote past birth. According to Buddhism, this inequality is due not only to heredity, environment, "nature and nurture", but also to Karma. In other words, it is the result of our own past actions and our own present doings. We ourselves are responsible for our own happiness and misery. We create our own Heaven. We create our own Hell. We are the architects of our own fate.

Perplexed by the seemingly inexplicable, apparent disparity that existed among humanity, a young truth-seeker approached the Buddha and questioned him regarding this intricate problem of inequality: "What is the cause, what is the reason, O Lord," questioned he, "that we find amongst mankind the short-lived and long-lived, the healthy and the diseased, the ugly and beautiful, those lacking influence and the powerful, the poor and the rich, the low-born and the high-born, and the ignorant and the wise?"

The Buddha's reply was:

"All living beings have actions (Karma) as their own, their inheritance, their congenital cause, their kinsman, their refuge. It is Karma that differentiates beings into low and high states."

He then explained the cause of such differences in accordance with the law of cause and effect. Certainly we are born with hereditary characteristics. At the same time we possess certain innate abilities that science cannot adequately account for. To our parents we are indebted for the gross sperm and ovum that form the nucleus of this so-called being. They remain dormant within each parent until this potential germinal compound is vitalised by the karmic energy needed for the production of the foetus. Karma is therefore the indispensable conceptive cause of this being.

The accumulated karmic tendencies, inherited in the course of previous lives, at times play a far greater role than the hereditary parental cells and genes in the formation of both physical and mental characteristics. The Buddha, for instance, inherited, likes every other person, the reproductive cells and genes from his parents. But physically, morally and intellectually there was none comparable to him in his long line of Royal ancestors. In the Buddha's own words, he belonged not to the Royal lineage, but to that of the Aryan Buddhas. He was certainly a superman, an extraordinary creation of his own Karma. According to the Lakkhana Sutta of *Digha Nikaya*, the Buddha inherited exceptional features, such as the 32 major marks, as the result of his past meritorious deeds.

The ethical reason for acquiring each physical feature is clearly explained in the Sutta. It is obvious from this unique case that karmic tendencies could not only influence our physical organism, but also nullify the potentiality of the parental cells and genes - hence the significance of the Buddha's enigmatic statement, - "We are the heirs of our own actions." Dealing with this problem of variation, the *Atthasalini*, being a commentary on the Abhidharma, states:

"Depending on this difference in Karma appear the differences in the birth of beings, high and low, base and exalted, happy and miserable. Depending on the difference in Karma appears the difference in the individual features of beings as beautiful and ugly, high-born or low born, well-built or deformed. Depending on the difference in Karma appears the difference in worldly conditions of beings, such as gain and loss, and disgrace, blame and praise, happiness and misery."

Thus, from a Buddhist point of view, our present mental, moral intellectual and temperamental differences are, for the most part, due to our own actions and tendencies, both past and present. Although Buddhism attributes this variation to Karma, as being the chief cause among a variety, it does not, however, assert that everything is due to Karma. The law of Karma, important as it is, is only one of the twenty-four conditions described in Buddhist Philosophy. Refuting the erroneous view that "whatsoever fortune or misfortune experienced is all due to some previous action", the Buddha said:

"So, then, according to this view, owing to previous action men will become murderers, thieves, unchaste, liars, slanderers, covetous, malicious and perverts. Thus, for those who fall back on the former deeds as the essential reason, there is neither the desire to do, nor effort to do, nor necessity to do this deed, or abstain from this deed."

It was this important text, which states the belief that all physical circumstances and mental attitudes spring solely from past Karma that Buddha contradicted. If the present life is totally conditioned or wholly controlled by our past actions, then certainly Karma is tantamount to fatalism or determinism or predestination. If this were true, free will would be an absurdity. Life would be purely mechanistic, not much different from a machine. Being created by an Almighty God who controls our destinies and predetermines our future, or being produced by an irresistible Karma that completely determines our fate and controls our life's course, independent of any free action on our part, is essentially the same. The only difference lies in the two words God and Karma. One could easily be substituted for the other, because the ultimate operation of both forces would be identical. Such a fatalistic doctrine is not the Buddhist law of Karma.

According to Buddhism, there are five orders or processes *(niyama)* which operate in the physical and mental realms.

They are:

1. Utu Niyama - physical inorganic order, e.g. seasonal phenomena of winds and rains. The unerring order of seasons, characteristic seasonal changes and events, causes of winds and rains, nature of heat, etc., all belong to this group.
2. Bija Niyama - order of germs and seeds (physical organic order), e.g. rice produced from rice-seed, sugary taste from sugar-cane or honey, peculiar characteristics of certain fruits, etc. The scientific theory of cells and genes and the physical similarity of twins may be ascribed to this order.
3. Karma Niyama - order of act and result, e.g., desirable and undesirable acts produce corresponding good and bad results. As surely as water seeks its own level so does Karma, given opportunity, produce its inevitable result, not in the form of a reward or punishment but as an

innate sequence? This sequence of deed and effect is as natural and necessary as the way of the sun and the moon.

4. Dhamma Niyama - order of the norm, e.g., the natural phenomena occurring at the advent of a *Bodhisattva* in his last birth. Gravitation and other similar laws of nature. The natural reason for being good and so forth may be included in this group.
5. Citta Niyama - order or mind or psychic law, e.g., processes of consciousness, arising and perishing of consciousness, constituents of consciousness, power of mind, etc., including telepathy, telaesthesia, retro-cognition, premonition, clairvoyance, clairaudience, thought-reading and such other psychic phenomena which are inexplicable to modern science.

Every mental or physical phenomenon could be explained by these all-embracing five orders or processes which are laws in themselves. Karma as such is only one of these five orders. Like all other natural laws they demand no lawgiver. Of these five, the physical inorganic order and the order of the norm are more or less mechanistic, though they can be controlled to some extent by human ingenuity and the power of mind. For example, fire normally burns, and extreme cold freezes, but man has walked scatheless over fire and meditated naked on Himalayan snows; horticulturists have worked marvels with flowers and fruits; Yogis have performed levitation.

Psychic law is equally mechanistic, but Buddhist training aims at control of mind, which is possible by right understanding and skilful volition. Karma law operates quite automatically and, when the Karma is powerful, man cannot interfere with its inexorable result though he may desire to do so; but here also right understanding and skilful volition can accomplish much and mould the future. Good Karma, persisted in, can thwart the reaping of bad Karma, or as some Western scholars prefer to say 'action influence', is certainly an intricate law whose working is fully comprehended only by a Buddha. The Buddhist aims at the final destruction of all Karma. The Pali term Karma literally means action or doing. Any kind of intentional action whether mental, verbal, or physical, is regarded as Karma. It covers all that is included in the phrase "thought, word and deed". Generally speaking, all good and bad action constitutes Karma. In its ultimate sense Karma means all moral and immoral volition. Involuntary, unintentional or unconscious actions, though technically deeds, do not constitute Karma, because volition, the most important factor in determining Karma, is absent.

The Buddha says:

"I declare, O Bhikkhus, that volition is Karma. Having willed one acts by body, speech, and thought." (*Anguttara Nikaya*)

Every volitional action of individuals, save those of Buddhas and Arahants, is called Karma. The exception made in their case is because they are delivered from both good and evil; they have eradicated ignorance and craving, the roots of Karma. "Destroyed are their germinal seeds *(Khina bija)*; selfish desires no longer grow," states the Ratana Sutta of Sutta nipata. This does not mean that the Buddha and Arahantas are passive. They are tirelessly active in working for the real well being and happiness of all. Their deeds ordinarily accepted as good or moral, lack creative power as regards themselves. Understanding things as they truly are, they have finally shattered their cosmic fetters – the chain of cause and effect.

Karma does not necessarily mean past actions. It embraces both past and present deeds. Hence in one sense, we are the result of what we were; we will be the result of what we are. In another sense, it should be added, we are not totally the result of what we were; we will not absolutely be the result of what we are.

The present is no doubt the offspring of the past and is the present of the future, but the present is not always a true index of either the past or the future; so complex is the working of Karma. It is this doctrine of Karma that the mother teaches her child when she says "Be good and you will be happy and we will love you; but if you are bad, you will be unhappy and we will not love you." In short, Karma is the law of cause and effect in the ethical realm.

KARMA AND VIPAKA

Karma is action, and *Vipaka*, fruit or result, is its reaction. Just as every object is accompanied by a shadow, even so every volitional activity is inevitably accompanied by its due effect. Karma is like potential seed: *Vipaka* could be likened to the fruit arising from the tree - the effect or result. Anisamsa and Adinaya are the leaves, flowers and so forth that correspond to external differences such as health, sickness and poverty - these are inevitable consequences, which happen at the same time. Strictly speaking, both Karma and *Vipaka* pertain to the mind.

As Karma may be good or bad, so may *Vipaka* - the fruit - is good or bad. As Karma is mental so *Vipaka* is mental (of the mind). It is experienced as happiness, bliss, unhappiness or misery, according to the nature of the Karma seed. *Anisamsa* are the concomitant advantages - material things such as prosperity, health and longevity. When *Vipaka*'s concomitant material things are disadvantageous, they are known as *Adinaya*, full of wretchedness, and appear as poverty, ugliness, disease, short life-span and so forth.

As we sow, we reap somewhere and sometime, in his life or in a future birth. What we reap today is what we have sown either in the present or in the past.

The *Samyutta Nikaya* states:

"According to the seed that's sown,

So is the fruit you reap there from,

Doer of good will gather good,

Doer of evil, evil reaps,

Down is the seed and thou shalt taste

The fruit thereof."

Karma is a law in itself, which operates in its own field without the intervention of any external, independent ruling agency. Happiness and misery, which are the common lot of humanity, are the inevitable effects of causes. From a Buddhist point of view, they are not rewards and punishments, assigned by a supernatural, omniscient ruling power to a soul that has done good or evil. Theists, who attempt to explain everything in this and temporal life and in the eternal future life, ignoring a past, believe in a 'postmortem' justice, and may regard present happiness and misery as blessings and curses conferred on His creation by an omniscient and omnipotent Divine Ruler who sits in heaven above controlling the destinies of the human race. Buddhism, which emphatically denies such an Almighty,

All merciful God-Creator and an arbitrarily created immortal soul, believes in natural law and justice which cannot be suspended by either an Almighty God or an All-compassionate Buddha. According to this natural law, acts bear their own rewards and punishments to the individual doer whether human justice finds out or not. There are some who criticise thus: "So, you Buddhists, too, administer capitalistic opium to the people, saying: "You are born poor in this life on account of your past evil karma. He is born rich on account of his good Karma. So, be satisfied with your humble lot; but do good to be rich in your next life. You are being oppressed now because of your past evil Karma. There is your destiny. Be humble and bear your sufferings patiently. Do well now. You can be certain of a better and happier life after death."

The Buddhist doctrine of Karma does not expound such ridiculous fatalistic views. Nor does it vindicate a postmortem justice. The All-Merciful Buddha, who had no ulterior selfish motives, did not teach this law of Karma to protect the rich and comfort the poor by promising illusory happiness in an after-life. While we are born to a state created by ourselves, yet by our own self-directed efforts there is every possibility for us to create new, favourable environments even here and now. Not only individually, but also, collectively, we are at liberty to create fresh Karma that leads either towards our progress or downfall in this very life.

According to the Buddhist doctrine of Karma, one is not always compelled by an 'iron necessity', for Karma is neither fate, nor predestination imposed upon us by some mysterious unknown power to which we must helplessly submit ourselves. It is one's own doing reacting on oneself, and so one has the possibility to divert the course of one's Karma to some extent. How far one diverts it depends on oneself. Is one bound to reap all that one has sown in just proportion?

The Buddha provides an answer:

"If anyone says that a man or woman must reap in this life according to his present deeds, in that case there is no religious life, nor is an opportunity afforded for the entire extinction of sorrow. But if anyone says that what a man or woman reaps in this and future lives accords with his or her deeds present and past, in that case there is a religious life, and an opportunity is afforded for the entire extinction of a sorrow." (*Anguttara Nikaya*)

Although it is stated in the *Dhammapada* that "not in the sky, nor in mid-ocean, or entering a mountain cave is found that place on earth where one may escape from (the consequences of) an evil deed", yet one is not bound to pay all the past arrears of one's Karma. If such were the case emancipation would be impossibility. Eternal recurrence would be the unfortunate result.

Ignorance *(avijja)*, or not knowing things as they truly are, is the chief cause of Karma. Dependent on ignorance arise activities *(avijja paccaya samkhara)* states the Buddha in the *Paticca Samuppada* (Dependent Origination). Associated with ignorance is the ally craving (*tanha*), the other root of Karma. Evil actions are conditioned by these two causes.

All good deeds of a worldling *(putthujana)*, though associated with the three wholesome roots of generosity *(alobha)*, goodwill *(adosa)* and knowledge *(amoha)*, are nevertheless regarded as Karma because the two roots of ignorance and craving are dormant in him. The moral types of Supramundane Path Consciousness *(magga citta)* are not regarded as Karma because they tend to eradicate the two root causes.

Who is the doer of Karma?

Who reaps the fruit of Karma?

Does Karma mould a soul?

In answering these subtle questions, the Venerable Buddhaghosa writes in the *Visuddhi Magga*:

"No doer is there who does the deed;

Nor is there one who feels the fruit;

Constituent parts alone roll on;

This indeed! Is right discernment"

For instance, the table we see is apparent reality. In an ultimate sense the so-called table consists of forces and qualities. For ordinary purposes a scientist would use the term water, but in the laboratory he would say H 2 0. In this same way, for conventional purposes, such terms as man, woman, being, self, and so forth are used. The so-called fleeting forms consist of psychophysical phenomena, which are constantly changing not remaining the same for two consecutive moments. Buddhists, therefore, do not believe in an unchanging entity, in an actor apart from action, in a perceiver apart from perception, in a conscious subject behind consciousness.

Who then, is the doer of Karma? Who experiences the effect? Volition, or Will *(cetana)*, is itself the doer, Feeling *(vedana)* is itself the reaper of the fruits of actions. Apart from these pure mental states *(suddha dhamma)* there is no-one to sow and no-one to reap.

CLASSIFICATION OF KARMA

(A) With respect to different functions, Karma is classified into four kinds:

1. Reproductive Karma

Every birth is conditioned by a past good or bad karma, which predominated at the moment of death. Karma that conditions the future birth is called Reproductive Karma. The death of a person is merely 'a temporary end of a temporary phenomenon'. Though the present form perishes, another form which is neither the same nor absolutely different takes its place, according to the potential thought-vibration generated at the death moment, because the Karmic force which propels the life-flux still survives. It is this last thought, which is technically called Reproductive *(janaka)* Karma that determines the state of a person in his subsequent birth. This may be either a good or bad Karma.

According to the Commentary, Reproductive Karma is that which produces mental aggregates and material aggregates at the moment of conception. The initial consciousness, which is termed the *patisandhi* rebirth consciousness, is conditioned by this Reproductive *(janaka)* Karma. Simultaneous with the arising of the rebirth-consciousness, there arise the 'body-decad', 'sex-decad' and 'base-decad' *(kaya-bhavavatthu dasakas)*. (decad = 10 factors).

a The body-decad is composed of:

2. The element of extension *(pathavi)*.
3. The element of cohesion *(apo)*.
4. The element of heat *(tajo)*.
5. The element of motion *(vayo)*.

b The four derivatives *(upadana rupa):*

1. Colour *(vanna)*.
2. Odour *(gandha)*.
3. Taste *(rasa)*.
4. Nutritive Essence *(oja)*

These eight (*mahabhuta* 4 + *upadana* 4 = 8) are collectively called *Avinibhoga Rupa* (indivisable form or indivisable matter).

c Vitality *(jivitindriya)* and Body *(kaya)*

These (*avinibhoga* 8 + *jivitindriya* 1 + Kaya 1 = 10) ten are collectively called "Body-decad" = *(Kaya dasaka)*.

Sex-decad and Base-decad also consist of the first nine, sex *(bhava)* and seat of consciousness *(vathu)* respectively (i.e.

eye, ear, nose, tongue, and body). From this, it is evident that the sex of a person is determined at the very conception of a being. It is conditioned by Karma and is not a fortuitous combination of sperm and ovum cells. The Pain and Happiness one experiences in the course of one's lifetime are the inevitable consequence of Reproductive Kamma.

Supportive Karma

That Karma which comes near the Reproductive *(janaka)* Kamma and supports it. It is neither good nor bad and it assists or maintains the action of the Reproductive (janaka) Karma in the course of one's lifetime. Immediately after conception till the death moment this Karma steps forward to support the Reproductive Karma. A moral supportive *(kusala upathambhaka)* Karma assists in giving health, wealth, happiness etc. to the being born with a moral Reproductive Karma. An immoral supportive Karma, on the other hand, assists in giving pain, sorrow, etc. to the being born with an immoral reproductive *(akusala janaka)* Karma, as for instance to a beast of burden.

Obstructive Karma or Counteractive Karma

Which, unlike the former, tends to weaken, interrupt and retard the fruition of the Reproductive Karma? For instance, a person born with a good Reproductive Karma may be subject to various ailments etc., thus preventing him from enjoying the blissful results of his good actions. An animal, on the other hand, who is born with a bad Reproductive Karma may lead a comfortable life by getting good food, lodging, etc., as a result of his good counteractive or obstructive *(upabidaka)* Karma preventing the fruition of the evil Reproductive Karma.

Destructive (Upaghataka) Karma

According to the law of Karma the potential energy of the Reproductive Karma could be nullified by a mere powerful opposing Karma of the past, which, seeking an opportunity, may quite unexpectedly operate, just as a powerful counteractive force can obstruct the path of a flying arrow and bring it down to the ground. Such an action is called Destructive *(upaghataka)* Karma, which is more effective than the previous two in that it is not only obstructive but also destroys the whole force. This Destructive Karma also may be either good or bad.

As an instance of operation of all the four, the case of Devadatta, who attempted to kill the Buddha and who caused a schism in the *Sangha* (disciples of the Buddha) may be cited. His good Reproductive Karma brought him birth in a royal family. His continued comfort and prosperity were due to the action of the Supportive Karma. The Counteractive or Obstructive Karma came into operation when he was subject to much humiliation as a result of his being excommunicated from the *Sangha*. Finally the Destructive Karma brought his life to a miserable end.

(B) There is another classification of Karma, according to the priority of effect:

Weighty *(Garuka)* Karma.

This is either weighty or serious – may be either good or bad. It produces its results in this life or in the next for certain. If good, it is purely mental as in the case of *Jhana* (ecstasy or absorption). Otherwise it is verbal or bodily. On the Immoral side, there are five immediate effective heinous crimes *(pancanantariya karma)*: Matricide, Patricide, and the murder of an Arahant, the wounding of a Buddha and the creation of a schism in the *Sangha*. Permanent Scepticism *(Niyata Micchaditthi)* is also termed one of the Weighty *(garuka)* Karmas.

If, for instance, any person were to develop the *jhana* (ecstasy or absorption) and later were to commit one of these heinous crimes, his good Karma would be obliterated by the powerful evil Karma. His subsequent birth would be conditioned by the evil Karma in spite of his having gained the *jhana* earlier. Devadatta lost his psychic power and was born in an evil state, because he wounded the Buddha and caused a schism in the *Sangha*.

King Ajatasattu would have attained the first stage of Sainthood *(Sotapanna)* if he had not committed patricide. In this case the powerful evil Karma acted as an obstacle to his gaining Sainthood.

- Proximate *(Asanna)* Karma Or Death-Proximate Karma

This is that which one does or remembers immediately before the moment of dying. Owing to the great part it plays in determining the future birth, much importance is attained to this deathbed (*asanna*) Karma in almost all Buddhist countries. The customs of reminding the dying man of good deeds and making him do good acts on his deathbed still prevails in Buddhist countries.

Sometimes a bad person may die happily and receive a good birth if he remembers or does a good act at the last moment. A story runs that a certain executioner who casually happened to give some alms to the Venerable Sariputta remembered this good act at the dying moment and was born in a state of bliss. This does not mean that although he enjoys a good birth he will be exempt from the effects of the evil deeds which he accumulated during his lifetime. They will have there due effect as occasions arise.

At times a good person may die unhappy by suddenly remembering an evil act of his or by harbouring some unpleasant thought, perchance compelled by unfavourable circumstances. In the scriptures, Queen Mallika, the consort of King Kosala, remembering a lie she had uttered, suffered for about seven days in a state of misery when she lied to her husband to cover some misbehaviour. These are exceptional cases. Such reverse changes of birth account for the birth of virtuous children to vicious parents and of vicious children to virtuous parents. As a result of the last thought moment being conditioned by the general conduct of the person.

- Habitual *(Accina)* Karma

It is that which on habitually performs and recollects and for which one has a great liking. Habits whether good or bad becomes ones second nature, tending to form the character of a person. At unguarded moments one often lapses into one's habitual mental mindset. In the same way, at the death-moment, unless influenced by other circumstances, one usually recalls to mind one's habitual deeds. Cunda, a butcher, who was living in the vicinity of the Buddha's monastery, died yelling like an animal because he was earning his living by slaughtering pigs.

King Dutthagamini of Ceylon (Sri Lanka) was in the habit of giving alms to the Bhikkhus (monks) before he took his own meals. It was his habitual Karma that gladdened him at the dying moment and gave him birth in the Tusita heaven.

- Reserve or Cumulative *(Katatta)* Karma

This literally means 'because done'. All actions that are not included in the aforementioned and those actions soon forgotten belong to this category. This is, as it were the reserve fund of a particular being.

(C) There is another classification of Karma according to the time in which effects are worked out:

1. Immediately Effective *(dittha dhammavedaniya)* Karma.
2. Subsequently Effective *(uppapajjavedaniya)* Karma.
3. Indefinitely Effective *(aparapariyavedaniya)* Karma.
4. Defunct or Ineffective *(ahosi)* Karma.

Immediately Effective Karma is that which is experienced in this present life. According to the *Abhidhamma* one does both good and evil during the *javana* process (thought-impulsion), which usually lasts for seven thought-moments. The effect of the first thought-moment, being the weakest, and one may reap in this life itself. This is called the Immediately Effective Karma. If it does not operate in this life, it is called 'Defunct or Ineffective' Karma. The next weakest is the seventh thought-moment. Its effect one may reap in the subsequence birth. This is called 'Subsequently Effective' Karma.

This, too, is called Defunct or Ineffective Karma if it does not operate in the second birth. The effect of the intermediate thought-moments may take place at any time until one attains *Nibbana*. This type of Karma is known as 'Indefinitely Effective' Karma. No one, not even the Buddhas and Arahantas, is exempt from this class of Karma which one may experience in the course of one's wandering in *Samsara*. There is no special class of Karma known as Defunct or Ineffective, but when such actions that should produce their effects in this life or in a subsequent life do not operate, they are termed Defunct or Ineffective Karma.

(D) The last classification of Karma is according to the plane in which the effect takes place, namely:

1. Evil Actions *(akusala kamma)* which may ripen in the sentient planes *(kammaloka)*. (Six celestial planes plus one human plane plus four woeful planes = eleven *kamaloka* planes.) Here are only four woeful *kamalokas.*
2. Good Actions (*kusala kamma*) which may ripen in the sentient planes except for the four woeful planes.
3. Good Actions *(kusala kamma)* which may ripen in the Realm of Form *(rupa brahamalokas)*. There are four *Arupa Brahma Lokas.*

QUESTIONS ON THE THEORY OF KARMA

Question: Do the Karmas of parents determine or affect the Karmas of their children? Answer: Physically, the Karma of children is generally determined by the Karma of their parents. Thus, healthy parents usually have healthy offspring, and unhealthy parents have unhealthy children. On the effect or how the Karma of their children is determined: the child's Karma is a thing apart of itself – it forms the child's individuality, the sum-total of its merits and demerits accumulated in innumerable past existences. For example, the Karma of the Buddha-to-be, Prince Siddhartha was certainly not influenced by the joint Karma of his parents, King Suddhodana and Queen Maya. The glorious and powerful Karma of our Buddha-to-be transcended the Karma of his parents which jointly were more potent than his own.

Question: If the Karma of parents does not influence those of their children, how would the fact is explained that parents who suffer from certain virulent diseases are apt to transmit these evils to their offsprings?

Answer: Where a child inherits such a disease it is due to the force of the parents' characteristics because of the force of the latter's Utu (conditions favourable to germination). Take, for example, two seeds from a sapling; plant one in inferior, dry soil; and the other in rich, moist soil. The result is that the first seed will sprout into a sickly sapling and soon show symptoms of disease and decay; while the other seed will thrive and flourish and grow up to be a tall and healthy tree.

It will be observed that the pair of seeds taken from the same stock grows up differently according to the soil into which they are put. A child's past Karma may be compared to the seed: the physical disposition of the mother to the soil; and that of the father to the moisture, which fertilised the soil. Roughly speaking, to illustrate our subject, we will say that, representing the sapling's germination, growth, and existence as a unit, the seed is responsible for one-tenth of them, the soil for six-tenths, and the moisture for the remainder, three-tenths. Thus, although the power of germination exists potentially in the seed (the child), its growth is powerfully determined and quickened by the soil (the mother) and the moisture (the father).

Therefore, even as the conditions of the soil and moisture must be taken as largely responsible factors in the growth and condition of the tree. So must the influences of the parents (or progenitors, as in the case of the animal world) be taken into account in respect to the conception and growth of their offspring. The parents' share in the Karma determining the physical factors of their issue is as follows: If they are human beings, then their offspring will be a human being. If they are cattle then their issue must be of their species. If the human being is Chinese, then their offspring must be of their race. Thus, the offspring are invariably of the same genera and species, etc., as those of the progenitors.

It will be seen from the above that, although a child's Karma is very powerful in itself, if cannot remain wholly uninfluenced by those of it parents. It is apt to inherit the physical characteristic of its parents. Yet, it may occur that the child's Karma, being superlatively powerful, the influence of the parent's joint Karma cannot overshadow it. Of course, it need hardly be pointed out that the evil influences of parents can also be counteracted by the application of medical science.

All beings born of sexual cohabitation are the resultant effects of three forces:

1. The old Karma of past existence;
2. The seminal fluid of the mother, and
3. The seminal fluid of the father.

The physical dispositions of the parents may, or may not, be equal in force. One may counteract the other to a lesser or greater extent. The child's Karma and physical characteristics, such as race, colour, etc., will be the produce of the three forces.

Question: On the death of a sentient being, is there a 'soul' that wanders about at will?

Answer: When a sentient being leaves one existence, it is reborn either as a human being, a celestial being, (*Deva* or Brahama), and inferior animal, or a denizen of one of the regions of hell. The sceptics and the ignorant people held that there are intermediate stages – *antrabhava* – between these; and that there are being who are neither of the human, the celestial, the Deva or the Brahma worlds nor of any one of the stages of exist recognised in the scriptures – but are in an intermediate stage. Some assert that these transitional stages are possessed of the Five Khandhas (Five Aggregates: they are Matter *(rupa)*; Feeling *(vedana)*; Perception *(sanna)*; 4. Mental-activities *(sankhara)*; and Consciousness *(vinnana)*.

Some assert that these beings are detached 'souls' or spirits with no material encasement, and some again, that they are possessed of the faculty of seeing like Devas, and further, that they have power of changing at will, at short intervals, from one to any of the existence mentioned above. Others again hold the fantastic and erroneous theory that these beings can, and so, fancies them to be in other than the existence they are actually in. Thus, to take for example one such of these suppositious beings. He is a poor person – and yet he fancies himself to be rich. He may be in hell - and yet he fancies himself to be in the land of the Devas, and so on. This belief in intermediate stages between existences is false, and is condemned in the Buddhist teachings.

A human being in this life who, by his Karma is destined to be a human being in the next, will be reborn as such; one who by his Karma is destined to be a Deva in the next will be appear in the land of the Devas; and one whose future life is to be in Hell, will be found in one of the regions of hell in the next existence.

The idea of an entity or soul or spirit 'going', 'coming', 'changing' or 'transmigrating' from one existence to another is an idea entertained by the ignorance and materialistic, and is certainly not justified by the *Dhamma*s that there is no such thing as 'going', 'coming', 'changing', etc., as between existences. The conception, which is in accordance with the *Dhamma*, may perhaps be illustrated by the picture thrown out by a cinema projector, or the sound of emitted by the gramophone, and their relation to the film or the sound-box and records respectively. For example, a human being dies and is reborn in the land of Devas.

Though these two existences are different, yet the link or continuity between the two at death is unbroken in point of time. The same is true in the case of a man whose further existence is to be in hell. The distance between Hell and the abode of man appears to be great. Yet, in point of time, the continuity of 'passage' from the one existence to the other is unbroken, and no intervening matter or space can interrupt the trend of a man's Karma from the world of human beings to the regions of Hell. The 'passage' from one existence to another is instantaneous, and the transition is infinitely quicker than the blink of an eyelid or a lightening-flash. Karma determines the realm of rebirth and the state of existence in that realm of all transient being (in the cycle of existences, which have to be traversed till the attainment, at last, of *Nibbana*).

The results of Karma are manifold, and may be affected in many ways. Religious offerings *(dana)* may obtain for a man the privilege of rebirth as a human being, or as a deva, in one of the six deva worlds according to the degree of the merit of the deeds performed, and so with the observance of religious duties *(sila)*. The *jhanas* or states of absorption are found in the Brahma world or Brahmalokas up to the summit, the twentieth Brahma world: And so with bad deeds, the perpetrators of which are to be found, grade by grade, down to the lowest depths of Hell. Thus are Karma, past, present and future were, are, and will ever be the sum total of our deeds, good, indifferent or bad. As was seen from the foregoing, our Karma determines the changes of our existences. "Evil spirits" are, therefore, not beings in intermediate or transitional stages of existence, but are really very inferior beings, and they belong to one of the following five realms of existence:

1. World of Men
2. The Lowest plane of deva-world
3. The region of hell
4. Animals below men, and
5. *Petas* (ghosts).

Number 2 and 5 are very near the world of human beings. As their condition is unhappy and they are popularly considered evil spirits. It is not true that all who die in this world are reborn as evil spirits; nor is it true that beings that die sudden or violent deaths are apt to be reborn in the lowest plane of the world of devas.

Question: Is there such a thing as a human being who is reborn and who is able to speak accurately of his or her past existence?

Answer: Certainly, this is not an uncommon occurrence, and is in accordance with the tenets of Buddhism in respect to Karma.

The following (who form, an overwhelming majority of human beings) are generally unable to remember there past existences when reborn as human beings: Children who die young. Those who die old and senile, those who are addicted to the drug or drink habit, those whose mothers, during their conception, have been sickly or have had to toil laboriously, or have been reckless or imprudent during pregnancy. The children in the womb, being stunned and started, lose all knowledge of their past existence. The following are possessed of a knowledge of their past existences, viz: Those who are not reborn (in the human world) but proceed to the world of the *devas*, of Brahmas, or to the regions of Hell, remember their past existences.

Those who die suddenly deaths from accidents, while in sound health, may also be possessed of this faculty in the next existence, provided that their mothers, in whose womb they are conceived, are healthy. Again, those who live steady, meritorious lives and who in their past existences have striven to attain, often attain it. Lastly the Buddha, the Arahantas and Ariyas attain this gift which is known as *pubbenivasa abhnna* (Supernatural Power remembering previous existences).

Question: Which are the five Abhinna? Are they attainable only by the Buddha?

Answer: The five Abhinna (Supernatural Powers): Pali - *abhi*, excellent, *nana*, wisdom) are:

Iddhividha = Creative power;

Dibbasola = Divine Ear;

Cetopariya nana = Knowledge of others' thoughts;

Pubbenivasanussati = Knowledge of one's past existence;

Dibbacakkhu = The Divine eye.

The Abhinna are attainable not only by the Buddha, but also by Arantas and Ariyas, by ordinary mortals who practise according to the Scriptures (as was the case with hermits etc, who flourished before the time of the Buddha and who were able to fly through the air and traverse different worlds). In the Buddhist Scriptures, we find, clearly shown, the means of attaining the five Abhinna. And even nowadays, if these means are carefully and perseveringly pursued, it would be possible to attain these. That we do not see any person endowed with the five Abhinna today is due to the lack of strenuous physical and mental exertion towards their attainment.

NATURE OF KARMA

In the working of Karma there are maleficent and beneficent forces and conditions to counteract and support this self-operating law. Birth *(gati)* time or condition *(kala)* substratum of rebirth or showing attachment to rebirth *(upadhi)* and effort *(payoga)* act as such powerful aids and hindrances to the fruition of Karma. Though we are neither the absolutely the servants nor the masters of our Karma, it is evident from these counteractive and supportive factors that the fruition of Karma is influenced to some extent by external circumstances, surroundings, personality, individual striving, and so forth.

It is this doctrine of Karma that gives consolation, hope, reliance and moral courage to a Buddhist. When the unexpected happens, and he meets with difficulties, failures, and misfortune, the Buddhist realises that he is reaping what he has sown, and he is wiping off a past debt. Instead of resigning himself, leaving everything to Karma, he makes a strenuous effort to pull the weeds and sow useful seeds in their place, for the future are in his own hands. He who believes in Karma does not condemn even the most corrupt, for them; too, have their chance to reform themselves at any moment. Though bound to suffer in woeful states, they have hope of attaining eternal Peace. By their own doings they have created their own Hells, and by their own doings they can create their own Heavens, too.

A Buddhist who is fully convinced of the law of Karma does not pray to another to be saved but confidently relies on him for his own emancipation. Instead of making any self-surrender or calling on any supernatural agency, he relies on his own will power, and works incessantly for the well-being and happiness of all.

This belief in Karma validates his effort and kindles his enthusiasm, because it teaches individual responsibility. To the ordinary Buddhist, Karma serves as a deterrent, while to an intellectual; it serves as in incentive to do good. He or she becomes kind, tolerant, and considerate. This law of Karma explains the problem of suffering, the mastery of so-called fate and predestination of other religions and about all the inequality of mankind.

The term '*Buddhism*' is now used to denote the teaching of the Buddha, a historical person who flourished some 25 centuries ago on the Indian subcontinent. This eaching has been described variously as a religion, a philosophy, a psychological system, an ethico-moral code, a socio-economic blue-print, and so on. No doubt all these aspects could be discerned in different parts of the Buddha's teaching, but the teaching is itself something more than all these combined. The term which Buddhists use to designate the teaching is *Dhamma* or *Dharma*.

This term comes from a root term meaning "to uphold", and means the basic law which "upholds" the universe. It is therefore sometimes translated simply as Law or Norm. It conveys some idea of the unity that informs the whole body of the Buddha's teaching. We shall use the words *Dhamma* and Buddhism as synonyms. The term "Basic Buddhism" is used in this work to denote those elements of Buddhism as currently propagated which could be attributed fairly unambiguously to the Buddha himself. It is a basic argument here that this teaching can not only be practised effectively in the modern world but also conforms to the modern scientific view of the world.

In seeking to establish the content of Basic Buddhism we have to start with a consideration of the different schools of Buddhism that have arisen in the course of history. The Buddha did not leave written records, and his disciples transmitted his teaching initially as an oral tradition. Quite early in its history several distinct schools of Buddhism arose based partly on the interpretation of common discourses, and partly on differing texts of the discourses themselves. There is a substantial degree of agreement between these diverse schools, and they have never exhibited an animosity towards each other comparable to the schisms that have characterised many other religions.

It is from the scriptures of these various schools of Buddhism, particularly from the Pali Canon, that the original message of the Buddha, which we term Basic Buddhism, has to be reconstructed. About three centuries after the death of the Buddha several different schools of Buddhism emerged, but the differences between them were slight and related to minor points. However towards the beginning of the Common Era (CE) some of these groups gave a new interpretation to the Buddha's teaching and called themselves the Mahayanana ("Greater Vehicle") School. They called the earlier schools the "Hinayana" (Lesser Vehicle) school. However this term was never accepted by the schools that were designated by it. Of these schools only one survives today.

This is the Theravada ("Doctrine of the Elders") school which claims to carry on the Buddhism of the early followers of the Buddha. This view is now generally accepted and the Mahayana is seen as a new innovation in Buddhism but still containing some of the essence of the original teaching. These two traditions have also been termed the Southern and Northern schools of Buddhism because of the geographical areas in which each prevailed. Each of these traditions has its own versions of the Buddhist scriptures. All Theravada groups subscribe to a common set of basic books (called the Pali Canon after the language, Pali, in which it is recorded). We shall however refer to the original Buddhism as Pali Buddhism rather than Theravada Buddhism.

Amongst the Mahayana there is a much greater diversity of schools, doctrines, languages and texts. Initially Sanskrit was the language of the Indian Mahayana schools, but many of these were later translated to Chinese and China soon became the centre of Mahayana Buddhism. From there it spread to many other countries including Korea, Japan (where the best known school of Buddhism is Zen) and Tibet (where a distinct variety of Mahayanana Buddhism called the Vajrayana or the "Diamond Vehicle" developed). In its fundamental doctrines basic Buddhism is closer to Pali Buddhism than to the Mahayana schools.

This is because the Pali Canon is the oldest compilation of the Buddha's teaching, and closest to the actual words of the Buddha. Its present form was settled at the Third Council of Buddhists held during the reign of King Asoka of Ancient India about 250 BCE. The Pali Canon was thus systemised quite early, and has changed very little, indeed if at all, since then. It was committed to writing in the first century BCE, and this preserved the texts from possible further verbal corruption. The Pali Canon (like some other Buddhist canons) consists of three sections (called *Piakas* or baskets) dealing with the *Vinaya* (monastic discipline), *Sutta* (doctrines) and the *Abhidhamma* (the analysis of the *Dhamma*).

While the principles and practice of basic Buddhism has to be sought in the Pali Canon (especially in the *Vinaya* and the *Sutta* piakas), actual Theravada theory shows some development from early Buddhism. This took three directions:

1. Some of the material in the third section of the Canon, the *Abhidhamma Pitaka*, was composed at a later date, and employed a didactic and taxonomic method in analysing the psychological and philosophical concepts introduced by the Buddha. The empirical method it employed to verify the Buddha's teaching was meditative contemplation (especially insight meditation), and it excluded the use of other empirical methods such as those employed by modern science.
2. The commentatorial efforts of the great medieval scholastics like Buddhaghosa and Dharmapala tended to ossify the meaning and interpretation of the Buddha's discourses, which was taken to be authoritative interpretations of the *Dhamma*.
3. Some contemporary developments in the Mahayana came to influence not only the practices of Theravada, but also some aspects of Theravada doctrine as well. These developments must be taken into account in the reconstruction of the original message of the Buddha.

It must not be thought that Basic Buddhism should exclude everything found in the Mahayana teachings. While

Mahayana has little to contribute to the reconstruction of the theory of early Buddhism, it did retain some early Buddhist practices which play a subordinate role in Pali Buddhism but could play a useful role in modern Buddhist practice. Mahayana Buddhism shifted the Buddhist ideal from the Arahant of Theravada Buddhism to the *Bodhisattva*. The *Bodhisattva* was seen as a being who while being capable of enlightenment and release from *samsara*, wilfully postpones becoming fully liberated in order to help others.

A natural consequence of this view was that the primary Buddhist virtue was compassion (karuna). In contrast to this Theravada had regarded *metta* (loving-kindness) as the dominant virtue. There is a need to reinstate compassion in Buddhist practice at least to an extent equal to that given to *metta*. Another aspect of Mahayana that is important is the greater role given to the lay community in contrast to that of monks. Early Buddhism had denoted by the *Sangha* the community of all Buddhists who had made some progress in the *Dhamma*. This *Sangha* included both monks and lay persons, but Theravada Buddhism tended to be excessively centred on the monastic orders, and included in the *Sangha* only ordained monks, and sometimes reserved for them the exclusive role as teachers of the *Dhamma*.

Mahayana took a more flexible attitude. While the role of monks in Buddhism cannot be underrated, and they will continue to play an important part in contemporary Buddhism, it is clear that basic Buddhism should reinstate the role of the lay community. Basic Buddhism should not be seen as an innovation in Buddhism but rather as an attempt to go back to the roots of Buddhism, to what would have been the actual doctrines preached originally by the Buddha.

8

The Elimination of Defilements and the Path to Enlightenment

Buddhism is a philosophy / religion based upon the teachings of Siddhartha Gautama (566 - 486 B.C.). He was an Indian prince born in Lumbini (a town situated in what is now Nepal), destined for a privileged life. According to legend for his life, before his birth, Gautama had visited his mother during a vision, taking the form of a white elephant. During the birth celebrations, a seer announced that this baby would either become a great king or a great holy man. His father, wishing for Gautama to be a great king, shielded his son from religious teachings or knowledge of human suffering. At age 16, his father arranged his marriage to Yashodhara, a cousin of the same age. She gave birth to a son, Rahula.

Although his father ensured that Gautama was provided with everything he could want or need, Gautama was troubled and dissatisfied. At the age of 29, Gautama was escorted on four subsequent visits outside of the palace. Here Siddhartha came across an old crippled man, a sick man, a dead body and an ascetic. This is known as the Four Passing Sights which lead Siddhartha to recognise the reality of death and suffering and the cyclical nature of human existence (*samsara*). He then left the palace, abandoned his inheritance and became a wandering monk, seeking a solution to an end of suffering. He began with the Yogic path and although he reached high levels of meditative consciousness, he was not satisfied.

He abandoned asceticism and realised the power of the Middle Way. This is an important idea in Buddhist thought and practice and to seek moderation and avoid the extremes of self-indulgence and self-mortification. At the age of 35, meditating under a Bodhi tree, Siddhartha reached Enlightenment, awakening to the true nature of reality, which is Nirvana (Absolute Truth);

The dustless and stainless Eye of Truth (*Dhamma-cakkhu*) has arisen. He has seen Truth, has attained Truth, has known Truth, has penetrated into Truth, has crossed over doubt, and is without wavering. Thus with right wisdom he sees it as it is (*yatha bhutam*)... The Absolute Truth is *Nibbana*, which is Reality. (Buddha, from the Dhatuvibhanga-sutta (No. 140) of the *Majjhima-nikaya*)

Thus Siddhartha Gautama became known as the Buddha. 'Buddha' (from the ancient Indian languages of Pali and Sanksrit) means 'one who has awakened'. It is derived from the verbal root "budh", meaning "to awaken" or "to be enlightened", and "to comprehend".

The Buddha taught that the nature of reality was impermanent and interconnected. We suffer in life because of our desire to transient things. Liberation from suffering may come by training the mind and acting according to the laws of karma (cause and effect) i.e. with right action, good things will come to you. This teaching is known as the Four Noble Truths:

Dukkha: Suffering is everywhere

Samudaya: There is a cause of suffering, which is attachment or misplaced desire (*tanha*) rooted in ignorance.

Nirodha: There is an end of suffering, which is Nirvana (the possibility of liberation exists for everyone).

Maggo: There is a path that leads out of suffering, known as the Noble Eightfold Path (right view, right thought, right speech, right conduct, right vocation, right effort, right attention and right concentration).

METAPHYSICS OF BUDDHISM

Buddha was correct that the gift of truth excels all other gifts, for only truth allows us to act wisely. Buddha was very close to understanding Reality as he knew that Matter was both Impermanent and Interconnected; The world is continuous flux and is impermanent (Buddha) and as Fritjof Capra writes; The Eastern mystics see the universe as an inseparable web, whose interconnections are dynamic and not static (Capra). This impermanence / flux is caused by the continual wave Motion of Space (which causes both Matter and Time) and the Interconnection of all things is due to the Spherical In and Out Waves which interact with all other matter in the universe.

We hope you enjoy the following quotes on Buddhism. This is a long page, as I have sourced many interesting ideas and find a lot of truth in Buddhism. Do not believe in anything simply because you have heard it. Do not believe in anything simply because it is spoken and rumored by many. Do not believe in anything because it is found written in your religious books. Do not believe in anything merely on the authority of your teachers and elders. Do not believe in traditions because they have been handed down for many generations. But after observation and analysis, when you find anything that agrees with reason and is conducive to the good and benefit of one and all, then accept it and live up to it. (Siddhartha Gautama - The Buddha), 563-483 B.C.

BUDDHISM QUOTES ON BUDDHA / BUDDHISM RELIGION

I will teach you the Truth and the Path leading to the Truth. (Buddha)

One is one's own refuge, who else could be the refuge? The wise man makes an island of himself that no flood can overwhelm. (Buddha)

It is proper for you to doubt do not go upon report do not go upon tradition do not go upon hearsay....' (Buddha, Kalama Sutra)

Never by hatred is hatred appeased, but it is appeased by kindness. This is an eternal truth. (Buddha)

O Brahmana, it is just like a mountain river, flowing far and swift, taking everything along with it; there is no moment, no instant, no second when it stops flowing, but it goes on flowing and continuing. So Brahmana is human life, like a mountain river. (Buddha)

'Wherefore, brethren, thus must ye train yourselves: Liberation of the will through love will develop, we will often practice it, and we will make it vehicle and base, take our stand upon it, store it up, thoroughly set it going.' (Buddha)

For the first time in the history of the world, Buddhism proclaimed a salvation which each individual could gain from him or herself, in this world, during this life, without any least reference to God, or to gods either great or small. (Aldous Huxley)

The dustless and stainless Eye of Truth (*Dhamma-cakkhu*) has arisen. He has seen Truth, has attained Truth, has known Truth, has penetrated into Truth, has crossed over doubt, and is without wavering. Thus with right wisdom he sees it as it is (yatha bhutam) (Ancient Buddhist texts)

The subtle waves are infinite, producing wondrous sounds. They follow those who should hear the Dharma's discussion. (Gaathaas in Praise of the Buddha Amitaabha, Composed by Dharma Teacher T'an-luan, 1978)

Criticism is the deliverance of the human mind from entanglements and passions. It is freedom itself. This is the true Buddhist standpoint. (T.L.V Murti, The Central Philosophy of Buddhism)

The Pali word kamma or the Sanskrit word karma (from the root kr to do) literally means 'action', 'doing'. But in the Buddhist theory of karma it has a specific meaning: it means only 'volitional action' not all action. In Buddhist terminology karma never means its effect; its effect is known as the 'fruit' or the 'result' of karma. The theory of karma should not be confused with so-called 'moral justice' or 'reward and punishment'. The idea of moral justice arises out of the conception of a supreme being, a God, who sits in judgement, who is a law-giver and who decides what is right and wrong.

The theory of karma is the theory of cause and effect, of action and reaction; it is a natural law, which has nothing to do with the idea of justice or reward and punishment. Every volitional action produces its effects or results. If a good action produces good effects, it is not justice, or reward, meted out by anybody or any power sitting in judgement of your action, but this is in virtue of its own nature, its own law. This is not difficult to understand. But what is difficult is that, according to karma theory, the effects of a volitional action may continue to manifest themselves even in a life after death. (Walpola Rahula, *What the Buddha Taught*)

..The Buddha's metaphysical conception of the impermanence and interdependence of all things profoundly influences his teaching about the conduct of daily life and the nature of human salvation. (Collinson, *Fifty Eastern Thinkers*)

The Buddha taught an attitude of non-violence and an awareness of community and relatedness among all things. He condemned the rigid hierarchy of the Hindu estates, maintaining that inner virtue rather than birth or rank is to be valued, and he welcomed followers, both men and women, from all walks of life. (Cooper, 1996) The impermanence of all forms is the starting point of Buddhism. The Buddha taught that 'all compounded things are impermanent', and that all suffering in the world arises from our trying to cling to fixed forms- objects, people or ideas- instead of accepting the world as it moves and changes. (Capra, *The Tao of Physics*)

The most important characteristic of the Eastern world view- one could almost say the essence of it- is the awareness of the unity and mutual interrelation of all things and events, the experience of all phenomena in the world as manifestations of a basic oneness. All things are seen as interdependent and inseparable parts of this cosmic whole; as different manifestations of the same ultimate reality. (Capra, *The Tao of Physics*)

In Indian philosophy, the main terms used by Hindus and Buddhists have dynamic connotations. The word Brahman is derived from the Sanskrit root brih – to grow- and thus suggests a reality which is dynamic and alive. The Rig Veda uses the term 'Rita' to express the dynamic character of the universe, from the root ri- to move; its original meaning in the Rig Veda being 'the course of all things', 'the order of nature'. The order of nature was conceived by the Vedic seers, not as a static divine law, but as a dynamic principle which is inherent in the universe.

This idea is not unlike the Chinese conception of the Tao - 'the Way'- as the way in which the Universe works, i.e. the order of Nature. Like the Vedic seers, the Chinese sages saw the world in terms of flow and change. Both concepts, Rita and Tao, were later brought down from their original cosmic level to the human and interpreted in a moral sense; Rita as the universal law which all gods and humans must obey and Tao as the right way of life. (Capra, *The Tao of Physics*)

The Eastern mystics see the universe as an inseparable web, whose interconnections are dynamic and not static. The cosmic web is alive; it moves and grows and changes continually. Modern physics, too, has come to conceive of the universe as such a web of relations and, like Eastern mysticism, has recognised that this web is intrinsically dynamic. The dynamic aspect of matter arises in quantum theory as a consequence of the wave-nature of subatomic particles, and is even more essential in relativity theory, where the unification of space and time implies that the being of matter cannot be separated from its activity. The properties of subatomic particles can therefore only be understood in a dynamic context; in terms of movement, interaction and transformation.

It is always a question of knowing and seeing, and not that of believing. The teaching of the Buddha is qualified as ehi-passika, inviting you to 'come and see', but not to come and believe.

According to Buddhist philosophy there is no permanent, unchanging spirit which can be considered 'Self' or 'Soul' or

'Ego', as opposed to matter, and that consciousness (vinnana) should not be taken as 'spirit' in opposition to matter. This point has to be emphasised, because a wrong notion that consciousness is a sort of self or Soul that continues as a permanent substance through life, has persisted from the earliest time to the present day.

All the factors of our lives subsist, then, in a web of mutual causality. Our suffering is caused by the interplay of these factors, particularly by the delusion; aversion and craving that arise from our misapprehension of them. Hence, the Four Noble Truths: We create our own bondage by reifying and clinging to what is by nature contingent and transient. Being caused in this way, our suffering is not endemic. It can cease. The causal play can be reversed. This is achieved by seeing the true nature of phenomena, which is their radical interdependence. This is made possible by the cleansing of perception through meditation and moral conduct. (Joanna Macy, *World as Lover, World as Self*)

Confirming an intuitive sense I've always felt for the interconnectedness of all things, the Buddhist doctrine has provided me ways to understand the intricate web of co-arising that links one being with all other beings, and to apprehend the reciprocities between thought and action, self and universe. (Joanna Macy) While all the worlds and planes of existence teem with consciousness, human mentality presents a distinctive feature: the capacity to choose, to change its karma. That is why a human life is considered so rare and priceless a privilege. And that is why Buddhist practice begins with meditation on the precious opportunity that a human existence provides- the opportunity to wake up for the sake of all beings. The Dharma vision of a co-arising world, alive with consciousness, is a powerful inspiration for the healing of the Earth. It helps us to see two important things:

It shows us our profound imbeddedness in the web of life, thus relieving us of our human arrogance and loneliness. And, at the same time, it pinpoints our distinctiveness as humans, the capacity for choice.

BUDDHA REALITY

Sabbo pajjalito loko, sabbo loko pakampito.

The entire universe is nothing but combustion and vibration. (Buddha)

Observing, observing you will reach the stage when you experience that the entire physical structure is nothing but subatomic particles: throughout the body, nothing but kalapas (subatomic particles). And even these tiniest subatomic particles are not solid. They are mere vibration, just wavelets.

As you experience it yourself you experience that the entire material world is nothing but vibration. We have to experience the ocean of infinite waves surging within, the river of inner sensations flowing within, the eternal dance of the countless vibrations within every atom of the body. We have to witness our continuously changing nature. All of this is happening at an extremely subtle level. These kalapas (subatomic particles) according to the Buddha are in a state of perpetual change or flux. They are nothing but a stream of energies, just like the light of a candle or an electric bulb. The body (as we call it), is not an entity as it seems to be, but is a continuum of matter and life-force coexisting.

Flux / Impermanence

O Brahmana, it is just like a mountain river, flowing far and swift, taking everything along with it; there is no moment, no instant, no second when it stops flowing, but it goes on flowing and continuing. So Brahmana is human life, like a mountain river.' (Buddha)

'The world is continuous flux and is impermanent. (Buddha)

One thing disappears, conditioning the appearance of the next in a series of cause and effect. There is no unchanging substance in them. There is nothing behind them that can be called a permanent Self (*Atman*), individuality, or anything that can in reality be called 'I'.

There is no unmoving mover behind the movement. It is only movement. It is not correct to say that life is moving, but life is movement itself. Life and movement are not two different things. In other words there is no thinker behind the thought. Thought itself is the thinker. If you remove the thought, there is no thinker to be found. Here we cannot fail to notice how this Buddhist view is diametrically opposed to the Cartesian cogito ergo sum: 'I think, therefore I am.' (Rahula, *What the Buddha Taught*)

It is important to understand how things change over time and thus how they have come to exist and how their change may be adapted in the future. The Metaphysics of Space and Motion and the Spherical Wave Structure of Matter explains this change (motion causes change/time/flux) and interconnectedness, that all things exist in Space and are subtly inter-connected by their spherical waves to all other things within the Space of our finite spherical universe. Gautama's final breakthrough of awareness under the bodhi tree, the culminating insight of the enlightenment, was to survey the underlying evolutionary principles that drive the universe of phenomena. His vision was of a world in constant flux with nothing immutable in it, and of human experience as a stream of momentary mental states, with no stable central controlling 'Mind' set apart from those mental states.

Yet both the flux of the world and the stream of the mind flow on in patterned, law-governed ways. The conditioned process is complex, Gautama realized, but its principles can be understood; it can be influenced. According to Buddhism, every event or phenomena, including every event in the mind, arises in dependence on a network of other phenomena which are its conditions, and it in turn forms one of the conditions for innumerable other phenomena.

The details of just how phenomena are connected together are incredibly complex and subtle. (Cooper, 1996) This philosophy of 'becoming' is unique in the spiritual history of humanity, in so far as it explains everything that exists through the co-operation of only momentarily existing forces, arising and disappearing in functional dependence on each other. (Helmuth von Glasenapp)

These momentary forces, of arising and disappearing, are thus explained with the Metaphysic of Space and Motion. It is a property of Standing Waves that they successively appear and disappear as the two waves, flowing in opposite directions, combine then cancel each other out. Thus matter, as a SSW appears and disappears in Space (with the frequency of roughly one hundred billion billion times per second.) This appearing and disappearing must also apply to the Wave-Center. Thus the particle effect of the Wave-Center appears in a discrete point in Space, then disappears, then re-appears again as the next In-Waves meets at its Wave-Center.

BUDDHA NATURE

On Nature and Interconnectedness

One is one's own refuge, who else could be the refuge? Said, the Buddha. (*Dhammapada*. XII 4.)

Buddha taught, encouraged and stimulated each person to develop themselves and work out their own emancipation, for humans have the power to liberate themselves from all bondage through their own personal effort and intelligence.

It is always a question of knowing and seeing, and not that of believing. The teaching of the Buddha is qualified as ehi-passika, inviting you to 'come and see', but not to come and believe. (Walpola Rahula, *What the Buddha Taught*)

The Buddha says, you should do the work, for the *Tathagatas* only teach the way. (*Dhammapada*. XX 4.)

(*Tathagata* means 'One who has come to Truth'. This is the term usually used by the Buddha referring to himself and to the Buddhas in general.) (Walpola Rahula, *What the Buddha Taught*)

A true Buddhist is the happiest of all beings. He has no fears or anxieties. He is always calm and serene, cannot be upset or dismayed by changes or calamities, because he sees things as they are. The Buddha was never melancholy or gloomy. He was described by his contemporaries as 'ever-smiling' (mihita-pubbamgama). (Walpola Rahula, *What the Buddha Taught*)

Although there is suffering in life, a Buddhist should not be gloomy over it, should not be angry or impatient at it. One of the principal evils in life, according to Buddhism, is 'repugnance' or hatred. Repugnance (pratigha) is explained as 'ill will with regard to living beings, with regard to suffering and with regard to things pertaining to suffering. Its function is to produce a basis for unhappy states and bad conduct.'

Thus it is wrong to be impatient at suffering. Being impatient or angry at suffering does not remove it. On the contrary, it adds a little more to one's trouble, and aggravates and exacerbates a situation already disagreeable. What is necessary is not anger or impatience, but the understanding of the question of suffering, how it comes about, and how to get rid of it, and then to work accordingly with patience, intelligence, determination and energy. (Walpola Rahula, *What the Buddha Taught*)

BUDDHA ON NIRVANA

The Third Noble Truth is that there is liberation, emancipation, freedom from suffering, from the continuity of *Dukkha*. This is called the Noble Truth of the Cessation of *Dukkha* (*Dukkhanirodha-ariyasacca*), which is *Nibbana*, more popularly known in its Sanskrit form of Nirvana. (Walpola Rahula)

Now you will ask: But what is Nirvana?The only reasonable reply is that it can never be answered completely and satisfactorily in words, because human language is too poor to express the real nature of the Absolute Truth or Ultimate Reality which is Nirvana. Language is created and used by masses of human beings to express things and ideas experienced by their sense organs and their mind. A supramundane experience like that of the Absolute Truth is not of such a category.

Words are symbols representing things and ideas known to us; and these symbols do not and cannot convey the true nature of even ordinary things. Language is considered deceptive and misleading in the matter of understanding of the Truth. So the Lankavatara-sutra says that ignorant people get stuck in words like an elephant in the mud. Nevertheless, we cannot do without language.

NIRVANA

Let us consider a few definitions and descriptions of Nirvana as found in the original Pali texts: 'It is the complete cessation of that very 'thirst' (*tanha*), giving it up, renouncing it, emancipation from it, and detachment from it.' (*Mahavagga*)

'Calming of all conditioned things, giving up of all defilements, extinction of 'thirst', detachment, cessation, *Nibbana*.' (S I, p.136)

'O Bhikkhus, what is the Absolute (asamkhata, unconditioned)? It is the extinction of desire (*ragakkhayo*), the extinction of hatred (*dosakkhayo*), and the extinction of illusion (*mohakkhayo*). This, O Bhikkhus, is called the Absolute.'

The cessation of Continuity and becoming (Bhavanirodha) is *Nibbana*.' (Words of Musila, disciple of Buddha. S II (PTS), p.117) Nirvana is definitely no annihilation of self because there is no self to annihilate. If at all, it is the annihilation of the illusion, of the false idea of self.

NIRVANA AS ABSOLUTE TRUTH

We may get some idea of Nirvana as Absolute Truth from the Dhatuvibhanga-sutta (No. 140) of the *Majjhima-nikaya*. This extremely important discourse was delivered by the Buddha to Pukkusati, whom the Master found to be intelligent and earnest, in the quiet of night in a potter's shed.

The essence of the relevant portions of the sutta is as follows:

A man is composed of six elements: solidity, fluidity, heat, motion, space and consciousness. He analyses them and finds that none of them is 'mine', or 'me' or 'my self.' He understands how consciousness appears and disappears, how pleasant, unpleasnt and neutral sensations appear and disappear. Through this knowledge his mind becomes detached. Then he finds within him a pure equanimity (*upekha*) which he can direct towards the attainment of any high spiritual state. But then he thinks:

'If I focus this purified and cleansed equanimity on the Sphere of Infinite Space and develop a mind conforming thereto, that is a mental creation (*samkhatam*). If I focus this purified and cleansed equanimity on the Sphere of Infinite Consciousness, on the Sphere of Nothingness, or on neither the Sphere of Neither-perception nor Non-perception and develop a mind conforming thereto, that is a mental creation.'

Then he neither mentally creates nor wills continuity and becoming (*bhava*) or annihilations (*vibhava*). As he does not construct or does not will continuity and becoming or annihilation, he does not cling to anything in the world; as he does not cling, he is not anxious; as he is not anxious, he is completely calmed within (fully blown out within paccattam yeva parinibhayati). And he knows:

'Finished is birth, lived is pure life, what should be done is done, nothing more is left to be done.' (This expression means that now he is an *Arahant*).

Now when he experiences a pleasant, unpleasant or neutral sensation, he knows that it is impermanent, that it does not bind him, that it is not experienced with passion. Whatever may be the sensation, he experiences it without being bound to it (*visamyutto*).

'Therefore, O Bhikkhu, a person so endowed is endowed with the absolute wisdom, for the knowledge of the extinction of all *Dukkha* is the absolute noble wisdom.

His deliverance, founded on Truth, is unshakable. O Bhikkhu that which is unreality (*mosa dhamma*) is false; that which is reality (*amosa dhamma*) is *Nibbana* is Truth (Sacca). Therefore O *Bhikkhu*, a person so endowed is endowed with this Absolute Truth. For, the Absolute Truth (paramam ariyasaccam) is *Nibbana*, which is Reality.' (Buddha, from the Dhatuvibhanga-sutta (No. 140) of the *Majjhima-nikaya*)

Elsewhere the Buddha unequivocally uses the word Truth in place of *Nibbana*: 'I will teach you the Truth and the Path leading to the Truth.' Now, what is this Absolute Truth? According to Buddhism, the Absolute Truth is that there is nothing absolute in the world, that everything is relative, conditioned, impermanent, and that there is no unchanging, everlasting, absolute substance like Self, Soul or *Atman* within or without. This is the Absolute Truth.

It is incorrect to think that Nirvana is the natural result of the extinction of craving. Nirvana is not the result of anything. If it would be a result, then it would be an effect produced by a cause. It would be samkhata 'produced' and 'conditioned'. Nirvana is neither cause nor effect. It is not produced like a mystic, spiritual, mental state, such as *Dhyana* or *samadhi*. Truth and nirvana is the only thing you can do is see it, realise it. There is a path leading to the realisation of Nirvana. But Nirvana is not the result of this path. You may get to the mountain along a path, but the mountain is not the result, not an effect of the path. You may see a light, but the light is not a result of your eyesight.

People often ask: What is there after Nirvana? This question cannot arise, because Nirvana is the Ultimate Truth. If it is Ultimate there can be nothing after it. If there is anything after Nirvana, then that will be the Ultimate Truth and not Nirvana. Another question arises: What happens to the Buddha or an *Arahant* after his death, parinirvana? This comes under the category of unanswered questions (*avyakata*).

There is yet another popular question: If there is no Self, no *Atman*, who realises Nirvana? Before we go on to Nirvana, let us ask the question: Who thinks now, if there is no self? We have seen earlier that it is the thought that thinks that there is no thinker behind the thought. In the same way, it is wisdom (*panna*), realisation that realises. There is no other self behind the realisation. In the discussion on the origin of *Dukkha* we saw that whatever it may be- whether being, or thing, or system- if it is of the nature of arising; it has within itself the nature, the germ, of its cessation, its destruction. *Dukkha* arises because of 'thirst' (*tanha*) and it ceases because of wisdom (*panna*). 'Thirst' and Wisdom are both within the Five Aggregates.

Thus, the germ of their arising as well as that of their cessation is both within the Five Aggregates. This is the real meaning of the Buddhas well-known statement:

'Within this fathom-long sentient body itself, I postulate the world, the arising of the world, the cessation of the world, and the path leading to the cessation of the world.' This means that all the Four Noble Truths are found within the Five Aggregates, i.e. within us. This also means that there is no external power that produces the arising and cessation of *Dukkha*.

When wisdom is developed and cultivated according to the Fourth Noble Truth, it sees the secret of life, the reality of things as they are. When the secret is discovered, when the Truth is seen, all the forces which feverishly produce the continuity of *samsara* in illusion become calm and incapable of producing any more karma-formations, because there is no more illusion, no more 'thirst' for continuity. It is like a mental disease which is cured when the cause or the secret of the malady is discovered and seen by the patient.

He who has realised Truth, Nirvana, is the happiest being in the world. He is free from all 'complexes' and obsessions, the worries and troubles that torment others. His mental health is perfect. He does not repent the past, nor does he brood over the future. He lives fully in the present. Therefore he appreciates and enjoys things in the purest sense without self-projections. He is joyful, exultant, enjoying the pure life, his faculties pleased, free from anxiety, serene and peaceful. As he is free from selfish desire, hatred, ignorance, conceit, pride, and all such 'defilements', he is pure and gentle, full of universal love, compassion, kindness, sympathy, understanding and tolerance. His service to others is of the purest, for he has no thought of self. He gains nothing, accumulated nothing, because he is free from the illusion of self and the 'thirst' of becoming.

Nirvana is beyond logic and reasoning *(atakkavacara)*. Nirvana is 'to be realised by the wise within themselves'. (*paccattam veditabbo vinnuhi*)

BUDDHA ON MIND AND MATTER

Sabbo pajjalito loko, sabbo loko pakampito. The entire universe is nothing but combustion and vibration. With this awareness, one can observe and realize that the entire *pancakkhandha*, the five aggregates, are nothing but vibrations, arising and passing away. The entire phenomenon of mind and matter has this continuously ephemeral nature. This is the ultimate truth (paramattha saccaparamattha sacca) of mind and matter -permanently impermanent; nothing but a mass of tiny bubbles or ripples, disintegrating as soon as they arise (sabbo loko pakampitosabbo loko pakampito).

This realisation of the basic characteristic of all phenomena as *Anicca* (impermanent) leads one to the realisation of the characteristic of *Anatta* (not 'I', not 'me', not 'mine', not 'my soul'). The various sensations keep arising in the body whether one likes it or not. There is no control over them, no possession of them. They do not obey our wishes. This in turn makes one realize the nature of *Dukkha* (suffering). Through experience, one understands that identifying oneself with these changing impersonal phenomena is nothing but suffering. As you experience the reality of matter to be vibration, you also start experiencing the reality of the mind: vinnana (consciousness), sanna (perception), *vedana* (sensation) and *sankhara* (reaction). If you experience them properly with Vipassana, it will become clear how they work.

Buddha discovered the way: whenever you experience any sensation, due to any reason, you simply observe it. Every sensation arises and passes away. Nothing is eternal. When you practice Vipassana you start experiencing this. However unpleasant a sensation may be - look, it arises only to pass away. However pleasant a sensation may be, it is just a vibration-arising and passing. Pleasant, unpleasant or neutral, the characteristic of impermanence remains the same. You are now experiencing the reality of *Anicca*. You are not believing it because Buddha said so, or some scripture or tradition says so, or even because your intellect says so. You accept the truth of *Anicca* because you directly experience it.

This is how your received wisdom and intellectual understanding turn into personally experienced wisdom. Only this experience of *Anicca* will change the habit pattern of the mind. Feeling sensation in the body and understanding that everything is impermanent, you don't react with craving or aversion; you are equanimous. Practicing this continually changes the habit of reacting at the deepest level. By observing reality as it is, you become free from all your conditioning of craving and aversion. The Buddha described everything as made from mind and matter. He described the parts of the mind and the qualities of matter. These are called "elements" which is confusing today when we use the same word for chemical elements and I prefer the translation to be "properties". The 4 properties he described were likened to earth, air, fire and water (the Greeks must have got this from him as he sent arahants to all the known lands) but are to be understood as the qualities of hardness, cohesion, vibration and expansiveness. These are a correct description for a tensile aether, just like Maxwell arrived at later and which I was also convinced lay behind the structure of cycles and of the wave nature of matter.

The *Abhidhamma Pitaka* investigates and analyses Mind (*citta*) and Matter (*Rupa*), the two composite factors of the so-called a being. (Pali term '*Abhidhamma* ' is composed of two words 'Abhi' and '*Dhamma*'. Abhi means subtle, higher, ultimate, profound, sublime and transcendental, and *Dhamma* means Truth Reality or Doctrine)

PRIMARY ELEMENTS / PROPERTIES

According to the Buddhist conception, all inanimate objects are aggregates of the following five inherent elements, namely:

1 The Element of Solidity (*Pathavi*),
2 The Element of Fluidity (*Apo*),
3 The Element of Heat (*Tejo*),
4 The Element of Vibration (*Vaya*)
5 The Element of Space (*Akasa*).

In the case of animate objects, all living beings are also aggregates of six inherent elements, i. e. the above five with addition of mind.

Whatever in one's own body there exists of hardness or softness, such as the hairs, nails, teeth, skin, flesh, etc, is called one's own solid element. By realizing the true nature of the solid element, there cannot be found one's own I'ness or personality or ego (*Atta*), but only the element of solidity which is ever arising and passing away from growth to decay, from decay to death. In reality, this is not mine; this is not I; this is not my ego, but only the atom of physical phenomena.

Whatever in one's own body there exists of Liquidity or fluidity, such as blood, sweat, fat, tears etc, is called one's own fluid element. By realizing the true nature of the fluid element, there cannot be found one's I'ness or personality or ego (*Atta*), but only the element of fluidity which is ever changing from one form to another. In reality, this is not mine; this is not I; this is not my ego, but this is only the atoms of fluid phenomena. Whatever in one's own body there exists of hotness, such as that whereby one is heated, consumed, scorched, perishable, whereby that which has been eaten, drunk, is fully digested or wasted and so on, is called one's own heating element. By realizing the true nature of the he heating element, there cannot be found one's own I'ness or personality or ego (*atta*), but only the element of that which is ever warming (*usama*), digesting (*pacaka*), decaying (*jirana*), going up and down of temperature (*santappana*) and burning (*daha*). In reality, this is not mine; this is not I; am not my Ego, but this is only the atoms of firing phenomena.

Whatever in one's own body there exists of wind or vibration, such as the upward-going and downward-going winds, the winds of stomach and intestines, in-breathing and out-breathing and so on is called one's own Vibrating elements. By realizing the true nature of the vibrating element, there cannot be found one's own I'ness or personality or ego (*Atta*), but only the element of vibration which is ever moving, supporting and permeating from place to place. In reality, this is not mine; this is not I, this is not my Ego, but this is only the atoms of vibrating phenomena.

In the case of the Element of Space, there is, of course, the space between any two phenomena or elements, such as bone and flesh, or skin and flesh and so on. Here we realise that Ancient Indian Philosophy did not understand the true connection between the One Thing, Space and the many things, matter. They believed Space / *Akasa* are what exist between matter, rather than matter existing as a spherical standing wave in space. By taking the whole view of the physical phenomena to one-pointedness, one should understand, discern and realize that the body composed of hairs,bones, teeth, blood, sweat, wind etc, is nothing, but the particles or atoms of these four primary phenomenal element which are for ever and ever arising and passing away without any stop even a very short moment.

Being so, the so-called body named such and such with a conventional term is, in the sense of ultimate reality merely proton, neutron and electron of physical phenomena, but not infinite soul; nor mine; nor am I, nor my personality nor ego or self. Regarding the mind, there is no place where mind can be located. Evidently mind is not static thing, but a moving phenomenon. It is therefore, in reality, the process of consciousness arisen between sense organs and objects. When mind comes in contact with an object through any one of six sense-doors, a new mental phenomenon or consciousness arises and immediately it passes away. Even during such a very short moment of consciousness, the mental process has happened many times very swiftly.

So the comprehensive discernment of physical and mental phenomena in its real nature is called (*Vipassana Nana*) Insight knowledge. By realizing the true nature of the ultimate reality, one in able to be contented; contentment leads to lesser and lesser desire for sensual pleasure, from lesser desire to delight, then to rapture, absolute purity, happiness, one-pointedness of the mind, discernment in insight as it really is, banefulness in craving, will for emancipation from craving, realization of insight in absolute emancipation and then finally leads to the attainment of Ultimate Peaceful Happiness of *Nibbana*.

Therefore, a Buddhist must not only view these two conceptions correctly, i.e. (1) (*Kammassakata Nana*) Insight knowledge in the nature of action and its results (2) (Vipassana Nana) Insightful knowledge into the true nature of physical and mental phenomena i. e., the three characteristics of impermanence, etc, but also he devotes himself to the actual practice of the Teaching in order to attain the Ultimate Happiness of *Nibbana*.

KARMA OF BUDDHISM RELIGION

The Pali word kamma or the Sanskrit word karma (from the root kr to do) literally means 'action', 'doing'. But in the Buddhist theory of karma it has a specific meaning: it means only 'volitional action' not all action. Nor does it mean the result of karma as many people wrongly and loosely use it. In Buddhist terminology karma never means its effect; its effect is known as the 'fruit' or the 'result' of karma. Volition may relatively be good or bad, just as desire may relatively be good or bad. So karma may be good or bad relatively. Good karma produces good effects and bad karma bad effects.

'Thirst', volition, karma, whether good or bad, has one force as its effect: force to continue- to continue in a good or bad direction. Whether good or bad it is relative, and is within the cycle of continuity (*samsara*). An Arahant, though he acts, does not accumulate karma, because he is free from the false idea of self, free from the 'thirst' for continuity and becoming, free from all other defilements and impurities. For him there is no rebirth. The theory of karma should not be confused with so-called 'moral justice' or 'reward and punishment'. The idea of moral justice, or reward and punishment, arises out of the conception of a supreme being, a God, who sits in judgement, who is a law-giver and who decides what is right and wrong. The term 'justice' is ambiguous and dangerous, and in its name more harm than good is done to humanity.

The theory of karma is the theory of cause and effect, of action and reaction; it is a natural law, which has nothing to do with the idea of justice or reward and punishment. Every volitional action produces its effects or results. If a good action produces good effects, it is not justice, or reward, meted out by anybody or any power sitting in judgement of your action, but this is in virtue of its own nature, its own law. This is not difficult to understand. But what is difficult is that, according to karma theory, the effects of a volitional action may continue to manifest themselves even in a life after death.

BUDDHISM RELIGION ON NO SOUL

Buddhism stands unique in the history of human thought in denying the existence of such a Soul, Self, or *Atman*. According to the teaching of the Buddha, the idea of self is imaginary, false belief which has no corresponding reality, and it produces harmful thoughts of 'me' and 'mine', selfish desire, craving, attachment, hatred, ill-will, conceit, pride, egoism, and other defilements, impurities and problems. It is the source of all the troubles in the world from personal conflicts to wars between nations. In short, to this false view can be traced all the evil in the world. Two ideas are psychologically deep-rooted in man: self-protection and self-preservation. For self-protection man has created God, on whom he depends for his own protection, safety and security, just as a child depends upon a parent.

For self-preservation man has conceived of the idea of an immortal Soul or *Atman*, which will live eternally. In his ignorance, weakness, fear and desire, man needs these two things to console him. Hence he clings to them deeply and fanatically. The Buddha's teaching does not support this ignorance, weakness, fear and desire, but aims at making man enlightened by removing and destroying them. According to Buddhism, our ideas of God and soul are false and empty. Though highly developed as theories, they are all the same extremely subtle mental projections, garbed in an intricate metaphysical and philosophical phraseology. These ideas are so deep-rooted in man, and so near and dear to him, that he does not wish to hear, does not want to understand, any teaching against them.

The Buddha knew this quite well. He said his teaching was 'against the current' (patisotagami), against man's selfish desires. Just four weeks after his Enlightenment, seated under the banyan tree, he thought to himself:

I have realised this Truth which is deep, difficult to see, difficult to understand... comprehensible only by the wise. Men who are overpowered by passions and surrounded by a mass of darkness cannot see this Truth, which is against the current, which is lofty, deep, subtle and hard to comprehend.

With these thoughts in mind, the Buddha hesitated for a moment, whether it would not be in vain if he tried to explain to the world the Truth he had just realised. Then he compared the world to a lotus pond: In a lotus pool there are some lotuses still under the water; there are others which have risen only up to the water level; there are still others which stand above water and are untouched by it. In the same way in this world, there are men at different levels of development. Some would understand the Truth. So the Buddha decided to teach.

ANATTA OR NO-SOUL

The doctrine of *Anatta* or No-Soul is the natural result of, or, the corollary to, the analysis of the Five Aggregates and the teaching of Conditioned Genesis (Paticca-samuppada). What we call a being is composed of the Five Aggregates, and when these are analysed and examined, there is nothing behind them which can be taken as 'I', *Atman* or Self, or any unchanging abiding substance. That is the analytical method. The same result can be arrived at through the doctrine of Conditioned Genesis which is the synthetical method, and according to this nothing in the world is absolute. Everything is conditioned, relative and interdependent. This is the Buddhist theory of relativity.

CONDITIONED GENESIS

On this principle of conditionality, relativity and interdependence, the whole existence and continuity of life and its cessation are explained in a detailed formula which is called Paticca-samuppada 'Conditioned Genesis', consisting of twelve factors:

1. Through ignorance are conditioned volitional actions or karma-formations (*Avijapaccaya samkhara*).
2. Through volitional actions is conditioned consciousness (*Samkharapaccaya vinnanam*).
3. Through consciousness are conditioned mental and physical phenomena (*Vinnanapaccaya namarupam*)
4. Through mental and physical phenomena are conditioned the six faculties (i.e. five physical sense-organs and mind) (*Namarupapaccaya salayatanam*).
5. Through the six faculties is conditioned (sensorial and mental) contact (*Salayatanapaccaya phasso*).
6. Through (sensorial and mental) contact is conditioned sensation (*Phassapaccaya vedana*).
7. Through sensation is conditioned desire, 'thirst' (*Vedana-paccaya tanha*).
8. Through desire ('thirst') is conditioned clinging (*Tanha-paccaya upadanam*).
9. Through clinging is conditioned the process of becoming (*Upadanapaccaya bhavo*).
10. Through the process of becoming is conditioned birth (*Bhavapaccaya jati*).
11. Through birth are conditioned (12) decay, death, lamentation, pain, etc. (*Jatipaccaya jaramaranam.*)

This is how life arises, exists and continues. It should be clearly remembered that each of these factors is conditioned (*paticcasamuppanna*) as well as conditioning (*paticca samuppada*).

Therefore they are all relative, interdependent and interconnected, and nothing is absolute or independent; hence no first cause is accepted by Buddhism. Conditioned Genesis should be considered as a circle, and not as a chain.

THE DHAMMAPADA

WORDS OF TRUTH - SELECTIONS FROM THE DHAMMAPADA

Not to do any evil, to cultivate the good, to purify one's mind, this is the Teaching of the Buddhas. To speak no ill will, to do no harm, to practice self-restraint according to the fundamental precepts, to be moderate in eating, to live in seclusion, to devote oneself to higher consciousness, this is the Teaching of the Buddhas. Fools, men of little intelligence, give themselves over to negligence, but the wise man protects his diligence as a supreme treasure. Give not yourselves unto negligence; have no intimacy with sense-pleasures. The man who meditates with diligence attains much happiness. By endeavour, diligence, discipline and self-mastery, let the wise man make (of him) an island that no flood can overwhelm.

All (mental) states have mind as their forerunner, mind is their chief, and they are mind-made. If one speaks or acts with a defiled mind, then suffering follows:

All (mental) states have mind as their forerunner, mind is their chief, and they are mind-made. If one speaks or acts, with a pure mind, happiness follows one as one's shadow that does not leave one.

'He abused me, he beat me, he defeated me, and he robbed me': the hatred of those who harbour such thoughts is not appeased.

Hatred is never appeased by hatred in this world; it is appeased by love. This is an eternal Law. This fickle, unsteady mind; difficult to guard, difficult to control, the wise man makes straight, as the fletcher the arrow. Hard to restrain, unstable is this mind; it flits wherever it lists. Good is it to control the mind. A controlled mind brings happiness. He whose mind is unsteady, he who knows not the Good Teaching, he whose confidence wavers, the wisdom of such a person does not attain fullness.

Whatever harms a foe may do to a foe, or a hater to another hater, a wrongly-directed mind may do one harm far exceeding these.

Neither mother, nor father, nor any other relative, can do a man such good as is wrought by a rightly-directed mind.

That deed is not well done, which one regrets when it is done and the result of which one experiences weeping with a tearful face.

Make haste in doing good; restrain your mind from evil.

Whosoever offends an innocent person, pure and guiltless; his evil comes back on that fool like a fine dust thrown against the wind. The man of little learning (ignorant) grows like a bull; his flesh grows but not his wisdom.

If a man practices himself what he admonishes others to do, he himself, being well-controlled, will have control over others. It is difficult, indeed, to control oneself.

Oneself is one's own protector (refuge); what other protector (refuge) can there be? With oneself fully controlled, one obtains a protection (refuge) which is hard to gain.

Do not follow mean things. Do not dwell in negligence. Do not embrace false views.

Come; behold this world, how it resembles an ornamental royal chariot, in which fools flounder, but for the wise there is no attachment to it.

Happy indeed we live without hate amongst the hateful. We live free from hatred amidst hateful men.

From lust arises grief; from lust arises fear. For him who is free from lust there is no grief, much less fear.

He who holds back arisen anger as one checks a whirling chariot, him I call a charioteer; other folk only hold the reins.

Conquer anger by love, evil by good; conquer the miser with liberality, and the liar with truth.

Be on your guard against verbal agitation; be controlled in words. Forsaking wrong speech, follow right ways in words.

Be on your guard against mental agitation; be controlled in thoughts. Foresaking evil thoughts follow right ways in thoughts.

The wise are controlled in deed, controlled in thoughts, verily, they are fully controlled.

As rust, arisen out of iron, eats itself away, even so own deeds lead the transgressor to the states of woe.

Know this, O good man, that evil things are uncontrollable. Let not greed and wickedness drag you to suffering for a long time.

There is no fire like lust. There is no grip like hate. There is no net like delusion. There is no river like craving.

The fault of others is easily seen; but ones own is hard to see. Like chaff one winnows other's faults, but one's own one conceals as a crafty fowler disguises himself.

Not by silence does one become a sage (*muni*) if one be foolish and untaught. But the wise man who, as if holding a pair of scales, takes what is good and leaves out what is evil, is indeed a sage.

You yourselves should make the effort; the Awakened Ones are only teachers. Those who enter this Path and who are meditative are delivered from the bounds of Mara (Evil).

'All conditioned things are impermanent', when one sees this in wisdom, then one becomes dispassionate towards the painful. This is the Path to Purity.

Who strives not when he should strive, who, though young and strong, is given to idleness, who is loose in his purpose and thoughts, and who is lazy- that idler never finds the way to wisdom. Watchful of speech, well restrained in mind, let him do no evil with the body; let him purify these three ways of action, and attain the Path made known by the Sages.

The craving of the man addicted to careless living grows like a Maluva creeper. He jumps hither and thither, like a monkey in the forest looking for fruit.

Whosoever in this world is overcome by this wretched clinging thirst, his sorrow grows.

One should not despise what one receives, and one should not envy (the gain of) others. Those who envy others do not attain concentration.

The sun glows by day; the moon shines by night; in his armor the warrior glows. In meditation shines the Brahman. But all day and night shines with radiance the Awakened One.

THE EIGHTFOLD PATH AND THE FOUR NOBLE TRUTHS

In the Benares Sermon the Buddha's teaching begins with the enunciation of the Four Noble Truths. These truths are: that suffering is everywhere (known as the truth of *Dukkha*), that misplaced desire (attachment) is the cause of suffering; that its cure lies in removal of the cause (the Possibility of Liberation from Difficulties exists for everyone); and that the cause may be removed by following the Noble Eightfold Path.

Buddhism recognizes that humans have a measure of freedom of moral choice, and Buddhist practice has essentially to do with acquiring the freedom to choose as one ought to choose with truth: that is of acquiring a freedom from the passions and desires that impel us to distraction and poor decisions. In this end, the Buddhist dharma enjoins:

..to tread the Noble Eightfold Path, the course of conduct that can end suffering. The path requires one to live a life based on a right view, right thought, right speech, right conduct, right vocation, right effort, right attention and right concentration. The details of Buddhist practice are to be derived from this framework and worked out by reference to the principle of seeking the Middle Way in all things. In following the Middle

Way, extremes are repudiated since they constitute the kind of ties and attachments that impede progress towards release.

It is the nature of life that all beings will face difficulties; through enlightened truthful living one can transcend these difficulties, ultimately becoming fulfilled, liberated and free. The Noble Eight-Fold Path is the path of living in awareness. Mindfulness is the foundation. By practicing mindfulness, you can develop concentration, which enables you to attain understanding. Thanks to right concentration, you realize right awareness, thoughts, speech, action, livelihood and effort. The understanding which develops can liberate you from every shackle of suffering and give birth to true peace and joy. What the individual can do is to give a fine example, and to have the courage to uphold ethical values... in a society of cynics.

All our philosophy is dry as dust if it is not immediately translated into some act of living service. Everything he advocated he did: he believed firmly that the best recommendation for a philosophy or a religion is not a book, but the life it inspires. This truth is to be lived, it is not merely pronounced with the mouth. They have a practical aspect that is readily absorbed into daily life. At the same time they deal with certain large questions that have always fascinated humankind: questions concerning the soul, the self, free will, death, God, reality and the meaning of life. Buddhism is sensitively agnostic concerning these ultimate questions and so allows for the human sense of mystery and transcendence and the propensity to speculate and reason that are part of human consciousness in general.

Man is made by his belief. As he believes, so he is. The body and mind both exist as the Relative Motions of Wave-Centers of all matter in the Universes and are intimately interconnected. Yoga, as a practical philosophy, recognises the importance of harmony of body, mind and universe as being an interconnected whole / One. Yoga means 'union' as Fritjof Capra writes; the idea of the individual being linked to the cosmos is expressed in the Latin root of the word religion, religare (to bind strongly), as well as the Sanskrit yoga, which means union.

The Wave Structure of Matter should greatly aid in the practice of yoga as it explains how humans are structures of the universe, an inseparable part of the whole / one. An improvement in posture and breathing is not the sole or even the primary aim of yoga. Instead, it is either a therapeutic method of freeing the mind from false beliefs, or the insight into ultimate reality, the dharmas, achievable by this method. Yoga is an intrinsic and integrated system consisting of metaphysics, the philosophy of mind, the theory of knowledge, ethics and the philosophy of language.

Health is a balanced state of bodily elements and of all anatomical and physiological systems, where each part of the body functions at full potential. All impressions and reactions are known as 'mental fluctuations' or 'thought-waves', and yoga is the control of thought-waves in the mind. Yoga aids many problems currently existing in modern society. At a physical level, it gives relief from countless ailments. The practice of the postures strengthens the body and creates a feeling of well-being. From the psychological viewpoint, Yoga sharpens the intellect and aids concentration. It steadies the emotions and encourages a caring concern for others.

Above all, it gives hope. The practice of breathing techniques calms the mind. Its philosophy sets life in perspective. In the realm of the spiritual, Yoga brings awareness and the ability to be still. Through meditation, inner peace is experienced.Thus Yoga is a practical philosophy involving every aspect of a person's being. It teaches the evolution of the individual by the development of self-discipline and self-awareness. One is one's own refuge, who else could be the refuge? Said the Buddha. Buddha taught, encouraged and stimulated each person to develop themselves and work out their own emancipation, for humans have the power to liberate themselves from all bondage through their own personal effort and intelligence.

The Buddha says, you should do the work, for the *Tathagatas* only teach the way. (*Tathagata* means 'One who has come to Truth'. This is the term usually used by the Buddha referring to himself and to the Buddhas in general.) Almost all religions are based on faith- rather 'blind' faith it would seem. But in Buddhism emphasis is laid on 'seeing', knowing, understanding, and not on faith, or belief.

The question of belief arises when there is no seeing - seeing in every sense of the word. The moment you see, the question of belief disappears. If I tell you that I have a gem hidden in the folded palm of my hand, the question of belief arises because you do not see it yourself. But if I unclench my fist and show you the gem, then you see it for yourself, and the question of belief does not arise. So the phrase in ancient Buddhist texts reads: 'Realising, as one sees a gem (or a myrobalan fruit) in the palm'. It is always a question of knowing and seeing, and not that of believing. The teaching of the Buddha is qualified as ehi-passika, inviting you to 'come and see', but not to come and believe.

The expressions used everywhere in Buddhist texts referring to persons who realised the Truth are:

The dustless and stainless Eye of Truth (*Dhamma-cakkhu*) has arisen. He has seen Truth, has attained Truth, has known Truth, has penetrated into Truth, has crossed over doubt, and is without wavering. Thus with right wisdom he sees it as it is (*yatha bhutam*). With reference to his own Enlightenment the Buddha said: 'The eye was born, knowledge was born, wisdom was born, science was born, and light was born.' It is through knowledge or wisdom (*nana-dassana*), and not believing through faith. This was more and more appreciated at a time when Brahmanic orthodoxy intolerantly insisted on believing and accepting their tradition and authority as the only Truth without question. Once a group of learned and well-known Brahmins went to see the Buddha and had a long discussion with him. One of the group, a Brahmin youth of 16 years of age, named Kapathika, considered by them all to be an exceptionally brilliant mind, put a question to the Buddha:

'Venerable Gotama, there are the ancient holy scriptures of the Brahmins handed down along the line by unbroken oral tradition of texts. With regard to them, Brahmins come to the absolute conclusion: "This alone is Truth and everything else is false". Now, what does the venerable Gotama say about this?' The Buddha inquired: 'Among Brahmins is there any one single Brahmin who claims that he personally knows and sees that "This alone is Truth and everything else is false."?'

The young man was frank and said: 'No'. 'Then, it is like a line of blind men, each holding on to the preceding one; the first one does not see, the middle one also does not see, the last one also does not see. Thus, it seems to me that the state of the Brahmins is like that of a line of blind men.' Then the Buddha gave advice of extreme importance to the group of Brahmins: 'it is not proper for a wise man who maintains (lit. protects) truth to come to the conclusion: "This alone is Truth, and everything else is false".'

Asked by the young Brahmin to explain the idea of maintaining or protecting the truth, the Buddha said: 'A man has a faith. If he says, "This is my faith", so far as he maintains truth. But by that he cannot proceed to the absolute conclusion: "This alone is Truth, and everything else is false".' In other words a man may believe what he likes, and he may say 'I believe this'. So far as he respects truth. But because of his belief or faith, he should not say that what he believes is alone the Truth, and everything is false. The Buddha says: "To be *Digha Nikaya* to one thing (to a certain view) and to look down upon other things (views) as inferior- this wise men call a fetter."

Once the Buddha explained the doctrine of cause and effect to his disciples, and they said they saw it and understood it clearly. Then the Buddha said: 'Oh Bhikkhus, even this view, which is so pure and so clear, if you cling to it, if you fondle it, if you treasure it, if you are *Digha Nikaya* to it, then you don't understand that teaching is similar to a raft, which is for crossing over, and not for getting hold of.' The Buddha was not interested in discussing unnecessary metaphysical questions which are purely speculative and which create imaginary problems. He considered them as a 'wilderness of opinions'. It seems that there were some among his disciples who did not appreciate this attitude of his. For, we have the example of one of them, Malunkyaputta by name, who put to the Buddha ten well-known classical questions on metaphysical problems and demanded answers.

One day Malunkyaputta got up from his afternoon meditation, went to the Buddha, saluted him, sat on one side and said:

'Sir, when I was all alone meditating, this thought occurred to me: There are these problems unexplained, put aside and rejected by the Blessed One. Namely,

1 Is the universe eternal
2 Is it not eternal
3 Is the universe finite
4 Is it infinite
5 Is soul the same as body
6 Is soul one thing and body another thing
7 Does the *Tathagata* exist after death
8 Does he not exist after death
9 Does he both (at the same time) exist and not exist after death
10 Does he both at the same time not exist and not not-exist.

These problems the Blessed One does not explain to me. This (attitude) does not please me, I do not appreciate it. I will go to the Blessed One and ask him about this matter. If the Blessed One explains them to me, then I will continue to follow the holy life under him. If he does not explain them, I will leave the Order and go away. If the Blessed One knows that the universe is eternal, let him explain it to me so. If the Blessed One knows that the Universe is not eternal, let him say so. If the Blessed One does not know whether the Universe is eternal or not, etc., then for a person who does not know, it is straightfoward to say "I do not know, I do not see".'

The Buddha's reply to Malunkyaputta should do good to many millions in the world today who are wasting valuable time on such metaphysical questions and unnecessarily disturbing their peace of mind:

'Did I ever tell you, Malunkyaputta, "Come, Malunkyaputta, lead the holy life under me, I will explain these questions to you?"

'No sir.'

'Then, Malunkyaputta, even you, did you tell me: "Sir, I will lead the holy life under the Blessed One, and the Blessed One will explain these questions to me?" 'No sir.' 'Even now, Malunkyaputta, I do not tell you: "Come and lead the holy life under me, I will explain these questions to you". And you do not tell me either: "Sir, I will lead the holy life under the Blessed One, and he will explain these questions to me". Under these circumstances, you foolish one, who refuses whom? (i.e. both are free and neither is under obligation to the other.) 'Malunkyaputta, if anyone says: "I will not lead the holy life under the Blessed One until he explains these questions," he may die with these questions unanswered by the *Tathagata*...

Then the Buddha explains to Malunkyaputta that the holy life does not depend upon these views. Whatever opinion one may have about these problems, there is birth, old age, decay, death, sorrow, lamentation, pain, grief, distress, ' the Cessation of which (i.e. Nirvana) I declare in this very life." "Therefore, Malunkyaputta, bear in mind what I have explained as explained and what I have not explained as unexplained. What are the things that I have not explained? Whether the universe is eternal or not, etc, (those 10 opinions) I have not explained. Why, Malunkyaputta, have I not explained them? Because it is not useful, it is not fundamentally connected with the spiritual holy life, is not conducive to aversion, detachment, cessation, tranquility, deep penetration, full realisation, Nirvana. That is why I have not told you about them.

Then, what, Malunkyaputta, have I explained? I have explained *Dukkha*, the arising of *Dukkha*, the cessation of *Dukkha*, and the way leading to the cessation of *Dukkha*. Why, Malunkyaputta, have I explained them? Because it is useful, is fundamentally connected with the spiritual holy life, is conducive to aversion, detachment, cessation, tranquility, deep penetration, full realisation, Nirvana. Therefore I have explained them.' (It seems that this advice had the desired effect on Malunkyaputta, because elsewhere he is reported to have approached the Buddha again for instruction, following which he became an *Arahant*.)

This is the fundamental mistake of Buddhism. Reality can now be known, and it is extremely useful to all beings and to the future survival of this planet. As all Truth comes from Reality, we cannot be wise without knowing the Truth. Humanity can now understand what they are and how they are connected to the universe, thus destroying the separate notion of particles and self. The interconnection and impermanence of the Buddhist doctrine can now be explained with the Wave Structure of Matter and the Metaphysics of Space and Motion.

THE FOUR NOBLE TRUTHS

1. *Dukkha*
2. *Samudaya*, the arising or origin of *Dukkha*
3. *Nirodha*, the cessation of *Dukkha*
4. *Magga*, the way leading to the cessation of *Dukkha*.

THE FIRST NOBLE TRUTH: DUKKHA

Dukkha is generally translated by most scholars as the "Noble Truth of Suffering", and is interpreted to mean that life according to Buddhism is nothing but suffering and pain. Both translation and interpretation are misleading. Buddhism is neither pessimistic nor optimistic. If anything at all, it is realistic, for it takes a realistic view of life and of the world. It looks at things objectively (*yathabhutam*). It does not falsely lull you into living in a fool's paradise, nor does it frighten and agonise you with all kinds of imaginary fears and sins. It tells you exactly and objectively what you are and what the world is around you, and shows you the way to perfect freedom, peace, tranquility and happiness.

It is true that the Pali word *Dukkha* (or Sanskrit *duhkha*) in ordinary usage means 'suffering', 'pain', 'sorrow', or 'misery' as opposed to the word *sukha* meaning 'happiness', 'comfort' or 'ease'. But the term *Dukkha* as the First Noble Truth, which represents the Buddha's view of life and the world, has a deeper philosophical meaning and connotes enormously wider senses. It includes deeper ideas such as 'imperfection', 'impermanence', 'emptiness', 'insubstantiality'. It is difficult therefore to find one word to embrace the whole conception of the term *Dukkha* as the First Noble Truth, and so it is better to leave it untranslated, than to give an inadequate and wrong idea of it by conveniently translating it as 'suffering' or 'pain'. The Buddha does not deny happiness in life when he says there is suffering.

On the contrary he admits different forms of happiness, both the material and the spiritual, for laymen as well as monks. In the Anguttara-nikaya, one of the five original Collections of Pali containing the Buddha's discourses, there is a list of happinesses (*sukhani*), such as the happiness of family life and the happiness of a recluse, of sense pleasures and renunciation, of attachment and deattachment, physical and mental happiness. But all these are included in *Dukkha*. Even the very pure spiritual states of *Dhyana* (recueillement or trance) attained by the practice of higher meditation, free from even a shadow of suffering in the accepted sense of the world, states which may be described as unmixed happiness, as well as the state of *Dhyana* which is free from sensations both pleasant (*sukha*) and unpleasant (*Dukkha*) and is only pure equanimity and awareness- even these very high spiritual states are included in *Dukkha*.

In one of the suttas of the Majjhima-nikaya (again one of the five original Collections), after praising the spiritual happiness of these *Dhyanas*, the Buddha says that they are 'impermanent, *Dukkha*, and subject to change' (*Anicca Dukkha* vipari*namaDhamma*). Notice the word *Dukkha* is explicitly used. It is *Dukkha*, not because there is 'suffering' in the ordinary sense of the word, but because 'whatever impermanent is *Dukkha*' (*yad aniccam tam dukkham*). The Buddha says with regard to life and the enjoyment of sense-pleasures, that one should clearly understand three things:

1 Attraction or enjoyment (*assada*)
2 Evil consequence or danger or unsatisfactoriness (*adinava*)
3 Freedom or liberation (*nissarana*).

When you see a pleasant, charming and beautiful person, you like them, you are attracted, you enjoy seeing that person again and again, and you derive pleasure and satisfaction from that person. This is enjoyment (*assada*). It is a fact of experience. But this enjoyment is not permanent, just as that person and all his (or her) attractions are not permanent either. When the situation changes, when you cannot see that person, when you are deprived of this enjoyment, you become sad, you may become unbalanced and unreasonable, even behave foolishly. This is the evil, unsatisfactory and dangerous side of the picture (*adinava*). This, too, is a fact of experience. Now if you have no attachment to the person, if you are completely detached, that is freedom, liberation (*nissarana*). These three things are true with regard to all enjoyment in life.

From this it is evident that it is no question of pessimism or optimism, but that we must take account of the pleasures of life as well as of its pains and sorrows, and also of freedom from them, in order to understand life completely and objectively. Only then is true liberation possible. The conception of *Dukkha* may be viewed from three aspects:

1 *Dukkha* as ordinary suffering (*Dukkha-Dukkha*)
2 *Dukkha* as produced by change (*viparinama-Dukkha*)
.3 *Dukkha* as conditioned states (*samkhara-Dukkha*)

All kinds of suffering in life like birth, old age, sickness, death, association with unpleasant people and conditions... all such forms of mental and physical suffering or pain, are included in *Dukkha* as ordinary suffering. A happy feeling, a happy condition in life, is not permanent, not everlasting. It changes sooner or later. When it changes it produces pain, suffering, and unhappiness. This vicissitude is included in *Dukkha* as suffering produced by change.

The third form of *Dukkha* as conditioned states is the most important philosophical aspect of the First Noble Truth, and it requires some analytical explanation of what we consider as a 'being', as an 'individual' or as 'I'.

What we call a 'being', or an 'individual', or 'I', according to Buddhist philosophy, is only a combination of ever-changing physical and mental forces or energies, which may be divided into five groups of aggregates (pancakkhandha). The Buddha says: 'In short these five aggregates of attachment are *Dukkha*'. Elsewhere he defines *Dukkha* as the five aggregates: 'Oh Bhikkhus, what is *Dukkha*? It should be said it is the five aggregates of attachment.'

The Five Aggregates:

1. Aggregate of Matter (*rupakkhandha*)
2. Aggregate of Sensation (*Vedanakkhandha*)
3. Aggregate of Perceptions (*sannakkhandha*)
4. Aggregate of Mental Formations (*samkharakkhandha*)
5. Aggregate of Consciousness

1. Aggregate of Matter (*Rupakkhandha*) included are the Four Great Elements (*cattari mahabhutani*), namely, solidity, fluidity, heat and motion, and also the Derivatives (*upadaya-rupa*) of the Four Great Elements.

   In the term 'Derivatives of Four Great Elements' are included our five material sense-organs, i.e. the faculties of eye, ear, nose, tongue and body, and their corresponding objects in the world, i.e. visible form, sound, odour, taste and tangible things, and also some thoughts or ideas or conceptions which are in the sphere of mind-objects (*dharmayatana*).
2. Aggregate of Sensation (*Vedanakkhandha*). All our sensations, pleasant or unpleasant or neutral, experienced through the contact of physical and mental organs with the external world. They are six of kinds: the sensations experienced through the contact of the eyes with visible forms, ear with sounds, nose with odour, tongue with taste, body with tangible objects and mind (the sixth faculty in Buddhist philosophy) with mind-objects or thoughts or ideas.

Mind is only a faculty or organ (*indriya*) like the ear or eye. It can be controlled and developed like any other faculty, and the Buddha speaks quite often of the value of controlling and disciplining these six faculties. Ideas and thoughts are not independent of the world experienced by these five physical sense faculties. In fact they depend on, and are conditioned by, physical experiences. Hence a person born blind cannot have ideas of colour, except through the analogy of sounds or some other things experienced through his other faculties. Ideas and thoughts which form part of the world are thus produced and conditioned by physical experiences and are conceived by the mind.

3. Aggregate of Perceptions (*Sannakkhandha*) like sensations, perceptions are also of six kinds, in relation to six internal faculties and the corresponding six eternal objects. It is the perceptions that recognise objects as physical or mental.
4. Aggregate of Mental Formations (*Samkharakkhandha*). In this group are included all volitional activities both good and bad. What is generally known as karma comes under this group. The Buddha's own definition of karma should be remembered here: 'O Bhikkhus, it is volition (*cetana*) that I call karma. Having willed, one acts through body, speech and mind.' Volition is 'mental construction, mental activity. Its function is to direct the mind in the sphere of good, bad or neutral activities.'

   Sensations and perceptions are not volitional actions. They do not produce karmic effects. It is only volitional actions- such as attention (*mana*sikara), will (*chanda*), determination (*adhimokkha*), confidence (saddha), concentration (*samadhi*), wisdom (*panna*), energy (*viriya*), desire (*raga*), repugnance or hate (*paatigha*), ignorance (*avijja*), conceit (*mana*), idea of self (sakkaya-ditthi) etc. - that can produce karmic effects. There are 52 such mental activities which constitute the Aggregate of Mental Formations.
5. Aggregate of Consciousness (*Vinnanakkhandha*) is a reaction or response which has one of the six faculties as its basis, and one of the six corresponding external phenomena

(visible form, sound, odour, taste, tangible things and mind objects) as its object.

According to Buddhist philosophy there is no permanent, unchanging spirit which can be considered 'Self' or 'Soul' or 'Ego', as opposed to matter, and that consciousness (vinnana) should not be taken as 'spirit' in opposition to matter. This point has to be emphasised, because a wrong notion that consciousness is a sort of self or Soul that continues as a permanent substance through life, has persisted from the earliest time to the present day.

The Buddha said, "There is no arising of consciousness without conditions," and "...Consciousness is named according to whatever condition through which it arises: on account of the eye and visible forms arises a consciousness, called visual consciousness..." (Mahatanhasamkhaya-sutta, M I (PTS)

What we call a 'being' or an 'individual' or 'I' is only a convenient name or a label given to a combination of these five groups. They are all impermanent, all constantly changing. 'Whatever is impermanent is *Dukkha* (*yad aniccam tam dukkham*). This is the true meaning of the Buddha's words: 'In brief the five Aggregates of Attachment are *Dukkha*.' They are not the same for two consecutive moments. Here A is not equal to A. They are in a flux of momentary arising and disappearing.

FLUX / IMPERMANENCE / MOTION .

The Buddha said, 'O Brahmana, it is just like a mountain river, flowing far and swift, taking everything along with it; there is no moment, no instant, no second when it stops flowing, but it goes on flowing and continuing. So Brahmana is human life, like a mountain river.' As the Buddha told Ratthapala: 'The world is continuous flux and is impermanent.'

One thing disappears, conditioning the appearance of the next in a series of cause and effect. There is no unchanging substance in them. There is nothing behind them that can be called a permanent Self (*Atman*), individuality, or anything that can in reality be called 'I'. Eberyonw will agree that neither matter, nor sensation, nor perception, nor any one of those mental activities, nor consciousness can really be called 'I'. But when these five physical and mental aggregates which are interdependent are working together in combination as a physio-psychological machine, we get the idea of 'I'. But this is only a false idea, a mental formation, which is nothing but one of those 52 mental formations, which is nothing but one of those 52 mental formations of the fourth Aggregate which we have discussed, namely, it is the idea of self (*sakkaya-ditthi*).

The Five Aggregates together, which we popularly call a 'being', are *Dukkha* itself (*samkhara-Dukkha*). There is no other 'being' or 'I', standing behind these five aggregates, who experiences *Dukkha*. There is no unmoving mover behind the movement. It is only movement. It is not correct to say that life is moving, but life is movement itself. Life and movement are not two different things. In other words there is no thinker behind the thought. Thought itself is the thinker. If you remove the thought, there is no thinker to be found. Here we cannot fail to notice how this Buddhist view is diametrically opposed to the Cartesian cogito ergo sum: 'I think, therefore I am.'

NO BEGINNING TO LIFE

According to the Buddha's teaching the beginning of the life-stream of living things is unthinkable. The believer in the creation of life by God may be astonished at this reply. But if you were to ask him, 'What is the beginning of God?' he would answer without hesitation 'God has no beginning,' and he would not be astonished by his reply.

The Buddha says: 'O Bhikkhus, this cycle of continuity (*samsara*) us without visible end, and the first beginning of beings wandering and running around, enveloped in ignorance (*avijja*) and bound down by the fetters of thirst (desire, *tanha*) is not the be perceived.' And further, referring to the ignorance which is the main cause of the continuity of life the Buddha states: 'The first beginning of ignorance is not to be perceived in such a way as to postulate that there was no ignorance beyond a certain point.' Thus it is not possible to say that there was no life beyond a certain definite point.

THE SECOND NOBLE TRUTH: SAMUDAYA 'THE ARISING OF DUKKHA'

The Second Noble Truth is that of the arising or origin of *Dukkha* (*Dukkhasamudaya-ariyasacca*). The most popular and well-known definition of the Second Truth as found in innumerable places in the original texts runs as follows:

'It is this "thirst" (craving, *tanha*) which produces re-existence and re-becoming (ponobhavika), and which is bound up with passionate greed (*nandiragasahagata*), and which finds fresh delight now here and now there (*tatratatrabhinandini*), namely,

1 Thirst for sense-pleasures (*kama-tanha*),

2 Thirst for existence and becoming (*bhava-tanha*) and

3 Thirst for non-existence (self-annihilation, *vibhava-tanha*).'

It is this 'thirst', desire, greed, craving, manifesting itself in different ways that gives rise to all forms of suffering and the continuity of beings. But it should not be taken as the first cause, for there is no first cause possible as, according to Buddhism, everything is relative and interdependent. Even this 'thirst', *tanha*, which is considered as the cause or origin of *Dukkha*, depends for its arising (*samudaya*) on something else, which is sensation (*vedana*), and sensation arises depending on contact (*phassa*), and so on and so forth goes the circle which is known as Conditioned Genesis (*Paticca- samuppada*).

So *Tanha*, 'thirst' is not the first or only cause of the arising of *Dukkha*. But it is the most palatable and immediate cause, the 'principle thing' and the 'all pervading thing'. Hence in certain places of the original Pali texts themselves the definition of samudaya or the origin of *Dukkha* includes other defilements and impurities (kilesa, *sasava, Dhamma*), in addition to *tanha*, thirst which is always given the first place. Within the necessarily limited space of our discussion, it will be sufficient if we remember that this 'thirst' has as its centre the false idea of self arising out of ignorance.

The term 'thirst' includes not only desire for, and attachment to, sense-pleasures, wealth and power, but also desires for, and attachment to, ideas and ideals, views, opinions, theories, conceptions and beliefs (*Dhamma-tanha*). According to the Buddha's analysis, all the troubles and strife in the world, from little personal quarrels in families to great wars between nations and countries, arise out of this selfish 'thirst'. From this point of view all economic, political, social problems are rooted in this selfish 'thirst'. As the Buddha told Rattapala: "The world lacks and hankers, and is enslaved to "thirst" (*tanhadaso*)."

KARMA AND REBIRTH

Everyone will admit that all the evils in the world are produced by selfish desire. This is not difficult to understand. But how this desire, 'thirst', can produce re-existence and re-becoming (*puno-bhavika*) is a problem not so easy to grasp. Here we must have some idea about the theory of karma and rebirth.

There are four Nutriments (*ahara*) in the sense of 'cause' or 'condition' necessary for the existence and continuity of beings:

1 Ordinary material food (*kabalinkarahara*)
2 Contact of our sense-organs (including mind) with the external world (*phassahara*)
3 Consiousness (*vinnanahara*) and
4 Mental volition or will (*manosancetanahara*).

Of these four, the last mentioned 'metal volition' is the will to live, to exist, to re-exist, and to continue, to become more and more. It creates the root of existence and continuity, striving forward by way of good and bad actions (*kusalakusalakamma*). It is the same as 'Volition' (*cetana*). We have seen earlier that volition is karma, as the Buddha himself defined it. Referring to 'Mental Volition' just mentioned above the Buddha says: 'When one understands the nutriment of mental volition one understands the three forms of 'thirst' (*tanha*)'.

Thus the terms 'thirst', 'volition', 'mental volition' and 'karma' all denote the same thing: they denote the desire, the will to be, to exist, to re-exist, to become more and more, to grow more and more, to accumulate more and more. This is the arising of *Dukkha*, and this is found within the Aggregate of Mental Formations, one of the Five Aggregates which constitute a being. Here is one of the most important and essential points in the Buddha are teaching. We must therefore clearly and carefully mark and remember that the cause, the germ, of the arising of *Dukkha* is within *Dukkha* itself, and not outside; and we must equally well remember that the cause, the germ, of the cessation of *Dukkha*, of the destruction of *Dukkha*, is also within *Dukkha* itself, and not outside. This is what is meant by the well-known formula often found in original Pali texts:

Yam kinci samudaya dhammam sabbam tam nirodha dhammam 'Whatever is of the nature of arising, all that is of the nature of cessation.' A being, thing, or a system, if it has within itself the nature of arising, the nature of coming into being, has also within itself the nature, the germ, of its own cessation and destruction. Thus *Dukkha* (Five Aggregates) has within itself the nature of its own arising, and has also within itself the nature of its own cessation.

KARMA

The Pali word kamma or the Sanskrit word karma (from the root kr to do) literally means 'action', 'doing'. But in the Buddhist theory of karma it has a specific meaning: it means only 'volitional action' not all action. Nor does it mean the result of karma as many people wrongly and loosely use it. In Buddhist terminology karma never means its effect; its effect is known as the 'fruit' or the 'result' of karma. Volition may relatively be good or bad, just as desire may relatively be good or bad. So karma may be good or bad relatively. Good karma produces good effects and bad karma bad effects. 'Thirst', volition, karma, whether good or bad, has one force as its effect: force to continue- to continue in a good or bad direction. Whether good or bad it is relative, and is within the cycle of continuity (*samsara*). An Arahant, though he acts, does not accumulate karma, because he is free from the false idea of self, free from the 'thirst' for continuity and becoming, free from all other defilements and impurities. For him there is no rebirth.

The theory of karma should not be confused with so-called 'moral justice' or 'reward and punishment'. The idea of moral justice, or reward and punishment, arises out of the conception of a supreme being, a God, who sits in judgement, who is a law-giver and who decides what is right and wrong. The term 'justice' is ambiguous and dangerous, and in its name more harm than good is done to humanity. The theory of karma is the theory of cause and effect, of action and reaction; it is a natural law, which has nothing to do with the idea of justice or reward and punishment. Every volitional action produces its effects or results. If a good action produces good effects, it is not justice, or reward, meted out by anybody or any power sitting in judgement of your action, but this is in virtue of its own nature, its own law.

This is not difficult to understand. But what is difficult is that, according to karma theory, the effects of a volitional action may continue to manifest themselves even in a life after death. We have seen earlier that a being is nothing but a combination of physical and mental forces or energies. What we call death is the total non-functioning of the physical body. Do all these forces and energies stop altogether with the non-functioning of the body? Buddhism says 'No'. Will, volition, desire, thirst to exist, to continue, to become more and more, is a tremendous force that moves the whole world. This is the greatest force, the greatest energy in the world. According to Buddhism this force does not stop with the non-functioning of the body, which is death; but it continues manifesting itself in another form, producing re-existence which is called rebirth.

Now, another question arises: If there is no permanent, unchanging entity or substance like self or Soul (*Atman*), what is it that can re-exist or be reborn after death? Before we go on to life after death, let us consider what Life is, and how it continues now. What we call life, is the combination of the Five Aggregates, a combination of physical and mental energies.

These are continously changing. Every moment they are born and they die. Thus even now during this lifetime, every moment we are born and die, but we continue.

If we can understand that in this life we can continue without a permanent, unchanging substance like self or Soul, why can't we understand that those forces themselves can continue without a Self or a Soul behind them after the non-functioning of the body? When this physical body is no more capable of functioning, energies do not die with it, but continue to take some other shape or form, which we call another life. In a child all the physical, mental and intellectual faculties are tender and weak, but they have within them the potentiality of producing a full grown man. Physical and mental energies which constitute the so-called being have within themselves the power to take a new form, and grow gradually and gather force to the full.

As there is no permanent, unchanging substance, nothing passes from one moment to the next. So quite obviously, nothing permanent or unchanging can pass or transmigrate from one life to the next. It is a series that continues unbroken, but changes every moment. The series is, really speaking, nothing but movement. It is like a flame that burns through the night: it is not the same flame nor is it another. A child grows up to be a man of sixty. Certainly the man of sixty is not the same as the child of sixty years ago, nor is he another person. Similarly, a person who dies here and is reborn elsewhere is neither the same person, nor another (na ca so na ca anno). It is the continuity of the same series.

The difference between death and birth is only a thought-moment: the last thought-moment in this life conditions the first thought-moment in the so-called next life, which, in fact, is the continuity of the same series. During this life itself too, one thought-moment conditions the next thought-moment. So from the Buddhist point of view, the question of life after death is not a great mystery, and a Buddhist is never worried about this problem. As long as there is 'thirst' to be and to become, the cycle of continuity (*samsara*) goes on. It can stop only when its driving force, this 'thirst', is cut off through wisdom which sees Reality, Truth, and Nirvana.

THE THIRD NOBLE TRUTH: NIRODHA 'THE CESSATION OF DUKKHA'

The Third Noble Truth is that there is liberation, emancipation, freedom from suffering, from the continuity of *Dukkha*. This is called the Noble Truth of the Cessation of *Dukkha* (*Dukkhanirodha-ariyasacca*), which is *Nibbana*, more popularly known in its Sanskrit form of Nirvana. Now you will ask: But what is Nirvana? The only reasonable reply is that it can never be answered completely and satisfactorily in words, because human language is too poor to express the real nature of the Absolute Truth or Ultimate Reality which is Nirvana. Language is created and used by masses of human beings to express things and ideas experienced by their sense organs and their mind. A supramundane experience like that of the Absolute Truth is not of such a category.

Words are symbols representing things and ideas known to us; and these symbols do not and cannot convey the true nature of even ordinary things. Language is considered deceptive and misleading in the matter of understanding of the Truth. So the Lankavatara-sutra says that ignorant people get stuck in words like an elephant in the mud. Nevertheless, we cannot do without language.

THE FOURTH NOBLE TRUTH: MAGGA

The Path is the Way leading to the cessation of *Dukkha*. This is known as the 'Middle Path' because it avoids two extremes: one extreme being the search for happiness through sense-pleasures, which is 'low, common, unprofitable and the way of ordinary people'; the other being the search for happiness through self-mortification in different forms of asceticism, which is 'painful, unworthy, unprofitable.' The Buddha discovered through personal experience the Middle Path, 'which gives vision and knowledge, which leads to Calm, Insight, Enlightenment, Nirvana.' This Middle Path is generally known as the Noble Eightfold Path. (*Ariya-Atthangika-Magga*):

Right Understanding

Right Thought

Right Speech

Right Action

Right Livelihood

Right Effort

Right Mindfulness

Right Concentration

They are to be developed more or less simultaneously, as far as possible according to the capacity of each individual. They are all linked together and each helps the cultivation of the others. These eight factors aim at promoting and perfecting the three essentials of Buddhist training and discipline: namely:

(a) Ethical Conduct (*Sila*)

(b) Mental Discipline (*Samadhi*)

(c) Wisdom (*panna*).

Ethical Conduct (*Sila*) is built on the vast conception of universal love and compassion for all living beings, on which the Buddha's teaching, is based. The Buddha gave his teaching 'for the good of many, for the happiness of many, out of compassion for the world.' According to Buddhism, for a man to be perfect there are two qualities that should develop equally: compassion (*karuna*) on one side and wisdom (*panna*) on the other. Here compassion represents love, charity, kindness, tolerance and other noble qualities on the emotional side, or qualities of the heart, while wisdom would stand for the intellectual side or the qualities of the mind. If one develops the emotional neglecting the intellectual, one may become a good-hearted fool; while to develop only the intellectual side neglecting the emotional may turn one into a hard-hearted intellect without feeling for others. Therefore to be perfect, one has to develop both equally. That is the aim of the Buddhist way of life: in it compassion and wisdom are inseparably linked together.

Right Speech means abstention:

1 From telling lies
2 From backbiting and slander and talk that may bring hatred, enmity, disunity and disharmony among individuals or groups of people
3 From harsh, rude, impolite, malicious and abusive language and
4 From idle, useless, foolish gossip or babble.

When one abstains from these forms of wrong and harmful speech one naturally has to speak the truth, has to use words that are friendly and benevolent, pleasant and gentle, meaningful and useful. One should not speak carelessly: speech should be at the right time and place. If one cannot say something useful, one should keep 'noble silence.'

Right Action aims at promoting moral, honourable and peaceful conduct. That we should also help others to lead a peaceful and honourable life in the right way.

Right Livelihood means that one should abstain from making ones living through a profession that brings harm to others.

These three factors (Right Speech, Right Action, and Right Livelihood) of the Eightfold Path constitute Ethical Conduct. It should be realised that the Buddhist ethical and moral conduct aims at promoting a happy and harmonious life both for the individual and society. This moral conduct is considered as the indispensable foundation for all higher spiritual attainments. No spiritual development is possible without this moral basis.

MENTAL DISCIPLINE (SAMADHI)

Right Effort is the energetic will (1) to prevent evil and unwholesome states of mind from arising, and (2) to get rid of such evil and unwholesome states that have already arisen within a person and also (3) to produce, to cause to arise, good and wholesome states of mind not yet arisen, and (4) to develop and to bring to perfection the good and wholesome states of mind already present. Right Mindfulness is to be diligently aware to (1) activities of the body (*kaya*) (2) sensations and feelings (*vedana*) (3) the activities of the mind (*citta*) (4) ideas, thoughts, conceptions and things. (*Dhamma*)

The practice of concentration on breathing (*anapanasati*) is one of the well-known exercises, connected with the body, for mental development. One should be clearly aware of all forms of feeling and sensation, all movements of the mind, all ideas, thoughts and conceptions- of their true nature, how they appear and disappear, how they are developed, suppressed, destroyed and so on. These four forms of mental culture or meditation are treated in detail in the Satipatthana-sutta (Setting up of Mindfulness).

Right Concentration leading to the four stages of *Dhyana*. In the first stage of *Dhyana*, passionate desires and certain unwholesome thoughts like sensuous lust, ill-will, languor, worry, restlessness and skeptical doubt are discarded, and feelings of joy and happiness are maintained, along with certain mental activities. In the second stage, all intellectual activities are suppressed, tranquility and 'one-pointedness' of mind developed, and the feelings of joy and happiness are still retained.

In the third stage, the feeling of joy, which is an active sensation, also disappears, while the disposition of happiness still remains in addition to mindful equanimity. In the fourth stage of *Dhyana*, all sensations, even of happiness and unhappiness, of joy and sorrow, disappear, only pure equanimity and awareness remaining. Thus the mind is trained and disciplined and developed through Right Effort, Right Mindfulness and Right Concentration.

WISDOM (PANNA)

Right Thought denotes the thoughts of selfless renunication or detachment, thoughts of love and non-violence, which are extended to all beings. True wisdom is endowed with these noble qualities, and that all thoughts of selfish desire, ill-will, hatred and violence are the result of a lack of wisdom- in all spheres of life whether individual, social or political.

Right understanding of things is they are, of the Four Noble Truths. According to Buddhism there are two sorts of understanding: What we generally call understanding is knowledge, an accumulated memory, an intellectual grasping of a subject according to certain given data. This is called 'knowing accordingly' (*anubodha*). It is not very deep. Real deep understanding is called 'penetration' (*pativedha*), seeing a thing in its true nature, without name and label. This penetration is possible only when the mind is free from all impurities and is fully developed through meditation.

From this brief account of the Path, one may see that it is a way of life to be followed, practiced and developed by each individual. It is self-discipline in body, word and mind, self-development and self-purification. It has nothing to do with prayer, belief, worship or ceremony. It is a Path leading to the realisation of Ultimate Reality, to complete freedom, happiness and peace through moral, spiritual and intellectual perfection.

FREE WILL

The question of Free Will has occupied an important place in Western thought and philosophy. But according to Conditioned Genesis, this question cannot and does not arise in Buddhist philosophy. If the whole of existence is relative, conditioned and interdependent, how can alone be free? Will, like any other thought, is conditioned. So-called 'freedom' itself is conditioned and relative. There can be nothing absolutely free, physical or mental, as everything is interdependent and relative. If Free Will implies a will independent of conditions, independent of cause and effect, such a thing does not exist. How can a will, or anything for that matter, arise without conditions, away from cause and effect, when the whole law of existence is conditioned and relative, and is within the law of cause?

Here again, the idea of Free Will is basically connected with the ideas of God, Soul, Justice, reward and punishment. Not only is so-called free will not free, but even the very idea of Free Will is not free from conditions. According to the doctrine of Conditioned Genesis, as well as according to the analysis of being into Five Aggregates, the idea of an abiding, immortal substance in man or outside, whether it is called *Atman*, 'I', Soul, Self or Ego is considered only a false belief, a mental projection.

This is the Buddhist doctrine of *Anatta*, No-Soul or No-Self. In order to avoid confusion it should be mentioned here that there are two kinds of Truth: conventional and ultimate truth. When we use such expressions in our daily life as 'I', 'you', 'being', 'Individual' etc. we do not lie because there is no self as such, but we speak a truth conforming to the convention of the world. But the ultimate truth is that there is no 'I' or 'being' in reality. 'A person should be mentioned as existing only in designation (i.e. conventionally there is a being), but not in reality (or substance dravya)'.

According to the Buddha's teaching, it is wrong to hold the opinion 'I have no self' (annihilationist) as to hold the opinion 'I have self' (eternalist), because both are fetters, arising from the false idea 'I am'. The correct position with regard to the question of *Anatta* is not to take hold of any opinions or views, but to try to see things objectively as they are without mental projections, to see that what we call 'I' or 'being', is only a combination of mental and physical aggregates, which are working together interdependently in a flux of momentary change within the law of cause and effect, and that there is nothing permanent, everlasting, unchanging and eternal in the whole of existence.

Here naturally a question arises: If there is no *Atman* or Self, who gets the result of karma (actions)? No one can answer this question better than the Buddha himself: 'I have taught you to see conditionality everywhere in all things'. The teaching of *Anatta* dispels the darkness of false beliefs, and produces the light of wisdom. It is not negative, as Asanga aptly says: 'There is the fact of No-selfness' (*nairatmyastita*).

MEDITATION OR MENTAL CULTURE: BHAVANA

The Buddha said: 'O Bhikkhus, there are two kinds of illness. What are these two? Physical illness and mental illness and there seem to be people who enjoy freedom from physical illness even for a year or two. But O Bhikkhus, rare in this world are those who enjoy freedom from mental illness even for one moment, except from those who are free from mental defilements.'(i.e. Arahants)

The Buddhas teaching, particularly his way of 'meditation', aims at producing a state of perfect mental health, equilibrium and tranquility. The word meditation is a very poor substitute for the original term bhavana, which means 'culture' or 'development' i.e. mental culture or mental development. Bhavana aims at cleansing the mind of impurities and disturbances, such as lustful desires, hatred, ill-will, indolence, worries and restlessness, skeptical doubts and cultivating such qualities as concentration, awareness, intelligence, will, energy, the analytical faculty, confidence, joy, tranquility, leading finally to the attainment of highest wisdom which sees the nature of things as they are, and realises the Ultimate Truth, Nirvana.

There are two forms of meditation. One is the development of mental concentration (*samatha* or *samadhi*), of one-pointedness of mind, by various methods prescribed in the texts, leading up to the highest mystic states. All these mystic states, according to the Buddha are mind created, conditioned (*samkhata*). They have nothing to do with Reality, Truth, and Nirvana. Buddha discovered the other form of meditation known as vipassana, 'Insight' into the nature of things, leading to the complete liberation of the mind, to the realisation of Ultimate Truth, Nirvana. This is essentially Buddhist 'meditation', Buddhist mental culture. It is an analytical method based on mindfulness, awareness, vigilance, observation. The most important discourse ever given by the Buddha on mental development is called the Satipatthana-sutta 'The Setting-up of Mindfulness'.

The 'ways' of meditation are not cut off from life, nor do they avoid life, on the contrary, they are all connected with our life, our daily activities, our sorrow and joys, our words and thoughts, our moral and intellectual occupations. The discourse is divided into four main sections: the first section deals with our body (kaya), the second with our feelings and sensations (*vedana*), the third with the mind (*citta*), and the fourth with various moral and intellectual subjects (*Dhamma*). Whatever the form of 'meditation' may be, the essential thing is mindfulness or awareness (*sati*), attention or observation (*anupassana*).

People do not generally live in their actions, in the present moment. They live in the past or in the future. Though they seem to be doing something now, here, they live somewhere else in their thoughts, in their imaginary problems and worries, usually in the memories of the past or in desires and speculations about the future. Therefore they do not live in, nor do they enjoy, what they do at the moment. So they are unhappy and discontented with the present moment, with the work at hand, and naturally cannot give themselves fully to what they appear to be doing. You cannot escape life however you may try. Real life is in the present moment- not in the memories of the past which are dead and gone, not in the dreams of the future which is not yet born.

One who lives in the present moment lives the real life, and he is happiest. Asked why his disciples where so radiant, who lived a simple and quiet life with one meal a day, the Buddha replied; 'They do not repent the past, nor do they brood over the future. They live in the present. Therefore they are radiant. By brooding over the future and repenting the past, fools dry up like green reeds cut down in the sun.' A man who is in anger is not really aware, not really mindful that he is angry. The moment he becomes aware of that state of his mind, the moment he sees his anger, it becomes, as it were, shy and ashamed, and begins to subside.

You should examine its nature, how it arises, how it disappears. You should not think 'I am angry', or of 'my anger'. You should only be aware and mindful of the state of an angry mind. Then there is a form of 'meditation' on ethical, spiritual and intellectual subjects. All our studies, reading, discussions, conversation and deliberations on such subjects are included in this 'meditation'. To read this book, and to think deeply about the subjects discussed in it, is a form of meditation.

So according to this form of meditation, you may study, think and deliberate on:

The Five Hindrances

1. Lustful Desire, 2. Ill-will, hatred, anger, 3. Torpor and Languor, 4. Restlessness and worry, 5. Skeptical Doubts

These five are considered as hindrances to any kind of clear understanding, to any kind of progress. When one is overpowered by them and when one does not know how to get rid of them, them one cannot understand right and wrong, or good and bad.

One may also meditate on:

The Seven Factors of Enlightenment (Bojjhanga)

1. Mindfulness (*sati*)
2. Investigation and research (*Dhamma*-vicaya)(all religious, ethical, philosophical studies, reading, conversation)
3. Energy (*viriya*)(- to work with determination to the end)
4. Joy (*piti*)(the quality quite contrary to the pessimistic, gloomy or melancholic attitude of mind),
5. Relaxation (*passaddhi*) (-of both body and mind. One should not be stiff mentally, physically),
6. Concentration (*samadhi*)
7. Equanimity (upekkha)(able to face life in all its vicissitudes with calm of mind, tranquility)

To cultivate these qualities the most essential thing is a genuine wish, will or inclination.

Four Sublime States (Brahma-vihara)

(1) *Metta*- Extending universal, unlimited love and good will to all living beings without any kind of discrimination,

(2) *Karuna*- Compassion for all living beings who are suffering, in trouble and affliction,

(3) *Mudita-* Sympanthetic joy in others success, welfare and happiness,

(4) *Upekkha-* Equanimity in all vicissitudes of life.

If one understands the Buddha's teaching, that his teaching is the right Path and tries to follow it, then one is a Buddhist. But according to the unbroken age-old tradition in Buddhist countries, one is considered Buddhist if one takes the Buddha, the *Dhamma* (The Teaching) and the *Sangha* (the order of monks)- generally called the Triple Gem- as one's refuges and undertakes to observe the Five Precepts (Panca-*sila*)- the minimum moral obligations of a lay Buddhist:

1. Not to destroy life
2. Not to steal
3. Not to commit adultery
4. Not to tell lies
5. Not to take intoxicating drinks-

Receiting the formulas given in the ancient texts.

A man named Dighajanu once visited the Buddha and said:

'Venerable Sir, we are ordinary lay men, leading the family life with women and children. Would the Blessed One teach us some doctrines which will be conducive to our happiness in this world and hereafter?' The Buddha tells him that there are four things which are conducive to man's happiness in this world:

1. To be skilled, efficient, earnest and energetic in whatever profession he is engaged. (*utthana-sampada*)
2. Protect his income, which he has earned righteously, with the sweat of his brow. (*arakkha-sampada*)
3. Have good friends (*kalyana-mitta*) who are faithful, learned, virtuous, liberal and intelligent, who will help him along the right path away from evil
4. He should spend reasonably, in proportion to his income, neither too much nor too little i.e. not to hoard wealth avariciously, nor should he be extravagant, live within his means (*samajivikata*).

While encouraging material progress, Buddhism always lays great stress on the development of the moral and spiritual character for a happy, peaceful, contented society. The *Dhammapadatthakatha* records that the Buddha directed his attention to the problem of good government. For a country to be happy it must have a just government. How this form of just government could be realised is explained by the Buddha in his teaching of the 'Ten Duties of a King' (*dasa-raja-Dhamma*).

1. Liberality, generousity, charity.
2. A high moral character.
3. Sacrificing everything for the good of the people. Prepared to give up all personal comfort, name and fame in the interest of the people.
4. Honesty and Integrity.
5. Kindness and Gentleness.
6. Austerity in habits. Lead a simple life, not indulge in a life of luxury. Have self-control.
7. Freedom from hatred, ill-will, enmity. Bear no grudges.
8. Non-violence (*avihimsa*). Should try to promote peace by avoiding and preventing war and everything which involves violence and destruction of life.
9. Patience, forebearance, tolerance, understanding. Able to bear insults hardships and difficulties without losing his temper.
10. Non-opposition, non-obstruction. Not to oppose the will of the people. Rule in harmony with his people.

The Buddha says: 'Never by hatred is hatred appeased, but it is appeased by kindness. This is an eternal truth.'

Bibliography

Aiyappan, A., and P. R. Srinivasan, *Story of Buddhism with Special Reference to South India.* Madras, India: Government of Madras, 1960.

Auboyer, Jeannine, *Buddha: A Pictorial History of His Life and Legacy.* New York: Crossroad, 1983.

Banerji, Aparna, *Traces of Buddhism in South India.* Calcutta: Scientific Book Agency, 1970

Bapat, P. V., ed., *2500 Years of Buddhism.* New Delhi: Government of India, Publications Division, 1956.

Basham, A. L., *History and Doctrines of the Ajivikas.* London: Luzac, 1951.

Basu, N. N., *Modern Buddhism and Its Followers in Orissa.* Calcutta, 1911.

Bechert, Heinz and Richard Gombrich, eds., *The World of Buddhism: Monks and Nuns in Society and Culture.* London: Thames and Hudson, 1984.

Cabezon, Jose Ignacia, ed., *Buddhism, Sexuality, and Gender.* Albany: SUNY Press, 1992.

Charles S. Prebish, ed., *Buddhism: A Modern Perspective.* University Park: Pennsylvania State University Press, 1975.

Conze, Edward, *Buddhism: Its Essence and Development.* New York: Harper Torchbooks, 1965.

.... ed., *Buddhist Texts through the Ages.* New York: Harper Torchbooks, 1964.

Gellner, David, "Buddhism and Hinduism in the Nepal Valley," in Sutherland, Stewart, et.al., eds., *The World's*

Religions. Boston: G. K. Hall, 1988.

Horner, I. B., *The Living Thoughts of Gotama the Buddha.* London: Cassell, 1948.

Jayatilleke, K. N., *Early Buddhist Theory of Knowledge.* London: George Allen & Unwin, 1963.

Joseph M. Kitagawa and Mark D. Cummings, ed., *Buddhism and Asian History.* New York: Macmillan, 1987.

Joshi, Lalmani, *Studies in the Buddhistic Culture of India,* 2nd rev. ed. Delhi: Motilal Banarsidass, 1977.

Karetsky, Patricia Eichenbaum, *The Life of the Buddha: Ancient Scriptural and Pictorial Traditions.* Lanham: University Press of America, 1992.

Keown, Damein et.al., eds. *Buddhism and Human Rights.* London: Curzon, 1998.

Kohn, Michael H., trans., *The Shambhala Dictionary of Buddhism and Zen.* Boston: Shambhala, 1991.

Lamotte, Etienne, *History of Indian Buddhism: From the Origins to the Saka Era.* Louvain-La-Neuve: Institut Orientaliste, 1988.

Lopez, Donald S., Jr, ed., *Buddhist Hermeneutics.* Honolulu: University of Hawaii Press, 1988.

Lopez, Donald S., Jr., ed., *Buddhism in Practice.* Princeton: Princeton University Press, 1995.

Malalasekera, G. P., ed., *Encyclopedia of Buddhism.* Colombo: Government of Sri Lanka, 1961.

Mishra, V. B., *Religious Beliefs and Practices of North India during the Early Mediaeval Period.* Leiden, Netherlands: Brill, 1973.

Morgan, Kenneth W., ed., *The Path of the Buddha.* New York: Ronald Press, 1974.

Nakamura, Hajime, *Gotama Buddha.* Los Angeles: Buddhist Books International, 1977.

Ñanamoli, Bhikkhu, *The Life of the Buddha.* Kandy, Sri

Lanka: Buddhist Publication Society, 1972.

Narada Thera, *The Buddha and His Teachings*. Kandy, Sri Lanka: Buddhist Publication Society, 1988 (reprint).

Prebish, Charles S., ed. *Buddhist Ethics: A Cross-Cultural Approach*. Dubuque: Kendall/Hunt, 1992.

Thomas, E. J., *The Life of the Buddha as Legend and History*. London: Routledge & Kegan Paul, 1927.

Warder, A. K, *Outline of Indian Philosophy*. Delhi: Motilal Banarsidass, 1971.

Warder, A. K., *Indian Buddhism*, 2nd ed. rev. Delhi: Motilal Banarsidass, 1980.

Warren, Henry C., *Buddhism in Translations*. New York: Atheneum, 1963.

Index